First World War
and Army of Occupation
War Diary
France, Belgium and Germany

16 DIVISION
47 Infantry Brigade
Royal Munster Fusiliers
1st Battalion
1 November 1916 - 30 April 1918

WO95/1971/1

The Naval & Military Press Ltd
www.nmarchive.com
Published in association with The National Archives

Published by

The Naval & Military Press Ltd

Unit 10 Ridgewood Industrial Park,

Uckfield, East Sussex,

TN22 5QE England

Tel: +44 (0) 1825 749494

www.naval-military-press.com

www.nmarchive.com

This diary has been reprinted in facsimile from the original. Any imperfections are inevitably reproduced and the quality may fall short of modern type and cartographic standards.

Contents

Document type	Place/Title	Date From	Date To
Heading	WO95/1971/1		
Heading	16th Division 47th Infy Bde 1st Bn Roy. Munster Fus. Nov 1916-Apl 1918 Absorbed 8 Bn 1916 Nov From 48 Bde 16 Div to 57 Div 172 Bde		
Heading	War Diary For Month of November, 1916. Volume 1st R. Munster Fusiliers. App 18		
War Diary	Bait Head Division in the line	01/11/1916	06/11/1916
War Diary	Kimmel	07/11/1916	19/11/1916
War Diary	In the Field	20/11/1916	22/11/1916
War Diary	Curragh Camp	23/11/1916	30/11/1916
Operation(al) Order(s)	Operation Order No. 43 By Lieut-Col. A.W. Clerke D.S.O. Comdg. 1st. Royal Munster Fusiliers. Appendix A.	02/11/1916	02/11/1916
Operation(al) Order(s)	Operation Order No. 43 By Lieut-Col. A.W. Clerke D.S.O. Comdg. 1st. R M F. Appendix B.	05/11/1916	05/11/1916
Operation(al) Order(s)	Operation Order No. 44 By Lieut-Col. R.H. Monck-Mason, Comdg. 1st. Royal Munster Fusiliers. Appendix D.	13/11/1916	13/11/1916
Operation(al) Order(s)	Operation Order No. 45 By Lieut-Col. R.H. Monck-Mason, Comdg. 1st. R. Munster Fusiliers. Appendix F	21/11/1916	21/11/1916
Operation(al) Order(s)	Operation Order No 46 by Lieut Col. R.E. Monck Mason Commdg 1st Roy. Munster. Fus. Appendix H	29/11/1916	29/11/1916
Miscellaneous			
Heading	War Diary For Month of December, 1916 Volume 1st Royal Munster Fusiliers		
War Diary	Vierstraat Section	01/12/1916	03/12/1916
War Diary	Derry Camp (N. 32. Central)	04/12/1916	04/12/1916
War Diary	Left Sub-Section. Spanbroek Section.	05/12/1916	12/12/1916
War Diary	Derry Camp (N. 32 Central)	13/12/1916	20/12/1916
War Diary	Left Sub-Section. Spanbroek Section.	21/12/1916	28/12/1916
War Diary	Curragh Camp	29/12/1916	31/12/1916
Operation(al) Order(s)	Operation Order 48. By Lieut. Colonel. R.H. Monck-Mason. Commanding 1st Roy Munster Fusiliers. Appendix B.	04/12/1916	04/12/1916
Miscellaneous	Operation Orders By Lieut-Col. R.H. Monck-Mason, Comdg. 1st. Royal Munster Fusiliers. Appendix C	09/12/1916	09/12/1916
Operation(al) Order(s)	Operation Order No. 49 By Lieut-Col. R.H. Monck-Mason, Comdg. 1st. Royal Munster Fusiliers. Appendix D	11/12/1916	11/12/1916
Heading	War Diary for month of January, 1917. Volume 1st Ro. Munster Fusiliers		
War Diary	Curragh Camp	01/01/1917	05/01/1917
War Diary	Left Sub-Section Spanbroek Section	06/01/1917	13/01/1917
War Diary	Derry Huts	14/01/1917	20/01/1917
War Diary	Spanbroek Sector Left Sub Section	21/01/1917	25/01/1917
War Diary	Curragh Camp	26/01/1917	28/01/1917
War Diary	Spanbroek Sector	29/01/1917	31/01/1917
Operation(al) Order(s)	Operation Order No. 1. By Lieut-Col. R.E. Monck-Mason, Comdg. 1st. Royal Munster Fusiliers. Appendix A	04/01/1917	04/01/1917

War Diary			
Operation(al) Order(s)	Operation Order No. 3. By Captain H.T. Goodland, Commanding 1st. Royal Munster Fusiliers. Appendix B	12/01/1917	12/01/1917
Operation(al) Order(s)	Operation Order No. 4. By Captain T.A.N. Bolton, Commanding 1st. Royal Munster Fusiliers. Appendix C.	20/01/1917	20/01/1917
Operation(al) Order(s)	Operation Order No. 5. By Captain H.T. Goodland, Commanding 1st. Royal Munster Fusiliers. Appendix D.	26/01/1917	26/01/1917
Miscellaneous	Brigade Division Corps Date of Recommendation.		
Operation(al) Order(s)	47th Infantry Brigade Order No. 91. Appendix E	27/01/1917	27/01/1917
Miscellaneous	Issued through Signals at 6.p.m.		
Miscellaneous	Relief Table To Accompany 47th Inf. Bde. Order No. 91		
Miscellaneous	47th Inf. Bde. No. G. 1232. 6th Royal Irish Regt. 6th Connaught Rangers. 7th Leinster Regt. 1st Royal Munster Fusiliers.	25/01/1917	25/01/1917
Miscellaneous	47th Inf. Bde. No. G. 1235/1. 6th Royal Irish Regt. 6th Connaught Rangers. 7th Leinster Regt. 1st Royal Munster Fusiliers.	26/01/1917	26/01/1917
Heading	War Diary For Month Of February, 1917 Volume Unit:- 1st R. Munster Fusiliers		
War Diary	Spanbroek Sector Bde Support Front Liner	01/02/1917	06/02/1917
War Diary	Wakefield Camp	07/02/1917	14/02/1917
War Diary	Spanbroek Sector	15/02/1917	18/02/1917
War Diary	Spanbroek Sector Right Sub Section	19/02/1917	22/02/1917
War Diary	Wakefield Camp	23/02/1917	28/02/1917
Operation(al) Order(s)	Operation Order No. 7. By Captain. H.T. Goodland, Commanding 1st Royal Munster Fusiliers. Appendix A	02/02/1917	02/02/1917
Operation(al) Order(s)	Operation Order No. 8. By Captain. H.T. Goodland, Commanding 1st Royal Munster Fusiliers. Appendix B	05/02/1917	05/02/1917
Operation(al) Order(s)	Operation Order No. 9. By Captain. H.T. Goodland, Commanding 1st Royal Munster Fusiliers. Appendix "C"	13/02/1917	13/02/1917
Miscellaneous	Operation Order By Captain. H.T. Goodland, Commanding 1st Royal Munster Fusiliers. Appendix 'D'	00/02/1917	00/02/1917
Operation(al) Order(s)	Operation Order No. 11 By Captain. H.T. Goodland, Commanding 1st Royal Munster Fusiliers. Appendix E	18/02/1917	18/02/1917
Miscellaneous	Operation Order By Captain. H.T. Goodland, Commanding 1st Royal Munster Fusiliers. Appendix "F"	21/02/1917	21/02/1917
Heading	War Diary For Month Of March, 1917 Volume Unit:- 1st Btn. Royal Munster Fusiliers		
War Diary	Wakefield. Camp	01/03/1917	01/03/1917
War Diary	Spanbroek Section Right. Sub-Sector.	02/03/1917	06/03/1917
War Diary	Doctors House	07/03/1917	09/03/1917
War Diary	Right Sub-Section Spranbrock Molen Section	10/03/1917	12/03/1917
War Diary	Derry Huts	13/03/1917	14/03/1917
War Diary	Berthon Area	15/03/1917	31/03/1917
Operation(al) Order(s)	Operation Order By Major H.T. Goodland, Commanding 1st Battn Royal Munster Fusiliers.	01/03/1917	01/03/1917
Miscellaneous	Operation Order By Major H.T. Goodland, Commanding 1st Battn Royal Munster Fusiliers.	01/03/1917	01/03/1917
Miscellaneous	Operation Order By Major H.T. Goodland, Commanding 1st Battn Royal Munster Fusiliers.	05/03/1917	05/03/1917
Miscellaneous	Operation Order By Lieut-Colonel R.H. Monck-Mason. Commanding 1st Royal Munster Fusiliers.	09/03/1917	09/03/1917

Operation(al) Order(s)	Operation Order No. 16. By Lieut-Colonel R.H. Monck-Mason. Commanding 1st Royal Munster Fusiliers.	09/03/1917	09/03/1917
Operation(al) Order(s)	Operation Order No. 17 By Major H.T. Goodland. Commanding 1st Battn, Royal Munster Fusiliers.	13/03/1917	13/03/1917
Operation(al) Order(s)	Operation Order No. 18 By Major H.T. Goodland. Commanding 1st Battn, Royal Munster Fusiliers.	13/03/1917	13/03/1917
Heading	War Diary For Month Of April, 1917. Volume:- Unit:- 1st R. Munster Fus.		
War Diary	Birr Barracks, Locre	01/04/1917	01/04/1917
War Diary	Left Sub-Section Vierstraat Sector.	02/04/1917	04/04/1917
War Diary	In Supports Rossignol	05/04/1917	09/04/1917
War Diary	Vierstraat Sector. Left Sub Section.	10/04/1917	15/04/1917
War Diary	Butterfly Farm. N 19 A.6.2	16/04/1917	19/04/1917
War Diary	Tallyho Camp X 5 A 5.2	20/04/1917	24/04/1917
War Diary	Kemmel Shelters N. 19. C.8.2	25/04/1917	30/04/1917
Miscellaneous	Operation Orders By Lieut-Colonel R.H. Monck-Mason, Commanding, 1st Royal Munster Fusiliers. Appendix A.	31/03/1917	31/03/1917
Miscellaneous	Operation Orders By Lieut-Colonel R.H. Monck-Mason, Commanding, 1st Royal Munster Fusiliers.		
Miscellaneous	Page 2 (a) 1st. Royal Munster Fusiliers will relieve the 8th. Bn. Royal Inns. Fusiliers in the sub-section. in the le		
Miscellaneous	Operation Orders By Lieut-Colonel R.H. Monck-Mason, Commanding 1st Royal Munster Fusiliers. Appendix B	03/04/1917	03/04/1917
Miscellaneous	Operation Orders By Lt-Colonel R.H. Monck-Mason, Comdg 1st Bn. Royal Muns. Fusiliers. In the Field Appendix C	09/04/1917	09/04/1917
Miscellaneous	Operation Orders By Major H.T. Goodland Comdg. Royal Munster Fusiliers. In the Field Appendix "D"	14/04/1917	14/04/1917
Miscellaneous	Operation Orders By Major H.T. Goodland Comdg. Royal Munster Fusiliers. In the Field Appendix "E"	18/04/1917	18/04/1917
Operation(al) Order(s)	Operation Orders By Major H.T. Goodland Comdg. Royal Munster Fusiliers. In the Field	17/04/1917	17/04/1917
Miscellaneous	Operation Orders By Major H.T. Goodland Comdg. Royal Munster Fusiliers. In the Field Appendix F.	24/04/1917	24/04/1917
Operation(al) Order(s)	Operation Orders No. 27 By Lt. Colonel R.H. Monck-Mason Comdg. 1st. Royal Muns. Fuslrs. In the Field Appendix "G"	28/04/1917	28/04/1917
Heading	War Diary: Volume:- For Month Of May, 1917. Unit:- 1st Royal Munster Fusiliers Vol 15		
War Diary	Kemmel Shelters	01/05/1917	01/05/1917
War Diary	Doncaster Huts	02/05/1917	05/05/1917
War Diary	Left Sub-Section Vierstraat Sector.	06/05/1917	10/05/1917
War Diary	Curragh Camp	11/05/1917	11/05/1917
War Diary	Rouge Croix Caestre	12/05/1917	16/05/1917
War Diary	Wallon Cappel	17/05/1917	17/05/1917
War Diary	Longuenesse	18/05/1917	18/05/1917
War Diary	Bayenghem Les Seninghem	19/05/1917	29/05/1917
War Diary	Arques	30/05/1917	30/05/1917
War Diary	Wallon Cappel	31/05/1917	31/05/1917
Heading	War Diary For Month Of June, 1917. Volume:- Unit:- 1st Battn. Royal Munster Fuslrs. Vol 16		
War Diary	Clare Camp	01/06/1917	03/06/1917
War Diary	Vierstraat Switch Trench System	04/06/1917	04/06/1917
War Diary	Vierstraat Switch	04/06/1917	06/06/1917

War Diary	Vierstraat	07/06/1917	08/06/1917
War Diary	Butterfly Farm	09/06/1917	12/06/1917
War Diary	Metteren Area	13/06/1917	16/06/1917
War Diary	Butterfly Farm	17/06/1917	17/06/1917
War Diary	Metteren Area	18/06/1917	19/06/1917
War Diary	Ecke Area	20/06/1917	21/06/1917
War Diary	Esquelbecq Area	22/06/1917	24/06/1917
War Diary	Zegers Cappel	25/06/1917	30/06/1917
Miscellaneous	47th. Infy. Bde. No. G. 3365 Report on the Wytschaete Operation June 1917	12/06/1917	12/06/1917
Miscellaneous	Officers		
Miscellaneous	Report On Operations Leading To The Capture Of Wytschaete by The 1st. Royal Munster Fusiliers	03/06/1917	03/06/1917
Miscellaneous	Appendix 2 Nominal Roll of Officers who took part in the Offensive		
Miscellaneous	To/Headquarters, 47th. Infantry Brigade. Report on "Tanks" Supporting 1st. R.M. Fus. in the Action on 7th. June.	07/06/1917	07/06/1917
Map	C		
Diagram etc			
Miscellaneous	Conversion Table Minutes-Hours		
Map	A.6. IX Corps Topo Sec: 5:6:17 9.C.T.M.15		
Heading	War Diary For Month of July, 1917. Volume:- 20 Unit:- 1st Ro. Munster Fuslrs. Vol 17		
War Diary	Zeggers Cap	01/07/1917	16/07/1917
War Diary	Tatinghem	17/07/1917	23/07/1917
War Diary	Winnezeele	24/07/1917	25/07/1917
War Diary	Watou	26/07/1917	30/07/1917
War Diary	Brandhoek 1/3 area Durham Redoubt	31/07/1917	31/07/1917
Operation(al) Order(s)	Operation Orders No. 43 By Lt. Col. R.H. Monck-Mason. D.S.O., Comdg, 1st Royal Munster Fusiliers. In-the-Field 15th July, 1917. App. A	15/07/1917	15/07/1917
Miscellaneous	March Table to accompany 1st R.M.F. O.O. No 43		
Operation(al) Order(s)	Operation Orders. No. 44. by Lt. Colonel R.H. Monck-Mason D.S.O. Comdg. 1st. Royal Muns. Fuslrs. In the Field 21-7-1917. App "B"	21/07/1917	21/07/1917
Operation(al) Order(s)	Operation Orders No. 45 By Lt. Colonel R.H. Monck-Mason Comdg. 1st. Royal Muns. Fus. In the Field 24.7.17. App 'C'	24/07/1917	24/07/1917
Miscellaneous	March Table to accompany Operation Order. No. 45		
Operation(al) Order(s)	Operation Orders No. 46 By Lt. Colonel R.H. Monck-Mason D.S.O. Comdg. 1st. Royal Muns. Fus. In the Field 29.7.17 App D	29/07/1917	29/07/1917
Operation(al) Order(s)	Operation Orders No. 47 By Lt. Colonel R.H. Monck-Mason D.S.O. Comdg. 1st. Royal Muns. Fus. In the Field 30.7.17 App E	30/07/1917	30/07/1917
Miscellaneous	March Table to accompany Operation Order No. 46 dated 29.7.17	29/07/1917	29/07/1917
Heading	War Diary. For Month Of August, 1917. Volume. Unit 1st Royal Munster Fusiliers Vol 18		
War Diary	Durham Redoubt (H.11. Central)	01/08/1917	01/08/1917
War Diary	Cambridge Trench I. 5.a. 10.70	02/08/1917	02/08/1917
War Diary	Right Support. (Ypres-Roolers Rly-D. 25.C. 65.70)	03/08/1917	05/08/1917
War Diary	Brandhoek No. 2 area	06/08/1917	10/08/1917
War Diary	Frezenberg (D. 25. C.4.7)	11/08/1917	13/08/1917
War Diary	Ecole (Ypres)	14/08/1917	14/08/1917

War Diary	Old German Line (Right 5/5)	15/08/1917	16/08/1917
War Diary	Vlamertinghe No 3 area	17/08/1917	18/08/1917
War Diary	Watou "B" Area	19/08/1917	19/08/1917
War Diary	Eecke	20/08/1917	20/08/1917
War Diary	Gomiecourt	21/08/1917	24/08/1917
War Diary	Moyenneville [A.5.a.8.8	25/08/1917	25/08/1917
War Diary	Support. N. of Bullecourt	26/08/1917	31/08/1917
Miscellaneous	47th Inf. Bde. No G. 3760 Appendix A	01/08/1917	01/08/1917
Heading	EVS		
Operation(al) Order(s)	Imbue Order No. P.1. Appendix B	02/08/1917	02/08/1917
Miscellaneous		15/08/1917	15/08/1917
Miscellaneous	1st Royal Munster Fusiliers M.H. 137 Appendix I		
Operation(al) Order(s)	47th Inf. Bde. Warning Order No. 145. Appendix C	02/08/1917	02/08/1917
Operation(al) Order(s)	Operation Orders No. 150 by Lt.-Col. R.H. Monck-Mason D.S.O. Comdg. 1st. Bn. Roy. Muns. Fus. In the Field 10/8/1917 Appendix E	10/08/1917	10/08/1917
Miscellaneous	Operation Order M.H. 195 Appendix E	14/08/1917	14/08/1917
Miscellaneous	1st Royal Munster Fusiliers Order M.H. 203 Appendix G		
Miscellaneous	V. Coy-2 guards	17/08/1917	17/08/1917
Operation(al) Order(s)	Operation Order No. 151 By Lt. Colonel R.H. Monck-Mason D.S.O. Comdg. 1st. Royal Muns. Fus. In the Field 18.8.17 Appendix J	18/08/1917	18/08/1917
Miscellaneous	March Table to accompany Battalion Order No. 151		
Operation(al) Order(s)	Operation Order No. 152 By Lt. Colonel R.H. Monck-Mason D.S.O. Comdg. 1st. Royal In the Field 20.8.17 Appendix K	20/08/1917	20/08/1917
Operation(al) Order(s)	Operation Orders No. 153 By Major J.W. Stacpoole Comdg. 1st Bn. Royal Munster Fusiliers. In the Field 20.8.17 Appendix L	20/08/1917	20/08/1917
Operation(al) Order(s)	Operation Orders No. 154 By Major J.W. Stacpoole Comdg. 1st Bn. Royal Munster Fusiliers. In the Field 24.8.17 Appendix H	24/08/1917	24/08/1917
Operation(al) Order(s)	Operation Orders No. 155 By Major J.W. Stacpoole Commanding. 1st Bn. Royal Munster Fusiliers. In the Field 26.8.17 Appendix N	26/08/1917	26/08/1917
Heading	War Diary For Month Of 1917, Volume Unit 1st Royal Munster Fusiliers Vol 19		
War Diary	3rd Army 6th Corps 16 Div. Front	01/09/1917	06/09/1917
War Diary	See Brigade Diaries	07/09/1917	11/09/1917
War Diary	Front Line	12/09/1917	15/09/1917
War Diary	Ervillers	16/09/1917	30/09/1917
Operation(al) Order(s)	Operation Orders No 1 By Lt. Col. R.H. Monck-Mason D.S.O. Comdg. 1st. R.M. Fusiliers. In the Field 10th. Sept. 17	10/09/1917	10/09/1917
Operation(al) Order(s)	Operation Orders No 2 By Lt. Col. R.H. Monck-Mason D.S.O. Comdg. 1st. Royal. Munster. Fusiliers. In the Field 15.9.17	15/09/1917	15/09/1917
Operation(al) Order(s)	Operation Orders No 3 By Lt.-Col. R.H. Monck-Mason D.S.O. Comdg. 1st. Royal. Munster. Fusiliers. In the Field 30/9/1917	30/09/1917	30/09/1917
Heading	War Diary For Month Of October, 1917. Unit 1st Ro. Munster Fusiliers Volume Number Vol 20		
War Diary	Enniskillen Camp Ervillers	01/10/1917	01/10/1917
War Diary	In Support Ecouste Sector	02/10/1917	17/10/1917
War Diary	Dysart Camp Ervillers	18/10/1917	24/10/1917

War Diary	Dysart Camp	25/10/1917	31/10/1917
Operation(al) Order(s)	Operation Orders No. 3 By Lt-Col. R.E. Monck-Mason. D.S.O. Comdg. 1st. Royal Munster Fusiliers. In the Field. 30/9/1917	30/09/1917	30/09/1917
Operation(al) Order(s)	Operation Order No. 4 By Lt. Col. R.E. Monck-Mason. D.S.O. Comdg. 1st. Royal Muns Fus. In the Field. 9.10.17	09/10/1917	09/10/1917
Operation(al) Order(s)	Operation Order No. 5 By Lt. Col. R.E. Monck-Mason. D.S.O. Comdg. 1st. Royal Muns Fusiliers. In the Field. 16.10.17	16/10/1917	16/10/1917
Heading	War Diary Of November, 1917. Volume:- Unite 1st Royal Munster Fusiliers Vol 21		
War Diary	Dysart Camp Ervillers	01/11/1917	02/11/1917
War Diary	Hendecourt Sector Croiselles Ecouste Line	03/11/1917	11/11/1917
War Diary	Left Sector	12/11/1917	13/11/1917
War Diary	Durrow Camp	14/11/1917	18/11/1917
War Diary	Left Sector	19/11/1917	20/11/1917
War Diary	Tunnel Trench	21/11/1917	22/11/1917
War Diary	Durrow Camp	23/11/1917	25/11/1917
War Diary	In. Line	26/11/1917	30/11/1917
War Diary		01/11/1917	30/11/1917
Operation(al) Order(s)	Operation Orders No 6 By Lt-Col. R.H. Monck-Mason D.S.O. Commanding 1st. Bn. Royal Munster Fus. In the Field 1/11/1917	01/11/1917	01/11/1917
Operation(al) Order(s)	Operation Orders No 7 By Lt-Colonel. R.H. Monck-Mason D.S.O. Commanding 1st. Bn. Royal Munster Fusiliers. In the Field 13/11/17	13/11/1917	13/11/1917
Operation(al) Order(s)	Operation Orders No 8 By Lt-Col. R.H. Monck-Mason D.S.O. Commanding 1st. Bn. Royal Munster Fusrs. In the Field 17/11/17	17/11/1917	17/11/1917
Operation(al) Order(s)	Operation Orders No 9 By Lt-Col. R.H. Monck-Mason D.S.O. Commanding 1st. Bn. Royal Munster Fus. In the Field 18/11/1917	18/11/1917	18/11/1917
Operation(al) Order(s)	Operation Orders No 10 By Lt-Col. R.H. Monck-Mason D.S.O. Commanding 1st. Bn. Royal Munster Fus. In the Field 19/11/17	19/11/1917	19/11/1917
Operation(al) Order(s)	Operation Orders No 12 By Lt. Col. R.H. Monck-Mason D.S.O. Comdg. 1st. Royal Muns. Fusiliers. In the Field 25.11.17	25/11/1917	25/11/1917
Operation(al) Order(s)	Operation Orders No. 13 By Major H.T. Goodland Comdg. 1st. Royal Munster Fusiliers. In the Field 29.11.17	29/11/1917	29/11/1917
Operation(al) Order(s)	Operation Orders No. 14 By Major H.T. Goodland Comdg. 1st. Royal Munster Fusiliers. In the Field 29.11.17	29/11/1917	29/11/1917
Miscellaneous	Report on Operations North of Bullecourt Part taken by 1st. Royal Munster Fusiliers.	27/11/1917	27/11/1917
Heading	War Diary For Month Of December, 1917 Volume:- Unit:- 1st Royal Munster Fusrs. Vol 22		
War Diary	Bullecourt & Tunnel Tr Front	01/12/1917	03/12/1917
War Diary	Beaulencourt	04/12/1917	06/12/1917
War Diary	Tincourt	07/12/1917	11/12/1917
War Diary	Line Left Sub-Sector	12/12/1917	15/12/1917
War Diary	In Line	16/12/1917	17/12/1917
War Diary	Lempire	18/12/1917	23/12/1917
War Diary	Tincourt	24/12/1917	29/12/1917

War Diary	In Line Right Sub-Sec. of Left Section	30/12/1917	31/12/1917
War Diary	I.R. Munster Fus.	01/12/1917	31/12/1917
Operation(al) Order(s)	Operation Orders No. 15 By Major H.T. Goodland Comdg. 1st. Royal Munster Fusiliers. In the Field 2.12.17	02/12/1917	02/12/1917
Heading	Adjustant		
Operation(al) Order(s)	Operation Orders No. 16 By Major H.T. Goodland Comdg. 1st. Royal Muns. Fusiliers In the Field 5.12.17	05/12/1917	05/12/1917
Operation(al) Order(s)	Operation Orders No. 17 By Lt. Colonel H.T. Goodland Comdg. 1st. Royal Munster. Fusiliers In the Field 10.12.17	10/12/1917	10/12/1917
Operation(al) Order(s)	Operation Orders No. 18 By Lt. Col H.T. Goodland Comdg. 1st. Royal Munster. Fusiliers In the Field 16.12.17	16/12/1917	16/12/1917
Operation(al) Order(s)	Operation Orders No. 19 By Lt. Colonel H.T. Goodland Commanding. 1st. Bn. Royal Munster. Fus. In the Field 22.12.17	22/12/1917	22/12/1917
Heading	War Diary For Month Of January, 1918. Volume:- Unit:- 1st R. Munster Fusiliers Vol. 23		
War Diary	Right Sub of Sector Left Sector	01/01/1918	01/01/1918
War Diary	Lempire Section	02/01/1918	04/01/1918
War Diary	St Emillie	05/01/1918	10/01/1918
War Diary	Hamel	11/01/1918	22/01/1918
War Diary	Left Sub-Sector of Right Sector	23/01/1918	26/01/1918
War Diary	Left Sub. Sec.	27/01/1918	28/01/1918
War Diary	Lempire	29/01/1918	31/01/1918
War Diary	Strength And Casualty Return I.R. Muns Fus. Appendix A	01/01/1918	31/01/1918
Operation(al) Order(s)	Operation Order No. 1 By Lt. Col H. Goodland Comdg. 1st Bn. Royal Munster Fusiliers In the Field 3.1.1918	03/01/1918	03/01/1918
Operation(al) Order(s)	Operation Order No. 2 By Lt. Colonel H.T. Goodland Comdg. 1st Royal Munster Fusiliers In the Field 9.1.18	09/01/1918	09/01/1918
Operation(al) Order(s)	Operation Order No. 3 By Lt. Colonel H.T. Goodland Comdg. 1st Royal Munster Fusiliers In the Field 21.1.18	21/01/1918	21/01/1918
Operation(al) Order(s)	Operation Order No. 4 By Lt. Colonel H.T. Goodland Comdg. 1st Royal Munster Fusiliers In the Field 27.1.17	27/01/1917	27/01/1917
Heading	War Diary. For Month Of February, 1918. Volume:- Unit:- 1st Btn. Ro. Munster Fusiliers Vol. 24		
Operation(al) Order(s)	Operation Orders No. 5 By Colonel H.T. Goodland Comdg. 1st. Bn. Royal Munster Fusiliers In the Field 2.2.18	02/02/1918	02/02/1918
Operation(al) Order(s)	Operation Orders No. 7 By Colonel H.T. Goodland Comdg. 1st. Bn. Royal Munster Fusiliers In the Field 7.2.18	07/02/1918	07/02/1918
Operation(al) Order(s)	Operation Orders No. 8 By Lt. Colonel R.R. Kane D.S.O. Comdg. 1st. Bn. Royal Munster Fusiliers In the Field 11.2.18	11/02/1918	11/02/1918
Operation(al) Order(s)	Operation Orders No. 9 By Lt. Colonel R.R. Kane D.S.O. Comdg. 1st. Bn. Royal Munster Fusiliers In the Field 20.2.18	20/02/1918	20/02/1918
Operation(al) Order(s)	Operation Orders No. 10 By Lt. Colonel R.R. Kane D.S.O. Comdg. 1st. Bn. Royal Muns Fusiliers In the Field 23.2.18	23/02/1918	23/02/1918

Operation(al) Order(s)	Operation Orders No. 11 By Lt. Colonel R.R. Kane D.S.O. Comdg. 1st. Bn. Royal Muns Fus In the Field 27.2.18	27/02/1918	27/02/1918
War Diary	Lempire (Left Sub-Sector, Right Sector)	01/02/1918	08/02/1918
War Diary	Lempire (Left Sub-Sector, Right Sector)	07/02/1918	12/02/1918
War Diary	Lempire (Right Subsection)	18/02/1918	20/02/1918
War Diary	Lempire	20/02/1918	28/02/1918
Miscellaneous	Patrol Orders By Lt. Colonel R.R. Kane D.S.O. Comdg. 1st. Royal Munster Fusiliers. In the Field 26.2.18	26/02/1918	26/02/1918
Heading	47th Brigade. 16th Division 1st-Battalion Royal Munster Fusiliers March 1918		
War Diary	Lempire	01/03/1918	01/03/1918
War Diary	Villers-Faucon	04/03/1918	08/03/1918
War Diary	Tincourt	09/03/1918	11/03/1918
War Diary	St Emile	14/03/1918	22/03/1918
War Diary	Villers-Faucon	22/03/1918	22/03/1918
War Diary	Tincourt Wood	23/03/1918	23/03/1918
War Diary	Doingt	23/03/1918	23/03/1918
War Diary	Bray	24/03/1918	24/03/1918
War Diary	Morecourt	25/03/1918	25/03/1918
War Diary	Mericourt	26/03/1918	26/03/1918
War Diary	Proyart	26/03/1918	27/03/1918
War Diary	Frameville	28/03/1918	28/03/1918
War Diary	Caix	28/03/1918	28/03/1918
War Diary	Demum	28/03/1918	28/03/1918
War Diary	Castel	28/03/1918	29/03/1918
War Diary	Wes	29/03/1918	29/03/1918
War Diary	Aubigny	29/03/1918	31/03/1918
Miscellaneous	Appendix I Officers Casualties 21st & 22nd Mar 1918	21/03/1918	21/03/1918
Heading	1/R Munsters April 1918 Went to 57 Div April 1918		
Miscellaneous	Division 52		
War Diary	Aubigny	01/04/1918	01/04/1918
War Diary	Bois de Vaire	01/04/1918	01/04/1918
War Diary	Hamelet	02/04/1918	03/04/1918
War Diary	Saleux	04/04/1918	04/04/1918
War Diary	Blangy	05/04/1918	05/04/1918
War Diary	Le Translay	06/04/1918	08/04/1918
War Diary	St. Quentin	09/04/1918	09/04/1918
War Diary	Eu.	10/04/1918	10/04/1918
War Diary	Arques	10/04/1918	10/04/1918
War Diary	Heuringhen	11/04/1918	11/04/1918
War Diary	Merck St. Levien	12/04/1918	12/04/1918
War Diary	Le Bouquet	13/04/1918	13/04/1918
War Diary	Wovrans	14/04/1918	15/04/1918
War Diary	Steenbeke	16/04/1918	20/04/1918
War Diary	Pas	20/04/1918	20/04/1918
War Diary	Henu	21/04/1918	30/04/1918
Miscellaneous	51		

16TH DIVISION
47TH INFY BDE

1ST BN ROY. MUNSTER FUS.

NOV 1916-APL 1918

ABSORBED 8 BN 1916 NOV

from 48 BDE 16 DIV

to 57 DIV 172 BDE

7061

W A R D I A R Y .

F O R

MONTH OF NOVEMBER, 1916.

VOLUME ————

1st. R. Munster Fusiliers.

apl '18

969

Instructions regarding War Diaries and Intelligence Summaries are contained in F. S. Regs., Part II. and the Staff Manual respectively. Title pages will be prepared in manuscript.

WAR DIARY
or
INTELLIGENCE SUMMARY.
(*Erase heading not required.*)

Army Form C. 2118.

November

1st R. M. F.

Place	Date	Hour	Summary of Events and Information	Remarks and references to Appendices
Batt Headquarters	1916 1st Nov		In the line quiet day Capt F. J. F. Lee + 1 O.R. Joined AWG	
in the line	2nd Nov		The Companies in front line were relieved at 2.30 PM Appendix A. Casualties killed 2 Sgts + 3 O.R. Wounded 1 O.R. to Hospital 2 O.R. These happened during the relief at the Junction, ASH. LANE —— FRONT. LINE by an enemy's T.M. Rejoined 1 O.R. AWG	Appendix A
" "	3rd Nov		Capt Carrigan Wounded in head 2/Lieut H Waring Wounded Shell shock 2 O.R. to Hosp rejoined 3 O.R. One of our Balloons that had broken loose came over the line drifting north. hour 3.00 PM. AWG	
" "	4th Nov		The enemy shelled TURNERSTOWN N. R. + S. P. 12. Killed 1 Sgt. Wounded 2/Lieut BS. Cumming + 18 O.R. rejoined 2 O.R. AWG	
" "	5th Nov		The enemy shelled TURNERSTOWN R. + S. P. 12 again causing no casualties + very little damage. Capt F. J. F. Lee went to Hospital. Wounded 1 O.R. Rejoined 1 O.R.	
" "	6th Nov		The Battalion were relieved by 7th Royal Irish Rifles + moved into Billets at Kemmel appendix B AWG Relief Commenced 2.00 PM " Complete 3.15.00 PM. Wounded 1 O.R. Rejoined 1 O.R.	Appendix B
Kemmel	7th Nov		In Billets AWG	

Albert W. Clarke Lt Col
1st R M Fus

2353 Wt. W2544/1454 700,000 5/15 D. D. & L. A.D.S.S./Forms/C. 2118.

Instructions regarding War Diaries and Intelligence Summaries are contained in F. S. Regs., Part II. and the Staff Manual respectively. Title pages will be prepared in manuscript.

WAR DIARY
or
INTELLIGENCE SUMMARY.
(Erase heading not required.)

Army Form C. 2118.

November — 1st R. M. F.

Place	Date	Hour	Summary of Events and Information	Remarks and references to Appendices
	1916			
Kemmel	8th Nov		In Billets putting up Bunks & repairing mens Quarters also Headquarters To Hospital 1 OR	
"	9th "		" " " " " " To Hospital 1 OR	
"	10th "		" " " " " "	
"	11		Reinforcements 15 OR To Hosp. 4 OR	
"	12th		Rejoined 2 OR To Hosp. 2 OR	
"	13th		" 1 OR " " 2 OR	
"	14th		The Batt relieved the 7th R.I.R in front line Bgd O appendix C, Batt O appendix D Relief commenced 3.0 Pm " Completed 4.15 Pm Rejoined 3 OR To Hosp 2nd Lieut Martin + 2 OR	Appendix C + D
"	15th "		Day quiet - Reinforcements 6 OR Rejoined 2 OR	
"	16th		Commanding Officer went to Bgd HQs to act for Brigadier, day quiet at 10.30 Pm our artillery bombarded enemys trenches, little retaliation	
"	17th "		Day quiet Rejoined 1 OR Wounded 1 OR	
"	18th "		Companies in front line were relieved by Compys in Support at 5.30 Pm. Reinforcements 13 OR Casualties Killed 1 OR To Hosp 1 OR	
	19th		Day quiet - Rejoined 2 Lieut Hartnett 15 T.M.B	

Albert Mc[illegible] Lt Col
[illegible] R.M.F.

Instructions regarding War Diaries and Intelligence Summaries are contained in F. S. Regs., Part II. and the Staff Manual respectively. Title pages will be prepared in manuscript.

WAR DIARY
or
INTELLIGENCE SUMMARY.
(Erase heading not required.)

Army Form C. 2118.

November — 1st R.M.F.

Place	Date	Hour	Summary of Events and Information	Remarks and references to Appendices
	1916			
In the Field	20th		Day quiet – Rejoined 1.O.R AWB	
" " "	21st		" " AWB	
" " "	22nd		Battalion were relieved by the 8th Royal Dublin Fus. and came into Billets at Canada Corner. CURRAGH CAMP. and came under Orders of 47th Brigade Bgd O. appendex E. Batt O appendex F Reinforcements 76.O.R. AWB	appendex E + F
CURRAGH CAMP	23rd		The 8th Batt R.M.F. were absorbed into this Batt. 21 Officers + 446.O.R. appendex E. ~~[illegible]~~ AWB	app...
"	24th		In Billets To Hosp 1.O.R AWB	
"	25th		" " Rejoined 4.O.R To Hosp 2.O.R AWB	
"	26th		" " ~~Rejoined~~ Reinforcements 20.O.R To Hosp 3.O.R AWB	
"	27th		" " Rejoined 1.O.R To Hosp 6.O.R AWB	
"	28th		" " To Hospital 4.O.R AWB	
"	29th		" "	
"	30th		Batt relieved the 6th Royal Irish Regt in the front line Batt O 29.11 [illegible] appendex H. Relief commenced 1.00 P.M. " Completed 6.55.00 P.M.	appendex H

Albert W. Clarke Lt Col
1st R.M. Fus

Appendix. A.

SECRET

OPERATION ORDER No. 43

By Lieut-Col. A. [illegible] D.S.O. Comdg. 1st. Royal Munster Fusiliers.

1 Company [illegible] E Company [illegible] front line, on relief
[illegible] Company [illegible] S.P.12.
2 Company [illegible] Company/[illegible] front line, on relief
[illegible] to garrison TURNERTOWN RIGHT
[illegible] TRENCH [illegible]
[illegible] 2.30 [illegible] will be [illegible]
[illegible] B. [illegible]

(signed) E.C. Conley, 2/Lieut.

2-11-16

A/Adjutant 1st Royal Munster Fusiliers.

SECRET 5. 11. 16 appendex B. Copy No:- 4

Operation Order No:- 43.

By Lieut.-Col. A. W. Blake D.S.O. Comdg. 1st R. M. F.

Ref. sheet 28 S.W. 1/20,000

1. The 1st Royal Munster Fusiliers will be relieved in the Left Sub-Section by the 7th Royal Irish Rifles, on 6th Nov. 1916.
   On relief the Battalion will move into Brigade Reserve and be disposed as follows:- X Y & Z Companies in billets in KEMMEL. Battn. H.Q. at WHITE HOUSE N.21.c.7.3 W Coy. ROSSIGNOL N.22.a. CENTRAL. Relief will commence at 2 p.m.
2. 2/Lieut. P. F. Martin, 1 N.C.O. & 1 man per coy., except W Coy., C.S.M. Rooney & Sgt. Murphy will report at 7th R.I.R. H.Q. KEMMEL at 12 noon 6-11-16, to take over billets.
3. All permanent working parties and Schemes of Work will be handed over on relief.
4. Handing over Certificates to be rendered to Battn. H.Q. by 10 a.m. 7-11-16.
5. Completion of relief to be immediately reported to Battn. H.Q. in code by wire.
6. Transport Officer will provide 3 limbers for transport of baggage from ROSSIGNOL ESTAMINET, also arrange for the removal of water carts. Water carts on being refilled to report to Battn. H.Q. KEMMEL.
7. X Y & Z Companies Cookers will report to Battn. H.Q. KEMMEL. W Coys. packs and blankets will be delivered at ROSSIGNOL, and X Y & Z Companies packs and blankets at KEMMEL 6-11-16.

Issued at:- 6.40 p.m.
5-11-16.

E. Rooney 2/Lieut.
A/Adjutant 1st R. Munster Fus.

SECRET

13-11-16

Operation Order No. 44

Copy No:-

By Lieut-Col. R. H. Monck-Mason, Comdg. 1st Royal Munster Fusiliers

Ref. sheet Wytschaete 28 S.W.

Appendix D.

1. The 1st R.M.F. will relieve the 7th R.I.R. in the Left Sub-section, 43rd Bde. front, at 3 p.m. to-morrow 14th inst.

2. Company Commanders will proceed at 9 a.m. to-morrow to reconnitre the trenches, with special attention to work at present in progress.

3. The Battn. will move off by companies from billets in the following order at times stated:-

   Z Company at 2-30 p.m. Y Coy. at 2-40 p.m. W Coy. at 2-50 p.m. X Coy. will move off from Rossignol 10 minutes after W Coy have passed. O's C. W, Y & Z Coys. will get Brigade time at 12 noon from Orderly Room.

4. Z & Y Coys. will be in the front line, W & X Coys. in support. Z Coy. will relieve Left Coy and Y the Right Coy. in front line. W Coy. will relieve Coy. in TURNERSTOWN RIGHT and FORT ROYAL with 3 Platoons in Turnerstown Right and 1 Platoon in Fort Mount Royal. X Coy. will relieve Coy. in S.P. 12.

5. An advance party comprising Sgt. Murphy, Sgt. Kelly and 1 N.C.O. or man per Coy. will report to C.S.M. Reaney outside Orderly Room at 11 a.m. and will proceed under C.S.M. Reaney to take over trench stores.

6. All particulars of permanent working parties and Schemes of Work will be obtained by O's C. Coys. on reliefs, and they will immediately inform the Adjutant what permenant working parties they have been handed over.

7. Movements East of N.20.d. will be by Platoons at intervals of 200 yds.

8. Completion of reliefs will be immediately reported to Battn. H.Q. in code by wire.

   Lists of trench stores taken over will be rendered to Battn. H.Q. by 12 noon 15th inst.

9. All baggage, packs and 1 blanket per man for return to Quartermaster's stores will be stacked outside W Coys. billets by 1 p.m. Baggage going to Battn. H.Q. Rossignol will be stacked at same time and place in a separate pile.

10. The Transport Officer will arrange to have necessary transport to remove baggage to Rossignol with the Rations and will take back baggage for Quartermaster's Stores in empty ration limbers.

Issued at:- 5-55 pm
13-11-16

Cecil H. Ekhaus, Captain,
A/Adjutant 1st R. Munster Fusiliers

SECRET 21.11.16 Appendix F Copy No:- 12

Operation Order No. 45.

By Lieut-Col. R. H. Monck-Mason Comdg. 1st R. Munster Fusiliers

Ref. sheet 28 S.W Ed. 3D 1/20000

1. The 1st R.M.F will be relieved in the Left Sub-section by the 8th R.D.F. on 22 inst.
On relief the Battn. will move into billets at Curragh Camp, Canada Corner, M.17.C.6.5. and come under the orders of the G.O.C. 47th Inf. Brigade.

2. Reliefs will be as follows:-
W & X Companies. "C" Company 8th R.D.F. will relieve W & X Coys. in the front line. Relieving Coy. will be at Rossignol Estaminet at 11 a.m. W Coy. will supply a guide to report at Battn. H.Q. at 10.45 a.m. On relief W & X Coys. will proceed to Battn. H.Q. Rossignol Estaminet and will remain till men have had dinners. Arrangements should be made by O.s.C. Companies to have cooks sent down after breakfast. After dinners companies will march to new billets. O.s.C. Companies will report at Headquarters before marching off.

Z. Coy. "A" Coy. 8th R.D.F. will relieve Z Coy. in S.P. 12. They will be at Rossignol Estaminet at 1.45 p.m. Z Coy. will supply a guide at Battn. H.Q. at 1.30 p.m.

Y. Coy. "B" Coy. 8th R.D.F. will relieve Y Coy. They will be at Rossignol Estaminet at 2 p.m. Y Coy. will supply a guide at 1.45 p.m.
On relief Y & Z Coys. will proceed to new billets. O.s.C. Coys. will report at Headquarters before marching off.

H.Q. Company All N.C.O.s and men of H.Q. Coy. in the trenches will immediately on relief report to Battn. H.Q. When the entire of H.Q. Coy. has been relieved they will march under the R.S.M. to their new billets.

3. Billeting party consisting of C.S.M. Harris, 1 N.C.O & 1 man per company and 1 N.C.O & 1 man from H.Q. Coy. under 2/Lieut. F.M. West will report at Battn. H.Q. at 10 a.m.

4. Advance parties of 8th R.D.F. will arrive at Rossignol Estaminet as follows:- C Coy. 9.30 a.m. A & B Coys. 10.30 a.m.
X Coy. will arrange for guide to be at Battn. H.Q. at 9.15 a.m. and Y & Z Coys. will arrange for guides at 10.15 a.m.
All stores will be handed over to Advance Parties.
All schemes of work will be handed over on relief.

5. Transport Officer will provide the necessary limbers for removal of baggage from Rossignol Estaminet after dusk on the evening 22nd inst. He will also arrange for removal of watercarts. All packs and the one blanket per man at Quartermasters Stores will be conveyed to Curragh Camp so as to be there on arrival of Battalion.
Horses for O.s.C. W & X Coys. will be at Kemmel at 1.30 p.m. Y & Z Coys. at Kemmel at 3.30 p.m.

Appendix F

6. Company Cookers will move to Curragh Camp in time to have tea ready for the Battalion on arrival.

7. Handing over Certificates will be rendered to Battn. H.Q. by 10 a.m. 23rd inst.

8. Completion of relief will be immediately reported to Battn. H.Q. in code by wire.

Issued at:- 6 p.m.
21-11-16

Cecil H. Exham Captain,
A/Adjutant 1st Royal Munster Fus.

Copy No. 1. W Company
" " 2 X "
" " 3 Y "
" " 4 Z "
" " 5 Lewis Gun Officer
" " 6 Commanding Officer
" " 7 2nd in Command
" " 8 Adjutant
" " 9 Brigade H.Q.
" " 10 8th R.D.F.
" " 11 R.S.M.
" " 12 File
" " 13 "
" " 14 Unit at Curragh Camp.
" " 15 Quartermaster
" " 16 Transport Officer
" " 17 Medical Officer

Operation Order No 46 appendix H

SECRET by 29.11.16

Lieut Col. R.E. Monck-Mason (Map. Ref. 28 S.W. 3.d)

Commdg 1st Roy. Munster Fus.

I. The Battalion will relieve the 6th Roy. Irish Regt. and a party of the 6th Connaught Rangers in the Front + Support Lines of the 47th Infantry Brigade Front on the 30th inst. Battalion Head Quarters will be at YORK HOUSE.

II DISPOSITIONS.

"W" Coy. will relieve the Front Line less 1 team of Lewis Gunners of 1 N.C.O. and 6 men who will remain at CURRAGH CAMP with "Z" Coy.

"X" Coy will relieve the garrison of VAN KEEP, S.P. 13, + Support Trench less 1 team of Lewis Gunners of 1 N.C.O. and 6 men who will remain at CURRAGH CAMP with "Z" Coy

"Y" Coy. will relieve the garrison of SANDBAG VILLA less Lewis Gun Team of 1 N.C.O. + 6 men who will remain at CURRAGH CAMP with "Z" Coy.

These three Lewis Gun Teams will be rationed by "Z" Coy.

"Z" Coy. will remain at CURRAGH CAMP + billets will be allotted by the Brigade.

"W" Coy in the Front Line will have two Lewis Gun Teams from "Z" and "Y" Coys, attached for duty while in the trenches.

These will be rationed by "W" Coy.

III DETAILS.

(a) An Advance Party consisting of 1 N.C.O. + 2 men from H.Qrs, "W" "X" + "Y" Coys + 2 Lewis Gun Teams from all Coys, All under an Officer to be detailed by "W" Coy. will parade outside Orderly Room at 9 a.m. to proceed to the line + take over Stores + Gun positions.

(b) "W" Coy. will parade on their Coy. Parade Ground + will move off at 1 p.m.
"X" Coy. will parade on their Coy. Parade Ground + will move off at 1.20 p.m.
"Y" Coy will parade on their Coy. Parade Ground + will move off at 1.40 p.m.

(c) Movements East of Locre will be by Platoons at 150 yards interval.

(d) Movements East of Beaver Farm will be by sections at 150 yards distance in daylight

(e) Copies of Trench Store Receipts will be sent to reach Battalion Head Quarters by 10 a.m. 1st December,

(f) Completion of reliefs will be reported by code to Battn. H.qrs.

Continued

4. TRANSPORT.

The Transport Officer will arrange for four extra limbers (H.Q, "W", "X" & "Y" Coys) to go up with the Rations on the night of the 30th inst. to carry up packs & blankets for the men of the Companies.

O.C. Coys will arrange in the event of blankets & packs being taken up to have them stacked outside the R.S.M's hut before their Companies move off. They will detail two men to remain with them & load them on the limbers. These men will come up with the limbers.

5. O.C. "Z" Coy. will detail an Officer to hand over the billets in CURRAGH CAMP & will obtain a certificate of cleanliness from the incoming Battn. The certificate will be rendered to Orderly Room by 12 noon 1st December

Sd/ C.H. Exham Capt. A/Adjutant
1st Royal Munster Fusiliers.

Copies to:-

1 and 2 War Diary.
3. Filed.
4. G.O.C.
5. 7th Royal Irish Rifles.
6. 1st Royal Munster Fusiliers.
7. 2nd Royal Dublin Fusiliers.
8. 8th Royal Dublin Fusiliers.
9. 9th Royal Dublin Fusiliers.
10. 48th Machine Gun Company.
11. 48th Trench Mortar Battery.
12. Staff Captain.
13. 48th Brigade Signals.
14. 48th Brigade Transport Officer.
15. 48th Brigade Supply Officer.
16. 155th Field Company, R.E.
17. 16th Division.
18. 16th Divisional Artillery.
19. Centre Group, 16th Divl. Artillery.
20. 16th Division "Q".
21. 47th Infantry Brigade.
22. 49th Infantry Brigade.
23. 250th Tunnelling Coy. R.E.
24. Y. 16. Trench Mortar Battery.
25. A.D.M.S., 16th Division.
26. 145th. Company, Army Service Corps.

WAR DIARY FOR MONTH OF DECEMBER, 1916.

VOLUME

1st Royal Munster Fusiliers

Vol 12/10

WAR DIARY
or
INTELLIGENCE SUMMARY.
(Erase heading not required.)

Army Form C. 2118.

Instructions regarding War Diaries and Intelligence Summaries are contained in F. S. Regs., Part II. and the Staff Manual respectively. Title pages will be prepared in manuscript.

December. 1st Royal Munster Fusiliers

Place	Date	Hour	Summary of Events and Information	Remarks and references to Appendices
VIERSTRAAT SECTION.	1.12.16		Enemy quiet. Our Lewis Gun dispersed an enemy party at N.18.3 in the support line at 8.30 AM. Total effective strength 48 officers 1069 OR. To Hospital 1 OR.	
	2.12.16		At 8.30 AM our Stokes Mortars fired on enemy front line opposite MAYO STREET. Enemy retaliated with aerial Torpedoes. At 10.30 & 11.30 AM our 18 pdrs. & 4.5" Hows were active against enemy support line in front of UNNAMED WOOD. 2 Lieuts WALSH & REIDY & 3 OR rejoined from Hospital. To Hospital 6 OR. Wounded 2 OR. Strength 48 officers & 1068 O.R.	
	3.12.16		At 2.55 & 3.10 pm. enemy Heavy Trench Mortars were active against our support line. Our 18 pdrs. 4.5" Hows & Heavies retaliated on their emplacements in front of UNNAMED WOOD. Strength 48 officers & 1063 OR. Wounded 1 OR. To Hospital 2 OR.	
DERRY CAMP (N.32. Central)	4.12.16		Slight artillery activity on both sides otherwise quiet. Strength 48 officers & 1060 OR. Reinforcements 3 O.R. To Hospital 1 OR. 2 Lt. FRASER was evacuated to United Kingdom. The Battalion was relieved by 8th Royal Dublin Fusiliers & proceeded to DERRY CAMP at N 32 Central.	

~~[See appendix A]~~

[signature] Lt. for OC. 1st R.M.F.

T2134. Wt. W708—776. 500000. 4/15. Sir J. C. & S.

Instructions regarding War Diaries and Intelligence Summaries are contained in F. S. Regs., Part II. and the Staff Manual respectively. Title pages will be prepared in manuscript.

WAR DIARY
or
~~INTELLIGENCE SUMMARY~~.
(*Erase heading not required.*)

Army Form C. 2118.

December. 1st Royal Munster Fusiliers —

Place	Date	Hour	Summary of Events and Information	Remarks and references to Appendices
LEFT SUB-SECTION. SPANBROEK SECTION.	5.12.16		The Battalion relieved the 9th Royal Inniskilling Fusiliers in LEFT SUBSECTION, SPANBROEK SECTION [See appendix B]. Strength 47 officers & 1063 O.R. Wounded 6 OR. To Hospital 2 OR. Rejoined from Hospital 1 OR.	
	6.12.16		Enemy quiet. At 3.15 pm. our Stokes Mortars were active against Enemy line in front of Battalion on our Right. The enemy retaliated with Aerial Torpedos on our line, breaching it in 3 places, at N.3.c.5.2. Strength 47 officers & 1056 OR. Reinforcements 5 OR. To Hospital 1 OR.	
	7.12.16		Enemy quiet. Strength 47 officers & 1060 OR. Lt. MATTERSON rejoined from Hospital. 2Lt. FORAN was evacuated to United Kingdom.	
	8.12.16		At 3 pm. our Medium & Light Trench Mortars in adjoining subsections. The enemy retaliated on our line with Heavy Trench Mortars, Field Guns, Aerial Torpedos & Rifle Grenades, blocking front line in 2 places & damaging PICADILLY. Our 18 pdrs. themselves retaliated on enemy T.M. emplacements. The bombardment ceased at 4.15 pm. A patrol was sent out during the night. Strength: 46 officers & 1060 OR. Killed 1 OR. To Hospital 2 OR. Rejoined from hospital 3 OR.	

[illegible signature]
Lt. Col. 1st R.M.F.

T2134. Wt. W708—776. 500000. 4/15. Sir J. C. & S.

Instructions regarding War Diaries and Intelligence Summaries are contained in F. S. Regs., Part II. and the Staff Manual respectively. Title pages will be prepared in manuscript.

WAR DIARY
or
INTELLIGENCE SUMMARY.
(Erase heading not required.)

Army Form C. 2118.

December — 1st Royal Munster Fusiliers

Place	Date	Hour	Summary of Events and Information	Remarks and references to Appendices
LEFT SUB-SECTION SPANBROEK SECTION	9.12.16		At 3 AM an enemy patrol consisting of 5 men were dispersed by our Lewis Guns at the BULL RING. About 5.30 pm enemy shelled [illegible] LONG WAY with heavy Trench Mortars. A patrol went out to reconnoitre our wire in front of the BULL RING. Y Coy. relieved Z Coy. in Front Line [see appendix C]. Strength: 46 officers + 1060 O.R. To Hospital 5 O.R. Rejoined from Hospital 4 O.R. [initials]	
	10.12.16		Slight enemy Artillery Trench Mortar activity during the afternoon. A patrol was sent out during the night. Strength: 46 officers + 1059 O.R. Killed 1 O.R. Wounded 1 O.R. Rejoined from Hospital 2 O.R. [initials]	
	11.12.16		At 11 AM & 3 pm our Stokes Guns were active & provoked retaliation from Enemy Heavy & Light Trench Mortars, which centred chiefly about LONG LANE, PICADILLY, & ULSTER ROAD. Our Artillery replied. [initials] Strength: 46 officers, 1059 O.R. Casualties: Nil.	
	12.12.16		Enemy quiet. The Battalion was relieved by the 7th Leinster Regt. & proceeded to DERRY CAMP on completion of relief [see appendix D]. Strength:- 46 officers + 1059 O.R. Lt MAHER & 2 OR rejoined from Hospital. To Hospital 2 O.R. [initials]	

[signature] Lt. for O.C. 1st R.M.F.

T2134. Wt. W708—776. 500000. 4/15. Sir J. C. & S.

Instructions regarding War Diaries and Intelligence Summaries are contained in F. S. Regs., Part II. and the Staff Manual respectively. Title pages will be prepared in manuscript.

WAR DIARY
or
INTELLIGENCE SUMMARY.
(Erase heading not required.)

Army Form C. 2118.

December — 1st Royal Munster Fusiliers

Place	Date	Hour	Summary of Events and Information	Remarks and references to Appendices
DERRY CAMP. (N.32 Central)	13.12.16		Parades under Coy. arrangements for inspection of rifles, ammunition, respirators, kit, feet. Equipment stripped & cleaned. Working parties found for battalions in line & 176 Coy. R.E. Strength: 46 officers & 1059 OR. Rejoined from Hospital 3 OR. To Hospital 1 OR. [initials]	
	14.12.16		Parades under Coy. arrangements, Working Parties as yesterday. 5 NCOs per Coy paraded for General Course under R.S.M. at 8.45 AM. Following were appointed Lewis Gun officers to their Coys:- W Coy. Lt. G.F. MAHER; X Coy. 2Lt. D.J. BAILEY M.C.; Y Coy. Lt. J.R. COLFER; Z Coy. 2Lt. W. HARRIS. M.C. X & Y Coys. proceeded to baths at LOCRE. Strength: 46 officers + 1061 OR. Rejoined from Hospital 2 O.R. To Hospital 5 O.R. [initials]	
	15.12.16		Parades under Coy. arrangements. Working parties as yesterday. Rifles, bayonets & scabbards of X Coy. inspected by Armourer Sergeant. Strength: 46 officers & 1058 OR. Rejoined from Hospital 1 OR. To Hospital 2 OR. Transferred to other Regiments 10 OR. [initials]	
	16.12.16		Parades under Coy arrangements. Working parties as yesterday. Rifles, bayonets & scabbards of Z Coy. inspected by Armourer Sergeant. Strength: 46 officers & 1047 OR. Reinforcements 12 OR. Rejoined from Hospital 2 OR. To Hospital 5 OR. [initials]	

[illegible signature] Lt. for O.C. 1st R.M.F.

T2134. Wt. W708—776. 500000. 4/15. Sir J. C. & S.

Instructions regarding War Diaries and Intelligence Summaries are contained in F. S. Regs., Part II. and the Staff Manual respectively. Title pages will be prepared in manuscript.

WAR DIARY
or
INTELLIGENCE SUMMARY.
(Erase heading not required.)

Army Form C. 2118.

December. 1st Royal Munster Fusiliers —

Place	Date	Hour	Summary of Events and Information	Remarks and references to Appendices
DERRY CAMP. (N.32 Central)	17.12.16		Divine Service as follows: R.C. at Church DRANOUTRE 9AM: C of E at DERRY CAMP 9.30 AM. 2nd Lt. FISHER & 1 OR. proceeded to 16th Divl. SCHOOL for Course of instruction in Bayonet fighting & Physical Training. Working parties as yesterday. Strength: 46 officers & 1056 OR. Rejoined from Hospital 1 OR. To Hospital 2 OR. To Base 1 OR. [initials]	
	18.12.16		Parades under Coy. arrangements. Working parties as yesterday. Rifles, bayonets, & Scabbards of [illegible] Coy inspected by Armourer Sergeant. Lt. MAHER & 1 OR. proceeded to TERDEGHEM to attend a Grenade course. Strength: 46 officers & 1054 OR. Capt. J. H. LAWLOR reported for duty with the Battalion. Reinforcements: 61 OR. To Hospital 1 OR. [initials]	
	19.12.16		Parades under Coy. arrangements. Working parties as yesterday. Rifles, bayonets, & Scabbards of [illegible] Coy. inspected by Armourer Sergt. Strength: 47 officers & 1114 OR. Killed 2 OR. Wounded 1 OR. Transferred 8 OR. To Hospital 4 OR. 2Lt. M. D. GREGAN to Hospital. 2Lt. A. E. MALE attached to 6 Connaught Rangers. [initials]	
	20.12.16		Following NCOs. & men of the Battalion were awarded the Military Medal: 9091 Pte. BATSON. W., 8316 Pte. HENNESSY. T., 4943 Pte. O'BRIEN P., 5278 L/C GILROY. J., 5830 Pte. KEANE P., 9172 Sgt. STRUTTON. J. [initials]	

[signature] Lt. for OC 1st R.M.F.

2353 Wt. W2544/1454 700,000 5/15 D. D. & L. A.D.S.S./Forms/C. 2118.

Army Form C. 2118.

WAR DIARY
or
INTELLIGENCE SUMMARY.
(Erase heading not required.)

Instructions regarding War Diaries and Intelligence Summaries are contained in F. S. Regs., Part II. and the Staff Manual respectively. Title pages will be prepared in manuscript.

December — 1st Royal Munster Fusiliers

Place	Date	Hour	Summary of Events and Information	Remarks and references to Appendices
DERRY CAMP. N.32 Central)	20.12.16		7744 Sgt. UNSWORTH, H., 5799 Cpl. GODFREY, H., 8576 C.Q.M.S. MURPHY, J., 9642 Pte. TWOMEY, M. Genl. Sir D. HAIG C in C visited the Camp. The Battalion relieved the 7th Leinster Regt. in LEFT SUB SECTION, SPANBROEK SECTION [See Appendix E]. Strength: 46 officers + 1099 O.R. To Hospital 3 O.R. Lt. POLLOCK was evacuated to United Kingdom. Lt. & Qmr. J. REGAN was transferred to 6th Royal Irish Regt. [initials]	
LEFT SUB-SECTION. SPANBROEK SECTION.	21.12.16		Our Lewis Guns dispersed an enemy party opposite N.30.1 killing one of their number. At 3.15 pm. our Medium Trench Mortars fired on enemy line opposite KINGSWAY provoking Trench Mortar & Artillery retaliation on DEAD MANS FARM + FRONT LINE. Our artillery replied. A patrol was sent out from N.30.2. Strength: 44 officers & 1096 O.R. Wounded 1 O.R. To Hospital 7 O.R. Rejoined from Hospital 2 O.R.	[initials]
	22.12.16		Enemy quiet. A patrol was sent out to examine the Enemy wire. Strength: 44 officers + 1090 O.R. To Hospital 2 O.R. Rejoined from Hospital 1 O.R. [initials]	
	23.12.16		Enemy quiet. At 5.30 pm. gas was released by 36th Divn. on our right. During retaliation the Enemy obtained several direct hits on our front line with 4.2's. A patrol was sent out. Strength: 44 officers + 1088 O.R. To Hospital 7 O.R. Rejoined from Hospital 5 O.R. [initials]	

M. H. FitzGerald
Lt. for O.C. 1st R.M.F.

2353 Wt. W2544/1454 700,000 5/15 D. D. & L. A.D.S.S./Forms/C. 2118.

Army Form C. 2118.

WAR DIARY
or
INTELLIGENCE SUMMARY.
(Erase heading not required.)

Instructions regarding War Diaries and Intelligence Summaries are contained in F. S. Regs., Part II. and the Staff Manual respectively. Title pages will be prepared in manuscript.

December — 1st Royal Munster Fusiliers

Place	Date	Hour	Summary of Events and Information	Remarks and references to Appendices
LEFT SUB-SECTION. SPANBROEK SECTION.	24.12.16		At 3 pm. our 4.5's bombarded the Enemy's rearward positions. X Coy. relieved W Coy. in the Front Line [Appendix F2]. Strength: 44 officers & 1085 OR. To Hospital 1 OR. Rejoined from Hospital 1 OR. [initials]	
	25.12.16		Enemy quiet. Sounds of Singing were heard in Enemy Line about 7.30 pm. A patrol went out from junction of PICADILLY & Front Line. Strength: 44 officers & 1085 men. To Hospital 2 OR. Rejoined from Hospital 4 OR. [initials]	
	26.12.16		At 7.10 AM. our snipers claim to have hit one of an enemy party seen looking over their parapet in front of the BULL RING. At 5 pm. enemy artillery was active on our Right & a Trench Mortar Engagement ensued. During the night our artillery was active against enemy rearward positions. A patrol was sent out N. of Sap in BULL RING & reported Enemy Wiring party at work. The party was dispersed by our Lewis Guns. Strength: 44 officers & 1087 OR. To Hospital 3 OR. Rejoined 5 OR. [initials]	
	27.12.16		Our Medium Right Trench Mortars bombarded the enemy line in front of Battalion on our left from 2.15 pm to 2.45 pm. & from 3 pm. to 3.30 pm. Enemy retaliated heavily during past period with Trench Mortars on Front Line LONG LANE & PICADILLY, with 4.2's on S.P. 7. [initials] Strength: 44 officers & 1089 OR	

[signature] Lt. Col. Cmdg 1st R.M.F.

Army Form C. 2118.

WAR DIARY
or
INTELLIGENCE SUMMARY.
(Erase heading not required.)

Instructions regarding War Diaries and Intelligence Summaries are contained in F. S. Regs., Part II. and the Staff Manual respectively. Title pages will be prepared in manuscript.

December. 1st Royal Munster Fusiliers.

Place	Date	Hour	Summary of Events and Information	Remarks and references to Appendices
LEFT SUB SECTION SPANBROEK SECTION.	28/12/16		Enemy quiet. The Battalion was relieved by the 7th Leinster Regt. Relief complete about 7 p.m. Proceeded to CURRAGH CAMP. Lieut. J.H. FITZGERALD to 2nd Army Sniping School. Strength: 44 officers, 1087 O.R.	
CURRAGH CAMP	29/12/16		Parades under Company arrangements. Thorough cleaning up and stripping of equipment. Strength: 44 officers and 1087 O.R.	
	30/12/16		Running Parades for all Companies. No. 5933 R.Q.M.S. P. CALVIN proceeds to 16th I.B. Depot for Transfer. 2 O.R. to Hospital. 1 O.R. to Machine-Gun Course at CAMIERS. Lieut. R.J. POLLOCK evacuated to U.K. Strength: 43 officers, 1084 O.R.	
	31/12/16		Divine Service as follows:- R.C. at HOSPICE LOCRE 9 a.m. C of E. at SCHERPENBERG HILL 9.30 a.m. Battalion Cross-country Run 11.30 a.m. No. 3813 L/Cpl. T. BRENNAN awarded Military Medal. 2 O.R. to Hospital. 2nd Lieut. W.D. McKEOWN & 1 O.R. to Course of Bayonet fighting and P.T. at 16th Divl. School. 2nd Lieuts. J.F. FULLIN & J.H. HARTLEY & 2 O.R. to General Course of Instruction at 16th Divl. School. Capt. H.T. GOODLAND reported for duty. Strength: 44 officers, 1082 O.R.	

Cecil [illegible] Capt
A/Adj for OC 1st RMun Fus

2353 Wt. W2544/1454 700,000 5/15 D. D. & L. A.D.S.S./Forms/C. 2118.

Appendix B.

Copy No. ____

SECRET.

OPERATION ORDER 48.

4.[illegible].16.

-BY-

Lieut. Colonel. R.H. MONCK-MASON, Commanding 1st ROYAL MUNSTER FUSILIERS.

1. The 1st ROYAL MUNSTER FUSILIERS will relieve the 9th ROYAL INNISKILLING FUSILIERS in the Left Sub-Section, 47th Brigade Front on the night of 5th/6th December 1916.

2. DISPOSITIONS.
"Z" Coy. 1st R.M.F. will take over the Front Line and ULSTER ROAD. The Leading Platoon will be at DAYLIGHT CORNER at 5.30 p.m. where it will be met by guides. Platoons will follow each other at 5 minutes interval and will be met by their guides at same place.
"Y" Coy. will take over S.P. 7, [illegible] DUGOUTS and [illegible]. The Leading Platoon will march off from DERRY CAMP five minutes after the last Platoon of "Z" Coy. has left. Platoon guides will be at DAYLIGHT CORNER.
"X" Coy. will take over BEEHIVE DUGOUTS and FORT EDWARD. Leading Platoon to leave DERRY CAMP 5 minutes after last Platoon of "Y" Coy. has left. Guides will be at DAYLIGHT CORNER.
"W" Coy. will be allotted billets behind the Line which will be notified to O.C. Coy. later.
Three Lewis Gun Teams each from "Z" and "Y" will parade on Main Road outside DERRY CAMP at 10.30 a.m. under Lieut J.F. [illegible] and will proceed to the trenches to take over positions and Stores.

3. An advance Party of 1 N.C.O. 10 signallers and 1 N.C.O. and 2 men each from H.Q., "X", "Y", and "Z" Coys all under Lieut M.H. Fitz-Gerald will parade on Main Road outside DERRY CAMP at 11 a.m. and proceed to trenches to take over Signal Stations and Stores.
Lieut. R.C. Conley with Sgt. Kelly will report at Bn. H.Q. at 10.45 a.m. tomorrow and will proceed to trenches with advance Party at 11 a.m. to take over Bombing Stores.

4. O.C. "X" Coy will proceed to the trenches at 10 a.m. on 5th inst. to reconnoitre the position to be held by his Coy.

5. Transport Lines and Quarter Master's Stores remain as at present.

6. Trench Store receipts to be sent to Bn. H.Q. by 10 a.m. 6th inst.

7. H.Q. 47th Inf. Bde. will close at [illegible] and will re-open at DRANOUTRE [illegible] at the same hour.

8. The Transport Officer will arrange for the removal on his return from rations, of all kit &c., left by the Battalion at DERRY CAMP for return to Q.Mr. Stores.

9. Completion of Relief will be wired in code to Bn. H. Qrs.

Sd/ [illegible] Capt. A/Adjt.
1st Bn. Royal Munster Fusiliers.

Copy No. 1. - C.O.
Copy No. 2. - 2nd in Comm
Copy No. 3. - Adjt.
Copy No. 4. - 47th Bde.
Copy No. 5. - 9th INNISKILLINGS
Copy No. 6. - "W" Coy.
Copy No. 7. - "X"
Copy No. 8. - "Y"
Copy No. 9. - "Z"
Copy No. 10 - R.S.M.
Copy No. 11 - Q.M.
Copy No. 12 - T.O.
Copy No. 13 - Bombing Offr.
Copy No. 14 - L.Gun Offr.
Copy No. 15/16 - FILED.

SECRET.

Appendix C.

OPERATION ORDERS

BY

Lieut-Col. [illegible] Monck-Mason, Comdg. 1st. Royal Munster Fusiliers.

Ref. sheet [illegible] Edition [illegible].

1. "Y" Company will relieve "[illegible]" Company in the front line, Left Sub-sector 47th Brigade front on the 9th inst.

2. "Y" Company will move from their present position at 5 p.m. Relief will be arranged between O,s.C. Companies.. O.C. "Y" Company will leave an officer to hand over stores. "[illegible]" Company on relief will take over the position held by "Y" Company .

3. Completeion of relief will be reported by code immediately to Battalion Headquarters.

(signed) [illegible] [illegible] , Capt. & Adjutant.

9-12-16. 1st. Royal Munster Fusiliers.

S E C R E T. Appendix D

OPERATION ORDER No. 49.
BY
Lieut-Col. R.H. Monck-Mason, Comdg. 1st, Royal Munster Fusiliers.

Ref. sheet 28 S.W. Edition 3d.

1. 1st. Royal Munster Fusiliers will be relieved by the 7th Leinster Rgt. in the Left Sub-Sector, 47th Infnatry Brigade front, on 12th inst.

2. DISPOSITIONS.

"A" Coy. 7th Leinster Rgt. will relieve "Y" Coy. 1st. R.M.F. in the front line and ULSTER ROAD, with 3 platoons in front line and 1 in ULSTER ROAD.
"B" Coy. 7th Leinster Rgt. will relieve "Z" Coy. 1st. R.M.F. in S.P.7 and PICCADILLY DUG-OUTS.
"C" Coy. 7th Leinster Rgt. will relieve "X" Coy. 1st. R.M.F. in S.P.8. FORT EDWARD and BEEHIVE DUG-OUTS, with 1 platoon in S.P.8, 2 platoons in FORT EDWARD and 1 platoon in BEEHIVE DUG-OUTS.
"H.Q." Coy. 7th Leinster Rgt. will relieve "H.Q." Coy. 1st. R.M.F. in NEWPORT DUG-OUTS.
Lewis Guns 7th Leinster Rgt. will relieve the guns of 1st. R.M.F in their present positions.

3. DETAIL.

(a) Lewis Gun teams 7th Leinster Rgt. will be at DAYLIGHT CORNER N.33.c.8.8. at 8 a.m. Lewis Gun Officer will arrange to have one guide for the four front line guns and one guide for each of the other positions at DAYLIGHT CORNER at that hour.
On relief Lewis Guns will proceed via KINGSWAY to DERRY CAMP.
(b) One guide per platoon from X Y & Z Coys and one guide from H.Q. Coy. will be at DAYLIGHT CORNER N.33.c.8.8. at 10 a.m.
Leading platoon of 7th Leinster Rgt. will be at DAYLIGHT CORNER at that hour.
O.C. "W" Coy. will arrange to hand over the hutments at CURRAGH CAMP occupied by his company and all details of 1st. R.M.F. to the 6th Royal Irish Rgt.
On relief all companies will preceed to DERRY CAMP, X Y & Z Coys. will preceed via KINGSWAY.
(c) Advance parties of 1 officer, 1 N.C.O. and 2 men from each company, and 1 officer, 1 N.C.O. and 2 men from H.Q. Coy. will be at DERRY CAMP at 9 a.m. to take over billets.
(d) Gum boots if any, will be returned to Brigade Store at DAYLIGHT CORNER.
(e) Handing over certificates for trench stores will be sent to Battn. H.Q. by 10 a.m. 13th inst.
(f) Completion of reliefs will be reported to Battn. H.Q. in code by wire.
(g) Transport Officer will arrange for the cookers to move off from CURRAGH CAMP and proceed to DERRY CAMP immediately after breakfast is finished.
He will also arrange for two limbers and the Mess Cart to be at DAYLIGHT CORNER at 3 p.m.

(signed) C.A. Exham, Capt. & Adjutant,
1st. Royal Munster Fusiliers.

11-12-16.

Copy No.1. C.O. 2. 2nd in command, 3,Adjutant. 4 L.G. Officer
5. Intell. Officer. 6. R.S.M. 7. Bde. H.Q. 8. File. 9. 7th Leinsters.
10. Qrmr. 11. Transport Off. 12. W Coy. 13 X Coy. 14 Y Coy.
15. Z Coy.

SECRET.

OPERATION ORDER No. 49.
BY
Lieut-Col. [illegible], Comdg. 1st, Royal Munster Fusiliers.

Ref. Sheet 28 [illegible] Edition 3d.

1. 1st. Royal Munster Fusiliers will be relieved by the 7th Leinster Rgt. in the [illegible] Sub-Sector, 47th Infantry Brigade front, on 12th inst.

2. [illegible]

"[illegible]" Coy. 7th Leinster Rgt. will relieve "Y" Coy. 1st. R.M.F. in the front line [illegible], with [illegible] platoons in front line and 1 in [illegible].
"B" Coy. 7th Leinster Rgt. will relieve "[illegible]" Coy. 1st. R.M.F. in S.P.7 and [illegible] DUG-OUTS.
"C" Coy. 7th Leinster Rgt. will relieve "Z" Coy. 1st. R.M.F. in S.P.8, FORT EDWARD and BERRIES DUG-OUTS, with 1 platoon in S.P.8, [illegible] FORT EDWARD and 1 platoon in BERRIES DUG-OUTS.
"H.Q." Coy. 7th Leinster Rgt. will relieve "H.Q." Coy. 1st. R.M.F. in [illegible] DUG-OUTS.
Lewis Guns 7th Leinster Rgt. will relieve the guns of 1st. R.M.F. in their present positions.

3. Detail.

(a) Lewis Gun teams 7th Leinster Rgt. will be at DAYLIGHT CORNER [illegible].c.8.8. at 8 a.m. Lewis Gun Officer will arrange to have one guide for the four front line guns and one guide for each of the other positions at DAYLIGHT CORNER at that hour.
On relief Lewis Guns will proceed via [illegible]WAY to DERRY CAMP.
(b) One guide per platoon from X Y & Z Coys and one guide from H.Q. Coy. will be at DAYLIGHT CORNER N.32.c.8.[illegible] at 10 a.m. Leading platoon of 7th Leinster Rgt. will be at DAYLIGHT CORNER at that hour.
O.C. "[illegible]" Coy. will arrange to hand over the hutments at CURRAGH CAMP occupied by his company and all details of 1st. R.M.F. to the 6th Royal Irish Rgt.
On relief all companies will proceed to DERRY CAMP, X Y & Z Coys. will proceed via KINGSWAY.
(c) Advance parties of 1 officer, 1 N.C.O. and 2 men from each company, and 1 officer, 1 N.C.O. and 2 men from H.Q. Coy. will be at DERRY CAMP at 9 a.m. to take over billets.
(d) Gum Boots if any, will be returned to Brigade Store at DAYLIGHT CORNER.
(e) Handing over certificates for trench stores will be sent to Battn. H.Q. by 10 a.m. 13th inst.
(f) Completion of reliefs will be reported to Battn. H.Q. in code by wire.
(g) Transport Officer will arrange for the cookers to move off from CURRAGH CAMP and proceed to DERRY CAMP immediately after breakfast is finished.
He will also arrange for [illegible] Limber and the Mess Cart to be at DAYLIGHT CORNER at 3 p.m.

(signed) [illegible], Capt. & Adjutant,
1st. Royal Munster Fusiliers.

11-12-16.

Copy No. 1. C.O. 2. 2nd in command, 3, Adjutant. 4 L.G. Officer
5. Intell. Officer. 6. R.S.M. 7. [illegible] 8. File. 9. 7th Leinsters.
10. Qrmr. 11. Transport Off. 12. W Coy. 13 X Coy. 14 Y Coy.
15. Z Coy.

W A R D I A R Y for month of JANUARY, 1917.

VOLUME ____

1st R. Munster Fusiliers

Vol XI

16/47

Instructions regarding War Diaries and Intelligence Summaries are contained in F. S. Regs., Part II. and the Staff Manual respectively. Title pages will be prepared in manuscript.

WAR DIARY
or
INTELLIGENCE SUMMARY.
(Erase heading not required.)

Army Form C. 2118.

1st Royal Munster Fusiliers.

Place	Date	Hour	Summary of Events and Information	Remarks and references to Appendices
CURRAGH CAMP	1/1/17		Companies at disposal of Coy. Commanders for morning parades. Afternoon: Inter-Coy. Football Match. 3973 Sergt. M. SHANTON and 3371 Pte. C. TURNER awarded Military Medal. Strength: 44 officers and 1088 O.R.	
	2/1/17	9.A.M.	Battalion under R.S.M.: Arms Drill	
		10.30 a.m.	By Companies: Saluting Drill. In afternoon W & Z. Coys. to Baths at LOCRE. Commanding Officer received congratulations from C.-in-C. on smartness of Guard on the occasion of his visit to CASSEL. Brigadier also congratulated C.O. on smartness of Brigade Guard. Inter-Company Football Match 2.30 P.M. Strength: 44 officers and 1087 O.R.	
	3/1/17		In Morning: Lewis Gun Teams at Brigade Training Ground. W & Z Coys: Route march. X and Y Coys: Bayonet-fighting and Rifle-exercises. Afternoon: X and Y Coys. to Baths. Final of Company Football Competition 2.30 P.M. No. 5974 Sergt. T.J. MURTAGH proceeds to Cadet School in ENGLAND. Capt. J.D. BUTLER reported for duty. Strength: 44 officers 1083 O.R.	
	4/1/17		Morning Parades under Company arrangements. Capt. CRICHTON, Lieut. M.H. FITZGERALD and No. 7261 R.S.M. CALLAGHAN awarded Military Cross. Draft of 12 O.R. reported for duty. Strength: 45 officers and 1079 O.R.	
	5/1/17		Battalion relieves 7th Leinster Regt. in the Left Sub-section [illegible] Coy in Front Line	Appendix A

T2134. Wt. W708—776. 500000. 4/15. Sir J. C. & S.

Instructions regarding War Diaries and Intelligence Summaries are contained in F. S. Regs., Part II. and the Staff Manual respectively. Title pages will be prepared in manuscript.

WAR DIARY
or
~~INTELLIGENCE SUMMARY.~~
(Erase heading not required.)

Army Form C. 2118.

1st Royal Munster Fusiliers.

Place	Date	Hour	Summary of Events and Information	Remarks and references to Appendices
			and ULSTER ROAD. Z Coy in S.P.7 and PICCADILLY DUGOUTS. W Coy in S.P.8 FORT EDWARD and BEEHIVE DUGOUTS. X take over billets in LURGAN CAMP. Relief complete 4.30 P.M.	
LEFT SUB-SECTION			Draft of 7 O.R. arrived. During relief enemy T.M. active on CLOGHER VALLEY. One man wounded. Strength: 45 officers 1090 O.R.	
SPANBROEK SECTION	6/1/17		Night quiet. Trench Mortars active at intervals during the morning. Our Artillery was active between 2 and 3 p.m. Enemy T.M.'s retaliated on BULLRING, doing little damage. S.P. 7 was also lightly shelled. Strength: 45 officers and 1083 O.R. Large working-parties on Front Line, which was in bad condition.	
do.	7/1/17		Between 3 a.m. and 4 a.m. enemy T.M.'s were active, enfilading BULL RING from both flanks. Direct hits were obtained on CASTLE BAY, the sap at BULL RING, and ULSTER ROAD. At 1 p.m. one of our planes was brought down in flames behind our lines by an enemy plane. At 4 p.m. enemy shelled RESERVE TRENCH and PICCADILLY with 4.2s for 20 minutes. At 5 p.m. enemy Artillery shelled DEADMAN's FARM, obtaining a direct hit on ULSTER ROAD, killing one man and wounding another. Our guns retaliated. Draft 23 O.R. To Base (under age) 1 O.R. Strength: 45 officers and 1081 O.R.	
do.	8/1/17		At about 1 a.m. enemy working party fired on and dispersed. Day passed quietly. Capt. T.A.N. BOLTON reported for duty. Usual working parties at work. Nothing special to report. Strength: 45 officers and 1101 O.R.	

T2134. Wt. W708—776. 500000. 4/15. Sir J. C. & S.

Instructions regarding War Diaries and Intelligence Summaries are contained in F. S. Regs., Part II. and the Staff Manual respectively. Title pages will be prepared in manuscript.

WAR DIARY
or
~~INTELLIGENCE SUMMARY~~
(Erase heading not required.)

Army Form C. 2118.

1st Royal Munster Fusiliers

Place	Date	Hour	Summary of Events and Information	Remarks and references to Appendices
EFT SUB-SECTION. SPANBROEK SECTION.	9/1/17		Enemy Artillery and T.M.s very active from 8 a.m. to 10 a.m. Our field guns replied effectively. Afternoon passed quietly. At 9 p.m. enemy wiring party was dispersed by our Lewis Gun at N 30. 1.5; two of the party were seen to fall. Lieut. I. G. MATTERSON evacuated to U.K. Capt. F. J. F. LEE proceeded to R.F.C. (Kite-balloon Section.) Z Coy relieved Y Coy. in Front Line, Y taking over positions in Support. Strength: 46 officers and 1102 O.R. Weather very dirty. Some snow.	
do.	10/1/17		Night passed quietly. Slight enemy T.M. activity during morning and early in afternoon on CLOUGHER VALLEY. At 3.40 p.m. four enemy aeroplanes flew over our lines and brought down the Kite Balloon at DRANOUTRE in flames. Returning over our line, one machine was apparently slightly damaged. Strength: 44 officers and 1098 O.R.	
do.	11/1/17		At 2 p.m. our Artillery engaged enemy front line. He replied with 77 mm. and T.M.s. He also fired with 4.2 shells on ULSTER ROAD. Our 18-pounders retaliated. A blind 5.9 fell in vicinity of ULSTER ROAD. Strength: 44 officers and 1098 O.R.	
do.	12/1/17		There was considerable Artillery activity on both sides, enemy T.M.s causing damage to CLOUGHER VALLEY. During bombardment enemy observed from aeroplane. Our Artillery opened fire in preparation for raid on our left at 7.30 p.m., and at intervals during the evening a heavy Artillery duel took place. We lost 3 men killed and 2 wounded. 2 Lieut. J.E. Walsh (sick) to Hospital.	

T2134. Wt. W708—776. 500000. 4/15. Sir J. C. & S.

Instructions regarding War Diaries and Intelligence Summaries are contained in F. S. Regs., Part II. and the Staff Manual respectively. Title pages will be prepared in manuscript.

WAR DIARY
or
INTELLIGENCE SUMMARY.
(Erase heading not required.)

1st Royal ~~Dublin~~ Munster Fusiliers.

Army Form C. 2118.

Place	Date	Hour	Summary of Events and Information	Remarks and references to Appendices
LEFT SUB-SECTION			1 O.R. to Cadet School in ENGLAND. Draft of 4 O.R. arrived. Strength: 44 officers and 1096 O.R.	
SPANBROEK SECTION	13/1/17		Morning quiet. Battalion relieved in Trenches by 7th Leinster Regt. and proceeds to DERRY HUTS. X Coy. relieved in LURGAN CAMP by D Coy 7th Leinster Regt. Relief complete at 5 p.m. Weather very severe. Strength: 44 officers and 1096 O.R.	appendix E
DERRY HUTS	14/1/17		Church Parades: R.C. 9 a.m. at LOCRE. C. of E. 5 p.m. Capt. H.T. GOODLAND proceeds to 2nd Army School, Capt. T.N. BOLTON acting O.C. Battalion. Eight working-parties found. Strength: 44 officers and 1092 O.R.	
do.	15/1/17		Companies employed in cleaning up and stripping equipment. W and X Coys to Divisional Baths at LOCRE. To Cadet School 1 O.R. Capt. A.P. PERRY reported for duty. Strength: 44 officers and 1093 O.R. Transferred to other Regts. 10 O.R.	
do.	16/1/17		Inspections of ammunition, gas helmets and feet. Nothing special to record. Strength: 46 officers and 1047 O.R. Heavy snowfall.	
do.	17/1/17		Kit and Steel Helmet inspections.	

T2134. Wt. W708—776. 500000. 4/15. Sir J. C. & S.

Army Form C. 2118.

WAR DIARY
or
~~INTELLIGENCE SUMMARY.~~
(Erase heading not required.)

1st Royal Munster Fusiliers

Instructions regarding War Diaries and Intelligence Summaries are contained in F. S. Regs., Part II. and the Staff Manual respectively. Title pages will be prepared in manuscript.

Place	Date	Hour	Summary of Events and Information	Remarks and references to Appendices
DERRY HUTS	18/1/17		Parades under Coy Commanders, Lectures for N.C.O's on elementary map reading. Strength:- Officers 45. OR 1054 Hospital 2 OR	
do	19/1/17		Parades under Coy Commanders. Strength Officers 45 O.R 1052 - a new Draft of 32 OR arrived. to hospital 2 OR.	
do	20/1/17		Church Parade. Strength Officers 45. OR 1080. Draft 16 OR. to hospital 1 OR.	
SPANBROEK SECTOR LEFT SUB SECTION	21/1/17		1st R.M.F. relieved 7th Leinsters in this sub section. Strength: Officers 45, OR 1095. From hospital 2 OR. Front quiet. 2 Prisoners of the 104th Res Saxon Regt taken opposite Cop of PICCADILLY by X Coy. During afternoon bombarded by T.M's. Supports shelled by 4·2's and field guns.	Appendix C
	22/1/17		Front line bombarded by T.M's & shelled by 4·2's & field guns. Strength - Officers 45. OR 1097. from hospital 2. Casualties:- OR. 1 wounded, 1 killed, 3 to hospital	
	23/1/17		Enemy active with T.M's and artillery. Strength: Officers	

T2134. Wt. W708–776. 500000. 4/15. Sir J. C. & S.

Instructions regarding War Diaries and Intelligence Summaries are contained in F. S. Regs., Part II. and the Staff Manual respectively. Title pages will be prepared in manuscript.

WAR DIARY
or
INTELLIGENCE SUMMARY.
(Erase heading not required.)

Army Form C. 2118.

Place	Date	Hour	Summary of Events and Information	Remarks and references to Appendices
SPANBROEK	23/1/17		45, OR 1094. From hospital 3.	
SECTOR LEFT SUB-SECTION	24/1/17		Supports & strong points heavily shelled. Strength Officers 45, OR 1097. from hospital OR 1. Casualties killed 1 OR. wounded 1 OR. to hospital 6.	
	25/1/17		Very quiet, Strength Officers 45 OR 1090 from hospital 3, wounded 1 OR. to hospital 12 OR.	
CURRAGH CAMP	26/1/17		The Bn was relieved in the line by the 7th Leinsters. On completion of relief, the Bn moved into Divisional Res: at CURRAGH CAMP. Strength Officers 45 OR 1096. Sec Lieut returned to duty from hospital. from hospital 5 OR. to hospital 4 OR.	Appendix D
	27/1/17		Coy kit inspections & bathing parade. Strength Officers 45, OR 1097. Sec Lieut J. E. Walsh returned to duty from hospital. New draft of 9 OR arrived. from hospital 3 OR. to hospital 4 OR.	
	28/1/17		Church Parade. Strength 45 Officers 1100 OR. New draft 12 OR. from hospital 2 OR. Killed (attached) T.M.s 3 ORs, to 51 R.	
SPANBROEK SECTOR.	29/1/17		The Bn moved into Bde Support. See appendix.	

T2134. Wt. W708—776. 500000. 4/15. Sir J. C. & S.

Army Form C. 2118.

Instructions regarding War Diaries and Intelligence Summaries are contained in F. S. Regs., Part II. and the Staff Manual respectively. Title pages will be prepared in manuscript.

WAR DIARY
or
~~INTELLIGENCE SUMMARY.~~

(Erase heading not required.)

Place	Date	Hour	Summary of Events and Information	Remarks and references to Appendices
	29/1/17		Strength Officers 45, OR 1115, from hospital 5 OR to hospital 10, OR	Appendix E
	30/1/17		Front Quiet. Strength: Officers 45 OR 1110, Sec Lieut J. W. Lane joined the Bn, from hospital 4 OR to hospital 9 OR	
	31/1/17		Sec Lieut J. H. Lawlor transferred to the machine gun Corps Strength:- Officers 45, OR 1105.	
			Ian Bolton Capt 1st R. M. Fus.	

2353 Wt. W2544/1454 700,000 5/15 D. D. & L. A.D.S.S./Forms/C. 2118.

Appendix A

Copy No._____

SECRET.

OPERATION ORDER No.1.
BY
Lieut-Col. R.H. Monck-Mason, Comdg. 1st. Royal Munster Fusiliers.

1. RELIEFS.

The 1st. R.M.F. will relieve the 7th Leinster Rgt. in the Left Subsect 47th Inf. Brigade front on the 5th inst.

2. DISPOSITIONS.

Y Coy. will relieve D Coy. 7th Leinster Rgt. in the front line and ULSTER ROAD, with 3 platoons in the front line and one platoon in ULSTER ROAD.
Z Coy. will relieve C Coy. 7th Leinster Rgt. in S.P.7 and PICCADILLY DUG-OUTS, with 3 platoons in S.P.7 and 1 platoon in PICCADILLY DUG-OUTS.
W Coy. will relieve B Coy. 7th Leinster Rgt. in S.P.8 FORT EDWARD and BEEHIVE DUG-OUTS, with 1 platoon in S.P.8, 2 platoons in FORT EDWARD and 1 platoon in BEEHIVE DUG-OUTS.
X Coy. will take over billets from A Coy. 7th Leinster Rgt. in DURHAM CAMP.
H.Q. Coy. will take over NEWPORT DUG-OUTS.
Lewis Guns of Y & Z Coys. will relieve the guns of the 7th Leinster Rgt. in the positions at present occupied by them

3. DETAIL.

(a) Lewis Guns of Y & Z Coys. will parade under Coy. Lewis Gun Officers on the main road outside CURRAGH CAMP and will move off at 9-30 a.m. to take over positions.
(b) Advance parties of one officer and one N.C.O. each from W X Y Z & H.Q. Coys. and necessary signallers will leave CURRAGH CAMP at 10 a.m. Parade outside Orderly Room.
(c) Y Z W X & H.Q. Coys. will parade on their parade grounds at 12-25 and will move off in the order named, with five minutes interval between each company. Y Coy. will move off at 12-30.
(d) Movements East of DRANOUTRE-LOCRE ROAD will be by platoons at 500 yards interval.
(e) Copies of trench store receipts will be handed in to Battalion H.Q. by 10 a.m. 6th inst.
(f) Gum Boots will be taken over as trench stores from the companies relieved.
(g) Completion of reliefs will be immediately reported in code to Battalion H.Q.
(h) Baggage will be stacked by 11 a.m. on the open space East of the Orderly Room in piles by companies, one pile for baggage going to the trenches and another pile for baggage being returned to Quartermaster's Stores.
Transport Officer will arrange the necessary transport.

(signed) G.H. Exham, Capt. & Adjutant,
1st. Royal Munster Fusiliers.

4-1-17.

Copy No. 1 C.O.
2 2nd in Comd.
3 Adjutant
4 Brigade
5 R.S.M.
6 W Coy.
7 X "
8 Y "
9 Z "
10 Qrmr.
11 M.O.
12 File
13 7th Leinster Rgt.

Army Form C. 2118.

Instructions regarding War Diaries and Intelligence Summaries are contained in F. S. Regs., Part II. and the Staff Manual respectively. Title pages will be prepared in manuscript.

WAR DIARY
or
INTELLIGENCE SUMMARY.
(Erase heading not required.)

Place	Date	Hour	Summary of Events and Information	Remarks and references to Appendices

T2134. Wt. W708–776. 500000. 4/15. Sir J. C. & S.

Appendix B.

SECRET. Copy No.____

OPERATION ORDER No.3.

By Captain H.T. Goodland, Commanding 1st. Royal Munster Fusiliers.

1. RELIEF.

1st. R.M.F. will be relieved by the 7th Leinster Rgt. in the Left Subsector, 47th Ibf. Brigade front, on the 13th inst.

2. DISPOSITIONS.

"A" Coy. 7th Leinster Rgt. will relieve "Z" Coy. 1st. R.M.F.
"B" Coy. 7th Leinster Rgt. will relieve "Y" Coy. 1st. R.M.F.
"C" Coy. 7th Leinster Rgt. will re.ieve "W" Coy. 1st. R.M.F.
"D" Coy. 7th Leinster Rgt. will re;ieve "X" Coy. 1st. R.M.F.
in LURGAN CAMP.

The leading platoon of "A" Coy. 7th Leinster Rgt. will be at entrance to REGENT STREET at 12-30 p.m.

3. ADVANCE PARTIES.

C.Q.M.S's. of W X Y & Z Coys. and Sgt. Gunnell for H.Q. Coy. will meet 2/Lieut. R.A. Mudie at DERRY CAMP at 10 a.m. to arrange billets.

4. DETAIL

(a) Gum boots will be handed over as trench stores, and O's.C. Coys. will see that correct receipts are obtained.

(b) Trench store receipts will be handed in to Battn. H.Q. by 10 a.m. 14th inst.

(c) Completion of relief will be immediately reported to Battn. H.Q. in code by wire.

(d) Any blankets, Officers' Mess kits etc., which are required to be taken down by transport to DERRY CAMP will be stacked at FORT EDWARD by 11 a.m. 13th inst.
O.C. "W" Coy. will leave a guard to look after this baggage.
Transport Officer will arrange transport.

(e) Dinners will be had at DERRY CAMP. Arrangements for cookers have been made.

(signed) C.H. Exham, Capt. & Adjutant,
1st. Royal Munster Fusiliers.

12-1-17.

Copy No.1. CO.
2 Adjutant
3 Bde.
4 R.S.M.
5 W Coy.
6 X "
7 Y "
8 Z "
9 Quartermaster
10 Transport Officer
11 File
12 7th Leinster Rgt.

Appendix 6

4.   Copy No.______

O P E R A T I O N   O R D E R   No.4.
BY
Captain T.A.N. Bolton, Commanding 1st. Royal Munster Fusiliers.

-0-0-0-0-0-0-0-0-0-0-0-0-0-0-0-0-0-0-0-0-0-0-0-0-0-0-0-

1. RELIEF.

The 1st. R.M.F. will relieve the 7th Leinster Rgt. in the Left Subsector, 47th Inf. Brigade front, to-morrow 21st. inst.

2. DISPOSITIONS.

"X" Coy. will relieve the front line company of the 7th Leinster Rgt. with three platoons in the front line and one platoon in ULSTER ROAD.
"W" Coy. will relieve the support company of the 7th Leinster Rgt., in S.P.7 and PICCADILLY DUG-OUTS, with 3 platoons in S.P.7 and 1 platoon in PICCADILLY DUG-OUTS.
"Y" Company will relieve the reserve company of the 7th Leinster Rgt., in S.P.8, FORT EDWARD, and RESERVE DUG-OUTS, with 1 platoon in S.P.8., 2 platoons in FORT EDWARD and 1 platoon in RESERVE DUG-OUTS.
"Z" Company will be billeted in the huts at present occupied by Y & Z Coys. in DERRY CAMP.
H.Q. Coy. will take over NEWPORT DUG-OUTS.
Lewis Guns of "W" & "X" Coys. will relieve the guns of the 7th Leinster Rgt. in the positions at present occupied by them.

3. DETAIL.

(a) Lewis Gun teams of "W" & "X" Coys. will parade on the main road outside the Guard Hut under Lieut. G.F. Maher ready to move off at 9-30 a.m. to take over positions.

(b) Advance parties of one officer and 1 N.C.O. from W X Y & H.Q. Coy. and the necessary signallers will leave DERRY CAMP at 10 a.m. Parade on the main road outside Guard Hut.

(c) Companies will move off from their parade grounds at DERRY CAMP at the following times:-

"X" Coy.	12 noon
"W" "	12-15 p.m.
"Y" "	12-30 p.m.
"H.Q."	12-45 p.m.

Company cooks of W X Y & H.Q. Coy. will be marched to the trenches by the Cook Sgt. when ready after dinners.

(d) Movements East of DRANOUTRE-LOCRE ROAD will be by platoons at 300 yards interval.

(e) Copies of Trench Store receipts will be handed in to Battalion H.Q. by 10 a.m. 22nd inst.

(f) Gum boots will be taken over as trench stores from the companies relieved. Great care should be taken in checking the numbers taken over.

(g) Completion of reliefs will be immediately reported to Batts. H.Q. in code by wire.

(h) All baggage will be stacked by 11 a.m. in piles by companies. Care should be taken that the piles of baggage going to the Quartermaster's Stores and those going to the line are kept separate. Transport Officer will arrange the necessary transport.

(signed) C.R. Exham, Capt. & A/Adjutant,

20-1-17.   1st. Royal Munster Fusiliers.

Appendix D

S E C R E T. Copy.No.066

O P E R A T I O N   O R D E R. NO.5.
BY
Captain.H.T.GOODLAND, Commanding, 1st Royal Munster Fusiliers.

1. The 1st ROYAL MUNSTER FUSILIERS will be relieved in the LEFT SUB-SECTION., 47th Brigade Section by the 7th LEINSTER REGT to-day 26th inst.

On completion of relief the 1st ROYAL MUNSTER FUSILIERS will proceed to CURRAGH CAMP. Movement East of DRANOUTRE-LOCRE ROAD to be by platoons at 300 yards interval.

One guide per platoon to be at entrance REGENT STREET at 3-30.p.m.

2.. Trench Store certificates will be sent to Orderly Room by 10.am., 27th inst.

3. Completion of relief to be wired in code to Battalion Headquarters.

4. The Transport Officer will arrange for four limbers, the mess cart and Maltese Cart to report at FORT EDWARD as early as possible for removal of baggage. (6-30.p.m.)

5. One N.C.O. and one man per Company and one N.C.O. and one man of Headquarter Company will report to 2/Lieut Lawlor at CURRAGH CAMP by 2.p.m. to take over quarters.

6. Acknowledge.

Sd/ E.C.COMLEY, 2/Lieut,A/Adjutant.,
1st Royal Munster Fusiliers.

26-1-17.

[M1121] W6378/M780 500m 9/16s G & S E. 369. Forms/W. 3121 3

Army Form W. 3121.

_____ Brigade. _____ Division. _____ Corps. _____ Date of Recommendation.

Schedule No. (to be left blank)	Unit	Regtl. No.	Rank and Name	Action for which commended	Recommended by	Honour or Reward	(To be left blank)

S E C R E T. Copy No. ......4....

Appendix E.

47th Infantry Brigade Order No. 91.

27th January, 1917.

Ref. WYTSCHAETE Map
1/10,000 Ed. 7. A.

1. On the 29th inst the Divisional front will be re-organised as a two Brigade Front., the right sectors being held by 47th and 49th Bdes. alternately, and the Left sector permanently by 48th Bde.

2. The front of the Right Brigade will be from DURHAM ROAD to BROADWAY N.24.c.20.65 exclusive.

3. The dividing line between the Right and Left Brigades will be from BROADWAY, LEFNING LANE (inclusive to Left Brigade) ALSTON HOUSE (N.22.b.6.2.) thence west to BRULOOZE CROSS RDS M.24.c.7.3.

4. The Right Sector will be called SPANBROEK, the Left VIERSTRAAT.

5. 47th Inf.Bde. will take over the Right Sector on 29th inst., two Battalions being in front line, one Battalion in support, and one Battalion in reserve.

6. Battalion fronts will be:-

Right Battalion. Bn. H.Q. NEWPORT DUGOUTS	DURHAM ROAD to 1 Bay N. of PICCADILLY (inclusive)
Left Battalion Bn. H.Q. FORT VICTORIA.	1 Bay N. of PICCADILLY (exclusive) to BROADWAY (exclusive).

7. The 47th M.G.Coy. and 47th T.M.Battery will remain in the Right Subsector and the 49th M.G.Coy. and 49th T.M.Battery in the Left Subsector.

8. 156th Fd.Coy. and 157th Fd.Coy. will work in the Right and Left Subsectors respectively.

9. Reliefs will be carried out in accordance with attached Table. Any other details being arranged direct between, Commanding Officers concerned.

10. Movement East of the DRANOUTRE - LOCRE road will be by platoons at 300 yds interval. The road running South from REGENT STREET to FORT EDWARD will not be used in daylight.

11. Bde. H.Q. will close at DRANOUTRE and re-open at LITTLE KEMMEL (N.20.d.3.3.) on completion of reliefs.

12. Completion of reliefs and arrivals in new positions will be wired in code to Bde. H.Q.

13. Any suggestions by Commanding Officers concerning readjustment of accommodation after new positions have been taken over will be forwarded to Bde. H.Q.

H Priestman
Captain,
Brigade Major, 47th Infantry Brigade

Issued through Signals at 6 p.m.

copy No. 1. 6th Royal Irish Regt.
2. 6th Connaught Rangers.
3. 7th Leinster Regt.
4. 1st Royal Munster Fusiliers.
5. 47th M.G.Company.
6. 47th T.M.Battery.
7. B.B.O.,
8. 108th Inf.Bde.
9. 49th Inf.Bde.
10. 48th Inf. Bde.
11. 16th Division.
12. 16th Division (G)
13. 156th Field Coy. R.E.
14. Spanbroek Group R.F.A.
15. Staff Captain.
16. Bde. Signals.
17. A.D.M.S.
18. B.T.O.
19. Bde. Supply Officer.
20. No. 2 Bde. Pioneers.
21. 157th Fd.Coy. R.E.
22. 49th T.M.Battery.
23. 171 Tunnelling Coy.
24. War Diary.
25.)
26.) retained.

RELIEF TABLE TO ACCOMPANY 47th INF. BDE. ORDER No. 91.

Unit.	From	To	In relief of	Hour of commencement of relief and remarks.
6th Royal Irish Regt.	Present Right Subsector.	Bde. Reserve H.Q. 2 Coys. DERRY HUTS 2 Coys. KEMMEL CHATEAU.	6th Conn.Rangers.	On relief by 7th Leinster Regt.
6th Conn. Rangers.	DERRY HUTS	New Left Subsector. 1 Coy. Front line 1 Coy. Front line 1 Coy. H.Q. and 3) platoons. S.P.11.) 1 platoon S.P.10 1 Coy. (H.Q. & 3 platoons REGENT ST. DUGOUTS. (1 platoon S.P.9.	1 Coy. 7/8 R.I.Fus: 8/R. Innis. Fus. 7/8 R.I.Fus. 8/R.Innis. Fus. 8/R.Innis. Fus.	Via VIA GELLIA) Via PALL MALL.) 11 a.m. 11.30 a.m.
7th Leinster Regt.	Present Left Subsector.	New Right Subsector by absorbing remainder of present Right Subsector. Final dispositions then being:- 2 Coys Front line 2 platoons S.P. 6 2 " S.P. 7 1 platoon S.P. 8 1 ", PICCADILLY DUG-outs. 2 platoons SHAMUS DUG-OUTS.	6th R. Irish Regt.	10 a.m.

P. T. O.

Unit.	From	To	In relief of	Hour of commencement of relief and remarks.
1st R.Munster Fus.	CURRAGH CAMP.	Bde. Support. H.Q. DOCTORS HOUSE 1 Coy. (LA POLKA FM. (SASKATCHEWAN	7/8 R.I.Fus.	
		1 Coy. (YOUNG ST. DUGOUTS. (FORT REGINA.	7/8 R.I.Fus.	12.30 p.m.
		2 Coys (FORT EDWARD. (COOKER FARM. (BEEHIVE DUGOUTS.	7/Leinster Regt.	

S E C R E T.   47th Inf. Bde. No. G. 1232.

6th Royal Irish Regt.
6th Connaught Rangers.
7th Leinster Regt.
1st Royal Munster Fusiliers.

In view of instructions received that there will shortly be a readjustment of the Brigade frontage, inter Battalion reliefs will take place to-morrow:-

Right Subsection:- Commencing relief about 2 p.m.
Left Subsection:- " " " 4 p.m.

Relief orders follow.

[signature]
Captain,
25-1-17. Brigade Major, 47th Infantry Brigade.

SECRET   47th Inf. Bde. No. G. 1235/1.

6th Royal Irish Regt.
6th Connaught Rangers.
7th Leinster Regt.
1st Royal Munster Fusiliers.

Reference Warning Order, G. 1235 dated 26-1-17, the following are the probable arrangements:0

1. The new Brigade front (para. 1.b) will now probably be divided into two sectors
    (a) From N.24.c.30.68 to PICCADILLY exclusive - Left Sector.
    (b) From PICCADILLY inclusive to DURHAM ROAD - Right Sector.

2. Each sector will be held by one battalion, one battalion being in Bde. Support and one battalion in Bde. Reserve.

Battn. H.Q. Left Sector:- FORT VICTORIA (N.28.c.3.6.)
" " Right " :- NEWPORT DUGOUTS.
" " Support Bn.:- DOCTOR'S HOUSE, KEMMEL. (N.21.d.6.6.)

3. The adjustment of front will be carried out on 29th inst. as follows:-

(i) 7th Leinster Regt. will take over Right Sector by absorbing front now held by 6th Royal Irish Regt. before 12 noon on 29th inst.

(ii) 6th Connaught Rangers will take over Left Sector from 49th Inf.Bde. on afternoon 29th inst.

(iii) 1st Royal Munster Fusiliers will take over positions of Battn. in support. (to be notified later)

(iv) 6th Royal Irish Regt will proceed to Bde. Reserve. (DERRY HUTS and KEMMEL CHATEAU)

4. Officers of units ~~####~~ concerned will acquaint themselves with the position of the front line they will take over.

5. As far as possible units will in the future be detailed to sectors as follows:-

7th Leinster Regt.) 1st R.M.F.)	Right Sector.	6th R.Irish Regt) 6th Conn.Rangers)	Left sector.

[signature]

Captain,
Brigade Major, 47th Infantry Brigade.

26-1-17.

W A R D I A R Y.

FOR MONTH OF FEBRUARY, 1917.

VOLUME ____________

UNIT:- 1st R. Munster Fusiliers.

Vol 12

Army Form C. 2118.

WAR DIARY
or
INTELLIGENCE SUMMARY.
(Erase heading not required.)

Instructions regarding War Diaries and Intelligence Summaries are contained in F. S. Regs., Part II. and the Staff Manual respectively. Title pages will be prepared in manuscript.

1st Royal Munster Fusiliers

Place	Date	Hour	Summary of Events and Information	Remarks and references to Appendices
SPANBROEK SECTOR R.	1/2/17		Strength – Officers 44. OR 1100 From Hospital 3 OR To base under age 1 To Hospital 1.	
BDE SUPPORT FRONT LINE	2/2/17		Strength – Officers 44. OR 1101. From Hospital 5 OR Wounded 1. Relieved the 7th Leinster Regt in the R. SUB SECTION in the front line	Appendix A
	3/2/17		Strength Officers 44. OR 1103 To Hospital 1 OR. Enemy artillery very active throughout the day. Our [illegible] fired on a [illegible] working party of about 20. Five of them fell	
	4/2/17		Strength Officers 44, OR 1102, To Hospital 4, Wounded 1. [illegible] with [illegible] during the afternoon. The enemy [illegible] during the night bring in his wounded. Night fairly quiet	
	5/2/17		Strength Officers 44 OR 1097. To Hospital [illegible] OR. [illegible] OR. Enemy very jumpy opposite our front. Enemy shelled our [illegible]	

2353 Wt. W2544/1454 700,000 5/15 D. D. & L. A.D.S.S./Forms/C. 2118.

Instructions regarding War Diaries and Intelligence Summaries are contained in F. S. Regs., Part II. and the Staff Manual respectively. Title pages will be prepared in manuscript.

WAR DIARY
or
INTELLIGENCE SUMMARY.
(*Erase heading not required.*)

1st Royal Munster Fusiliers

Army Form C. 2118.

Place	Date	Hour	Summary of Events and Information	Remarks and references to Appendices
SPANBROEK SECTOR FRONT LINE	5 2/17		During the night pamphlets were distributed in the Hun lines, printed in German – The Saxons are still opposing us.	
	6 2/17		Strength Officers 44. OR 1097. From Hospital OR 4 To Hospital 3 OR Wounded 1 OR The 49th Bde relieved the 47th Inf Bde, The latter went into Divisional Reserve The 2nd R. Irish Regt relieved the 1st R Munster Fus, the latter went into reserve at WAKEFIELD CAMP	App B
WAKEFIELD CAMP	7 2/17		Strength: Officers 44, OR 1097. The Companies were at the disposal of Company commanders.	~~App B~~
	8 2/17		Strength Officers 44. OR 1097 From Hospital 2 OR. To Hospital 5 OR. Kit inspections & Baths for men	
	9 2/17		Strength Officers 44, OR 1094 From Hospital 3 OR To Hospital 5 OR. 2/Lt Lane to Hospital, Musketry parades Physical training & Bayonet fighting	

2353 Wt W2544/1454 700,000 5/15 D. D. & L. A.D.S.S./Forms/C. 2118.

Instructions regarding War Diaries and Intelligence Summaries are contained in F. S. Regs., Part II. and the Staff Manual respectively. Title pages will be prepared in manuscript.

WAR DIARY
or
~~INTELLIGENCE~~ SUMMARY.

(Erase heading not required.)

Army Form C. 2118.

1st Royal Inniskilling Fusiliers

Place	Date	Hour	Summary of Events and Information	Remarks and references to Appendices
WAKEFIELD CAMP	10/2/17		Strength: Officers 44, OR 1092, From Hospital 4, To Hospital OR 7. Parades: Musketry, Route march, Parchment certificates were distributed to 32 officers and OR, for bravery in the field. The Battalion was paraded for the presentation.	
	11/2/17		Strength:- Officers 44 OR 1092 From Hospital 4 OR To Hospital 9 OR. Divine Service parades; Mass at 9am at DRANOUTRE Church, C of E at 11am at LOCRE.	
	12/2/17		Strength:- Officers 44. OR 1094. To Hospital 5 OR Parades. Platoon Drill, Bayonet fighting, Games, Company Drill, Practice taking cover against hostile aeroplanes.	
	13/2/17		Strength: Officers 44 OR 1089. From Hospital 1 OR. To Hospital 5 OR. Parades, Platoon Drill, Bayonet Fighting, Route March.	

Instructions regarding War Diaries and Intelligence Summaries are contained in F. S. Regs., Part II. and the Staff Manual respectively. Title pages will be prepared in manuscript.

WAR DIARY
or
~~INTELLIGENCE SUMMARY.~~
(Erase heading not required.)

Army Form C. 2118.

1st Royal Munster Fusiliers

Place	Date	Hour	Summary of Events and Information	Remarks and references to Appendices
WAKEFIELD	14 2/17		Strength Officers 44. OR 1084. Rejoined 2 OR, Hospital 4 OR.	
CAMP			The 47th Bde will relieve the 49th Bde in the SPANBROEK SECTION to-day	
SPANBROEK			The 1st R.M. Fus will relieve the 7th R Inniskilling Fus. in Bde Reserve in	
SECTOR			DERRY CAMP & KEMMEL CHATEAU.	APP. C
	15 2/17		Strength – Officers 44. OR 1082, From Hospital 2 OR. To Hospital 7 OR.	
			Rifle & Foot inspections inside Billets	
	16 2/17		Strength Officers 44. OR. 1077 To Hospital 1 OR. To U K. 1 OR.	
	17 2/17		Strength Officers 44. OR 1075, From Hospital 1 OR. To Hospital 3 Wounded 9 OR.	
			The enemy fired a lachrymatory shell at the CHATEAU, it struck the outer	
			wall & the brickwork injured 9 men.	
	18 2/17		Strength Officers 44. OR 1064. To Hospital 3 OR. Col Clarke to U.K. (1).	
			The 1st R M Fus will relieve the 7th Leinster Regt in the R. Sub Section today	App D
			Coys will have 2 platoons in front line & 2 in support, except W Coy who	

Instructions regarding War Diaries and Intelligence Summaries are contained in F. S. Regs., Part II. and the Staff Manual respectively. Title pages will be prepared in manuscript.

WAR DIARY
or
INTELLIGENCE SUMMARY.
(Erase heading not required.)

Army Form C. 2118.

1st Royal Munster Fusiliers

Place	Date	Hour	Summary of Events and Information	Remarks and references to Appendices
PANBROEK SECTOR RIGHT SUB SECTION	19 2/17		Strength Officers 43. OR 1061 Rejoined 2OR. To U.K. 2 Killed 2OR wounded 1OR Hospital 3OR. During the night our artillery was very active. The enemy sent up a number of very lights. At 7.15 am our artillery opened an intense bombardment on hostile trenches. The 6th Connaught Rangers raided the enemy trenches from our front. The enemy were prepared for them & had their front trench crowded with men and a number of machine guns. The Rangers were unable to get through. At 6.55 pm the enemy blew a camouflet.	
	20 2/17		Strength Officers 43 OR 1055 to hospital 1OR. Enemy shelled our supports, our Lewis gunners [illegible]. The enemy blew another camouflet at 5am.	
	21 2/17		Strength Officers 43. OR 1054. Officer killed 1. wounded 1OR. Hospital 2. 2/Lieut Baily was sniped at about 6 am.	
	22 2/17		Strength Officers 43. OR 1053. Draft 2OR. Killed 2OR. wounded 1OR [illegible] 1 OR. To hospital 2 OR. The 47th Bde relieved by the 49th Bde. The 7/8 R Irish Fus relieved the 1st R Mun Fus. The latter went into Divisional Reserve at [illegible]FIELD CAMP.	

2353 Wt. W2544/1454 700,000 5/15 D. D. & L. A.D.S.S./Forms/C. 2118.

Instructions regarding War Diaries and Intelligence Summaries are contained in F. S. Regs., Part II. and the Staff Manual respectively. Title pages will be prepared in manuscript.

WAR DIARY
or
INTELLIGENCE SUMMARY.
(Erase heading not required.)

Army Form C. 2118.

1st Royal Munster Fusiliers

Place	Date	Hour	Summary of Events and Information	Remarks and references to Appendices
WAKEFIELD CAMP	23 2/17		Strength Officers 43, OR 1049. Draft 1 officer OR 5. Companies at disposal of Company Commanders for cleaning equipment etc.	
	24 2/17		Strength Officers 44, OR 1052 From hospital 1 OR To hospital 4 OR. Companies at disposal of company commanders. The Baths at LOCRE are alloted to Bn.	
	25 2/17		Strength Officers 44 OR 1051 From hospital 1 OR, To hospital 5 OR. Divine service parade. Mass in the church at DRANOUTRE at 9 am C of E 9.30. The Bn paraded in the new formation at 2 pm	
	26 2/17		Strength Officers 42 OR 1047 From hospital 2 OR To hospital 2 OR. The Bn were inspected by the Bde commander in the new formation. The men presented a very smart appearance and were complimented by the Brigadier. Company Platoon Drill under the R.S.M at 11-30 am	
	27 2/17		Strength Officers 44, OR 1047. Draft 3 OR. Rejoined 4 OR. To hospital 3 OR. The Bn went on a route march of about 7 miles. They proceeded by Companies. Lieut G R Baldwin evacuated to U.K. 15/2/17 vide G.R.O. 423.	

2353 Wt. W2544/1454 700,000 5/15 D. D. & L. A.D.S.S./Forms/C. 2118.

Instructions regarding War Diaries and Intelligence Summaries are contained in F. S. Regs., Part II. and the Staff Manual respectively. Title pages will be prepared in manuscript.

WAR DIARY
or
INTELLIGENCE SUMMARY.
(Erase heading not required.)

Army Form C. 2118.

1st Royal Munster Fusiliers

Place	Date	Hour	Summary of Events and Information	Remarks and references to Appendices
WAKEFIELD CAMP	28/2/17		Strength Officers 43, OR 1051 Parades, Company drill, wearing gas helmets, Bayonet fighting. Bn in mass under R.S.M. for Rifle exercises	
			[illegible] Capt 1st R.M.F.	

2353 Wt. W2544/1454 700,000 5/15 D. D. & L. A.D.S.S./Forms/C. 2118.

Appendix A

SECRET.

OPERATION ORDER No.7.

BY

Captain.H.T.Goodland, Commanding 1st Royal Munster Fusiliers.

---

1. The 1st R.M.F., will relieve the 7th LEINSTER REGT in the Right Subsection SPANBROEK Sector on the 2nd inst.

2. "Y" Coy will relieve "A" Coy 7th LEINSTER REGT on front DURHAM ROAD to approx. N.35.9., with 2 platoons in the front line and 2 platoons in SHAMUS DUGOUTS.(Farm)
Coy H.Q. SHAMUS DUGOUTS with 2 Officers always in front line.

"W" Coy will relieve "D" Coy 7th LEINSTER REGT in front of REDAN AVENUE to approx. 50 yards right of KINGSWAY, with 2 platoons in front line and 1 platoon in S.P.6.
One platoon of this company will act as permanent garrison of S.P.6.
Bombing post in broken line N.35.9. will be served by this company.
Coy H.Q. S.P.6.

"Z" Coy will relieve "C" Coy 7th LEINSTER REGT on front PICCADILLY. REDAN AVENUE, with 3 platoons in front line and 1 platoon in ULSTER ROAD.
Coy H.Q. ULSTER ROAD.

"X" Coy will relieve "B" Coy 7th LEINSTER REGT with 1 platoon in S.P.8, 1 platoon in PICCADILLY DUGOUTS., and will furnish permanent garrison of 2 Platoons in S.P.7.
Coy H.Q. S.P.7.

3. RELIEFS.
Reliefs will commence at 4-30.p.m. Battalion H.Q. will be at NEWPORT DUGOUTS.
Certificates for trench stores handed over and taken over will be sent to Battalion H.Q. by 10.a.m. 3rd inst.

4. Completion of reliefs will be reported to Battalion H.Q. NEWPORT DUGOUTS in code by wire.

5. 1 Officer 1 N.C.O. per company and 1 N.C.O. and 1 man from H.Q.Coy will take over trench stores, and if necessary 1 N.C.O. and 1 man per Coy will be left behind to hand over trench stores.

6. Extra blankets will be dumped at the DOCTOR'S HOUSE & FORT EDWARD Transport Officer will arrange for removal by empty ration limbers.

Sd/ E.C.Comley, 2/Lieut,A/Adjutant.
1st Royal Munster Fusiliers.

2-2-17.

S E C R E T

OPERATION ORDER No. 8.

By

Captain. H. T. Goodland., Commanding 1st Royal Munster Fusiliers.

---

1. The 49th Infantry Brigade will relieve the 47th Infantry Brigade in the SPANBROEK SECTOR on the 6th inst.

2. The 1st ROYAL MUNSTER FUSILIERS willb be relieved in the RIGHT SUBSECTION by the 2nd ROYAL IRISH REGIMENT.

Reliefs to commence at 5-30.p.m.

"A" Coy 2nd ROYAL IRISH REGIMENT will relieve "X" Coy 1st R.M.F.
"C" Coy " " " " " " "[illegible]" " " "
"B" Coy " " " " " " "[illegible]" " " "
"D" Coy " " " " " " "[illegible]" " " "

Companies will detail one guide each to meet relieving Lewis Gun Team "X" & "Y" Coy guides to be at entrance of KINGSWAY and "[illegible]" & "[illegible]" Coy guides to be at entrance of REGENT STREET at 10.a.m.

Companies will also detail one guide per PLATOON "X" & "Y" Coy guides will be at entrance of KINGSWAY and "[illegible]" & "[illegible]" guides will be at entrance of REGENT STREET at 4-45.p.m.

On completion of relief the Battalion will move to [illegible] CAMP.

Movement East of [illegible] ROAD will be by platoons at [illegible] yards interval.

3. Trench Store reciepts to be sent to Battalion H.Q. by 10.a.m. 7th inst.

4. Completion of reliefs will be reported to Battalion H.Q. [illegible] by wire in code. Arrival in camp will be reported to O.R.

5. Lieut [illegible] and 1 N.C.O. and 1 man per company will report at Battalion H.Q. at 10-30.a.m. to recieve orders for taking over [illegible] CAMP.

C.Q.M.S.'s will report to Lieut [illegible] at [illegible] CAMP at 12.30 p.m.

Sd/ [illegible], 2/Lieut. A/Adjutant,
1st Royal Munster Fusiliers.

5-2-17.

Appendix "C"

S E C R E T.

O P E R A T I O N   O R D E R   No.9.

By

Captain H.T.Goodland., Commanding 1st Royal Munster Fusiliers.

****

1. 47th Inf.Brigade will relieve the 49th Inf. Brigade in the SPANBROEK SECTION on the 14th inst.

2. 1st R.M.F. will relieve the 7th ROYAL INNISKILLING FUSILIERS in Brigade Reserve in DERRY CAMP and KEMMEL CHATEAU.

3. "W" & " Z" Companies will relieve the companies at present in KEMMEL CHATEAU. "X" & "Y" Companies will relieve the companies at present in DERRY CAMP.
H.Q.Company, including pipers will be billeted in DERRY CAMP.
"W" Company will parade on the main road outside WAKEFIELD CAMP and will move off at 12 noon.
"Z" Company will parade on the main road outside WAKEFIELD CAMP AND WILL move off at 12-15.p.m.
The route to be followed by the above two companies will be via LOCRE.
"X" Company will parade on the main road outside WAKEFIELD CAMP and will move off at 12-30.p.m.
"Y" Company will parade on the main road outside WAKEFIELD CAMP and will move off at 12-45.p.m.
H.Q.Company will parade on the main road outside BATTALION.H.Q. at 1-10.p.m.

4. Movements East of LOCRE-DRANOUTRE ROAD will be by platoons at 300 yards distance.

5. Advance parties will be as follows:-
1.N.C.O. and 2 men each from "W" & "Z" Companies will parade outside WAKEFIELD CAMP at 10.a.m. under an Officer to be detailed by O.C. "W" Coy and will proceed to KEMMEL CHATEAD to take over billets and stores.
1.N.C.O. and 2 men each from "X" & "Y" Companies and 1.N.C.O. and 2 men from H.Q.Company, all under an Officer to be detailed by O.C. "X" Company, will parade outside WAKEFIELD CAMP at 10-30.a.m. and will proceed to DERRY CAMP to take over billets and stores.

6. Dinners will be at WAKEFIELD CAMP before Battalion moves off. O's.C. Companies will arrange.

7. Packs will be carried. Blankets and all baggage etc, will be stacked by 11-30.a.m. outside the guard room WAKEFIELD CAMP.
Transport Officer will arrange the necessary transport.

8. Lists of stores taken over will be rendered to Battalion H.Q. by 10.a.m. 15th inst.

9. Completion of reliefs will be immediately reported in B.A.B. Code to Battalion H.Q. by wire.

Sd/ C.H.Exham, Captain,A/Adjutant,

1st Royal Munster Fusiliers.

13-2-17.

Appendix D

SECRET. No. 10.

OPERATION ORDERS

By

Captain E.T.Goodland, Commanding 1st Royal Munster Fusiliers.

---

1. The 1st ROYAL MUNSTER FUSILIERS will relieve the 7th LEINSTER REGT in the Right Sub-Section., SPANBROEK SECTOR on the 18th inst.

2. "X" Coy.1st R.M.F. will relieve the right company 7th LEINSTER REGT on front from Junction of DURHAM ROAD and Front Line exclusive to approximately midway between N.36.8. and N.36,9., with 2 platoons in front line and 2 platoons in SHAMUS DUG-OUTS.

Company H.qrs will be in SHAMUS DUG-OUTS.
Route will be via KINGSWAY-SAPPER LANE-DURHAM ROAD.

"Y" Coy.1st R.M.F. will relieve the centre company 7th LEINSTER REGT on front from approximately midway between N.36.8. and N.36.9., to Junction REDAN AVENUE and Front Line inclusive with 2 platoons in the front line and 2 platoons in S.P.6.

One of these platoons will be detailed by the O.C.Coy as the garrison of S.P.6.

Coy.H.Q. will be at S.P.6.
Route via KINGSWAY.

"W" Coy 1st R.M.F. will relieve the left company 7th LEINSTER REGT on front from REDAN AVENUE exclusive to 1 bay north of Junction of PICCADILLY and Front Line inclusive, with 3 platoons in the front line and 1 platoon in ULSTER ROAD.

Coy H.Q. will be in ULSTER ROAD.
Route will be via REGENT STREET and PICCADILLY.

"Z" Coy 1st R.M.F. will relieve support company 7th LEINSTER REGT in S.P. 7.,PICCADILLY DUG-OUTS and S.P.8., with 2 platoons in S.P.7., 1 platoon in PICCADILLY DUG-OUTS and 1 platoon in S.P.8.

The 2 platoons in S.P.7., and 1 platoon in S.P.8., are garrisons of their respective strong points.

Coy.H.Q. will be at S.P.7.
Route will be via REGENT STREET and PICCADILLY.

Battalion Headquarters will be at NEWPORT DUG-OUTS. H.Q.Coy will move off at 5-15.p.m. and will proceed via REGENT STREET.

3. "W" Coy will be at entrance to REGENT STREET at 4-30.p.m.
"Y" Coy will be at entrance to KINGSWAY at 4-30.p.m.
"Z" Coy will be at entrance to REGENT STREET at 5.p.m.
"X" Coy will be at entrance to KINGSWAY at 5.p.m.
All movements will be at 300 yards interval between platoons.

4. Advance parties of 1 Officer, 1 N.C.O., and 2 men per company and 1 N.C.O and 2 men from H.Q.Coy will proceed in the morning to take over stores.

5. All Lewis Gun teams under their Company Lewis Gun Officer will proceed at 1.p.m. to take over their respective positions.

6. 2/Lieut J.H.Hartley and 1 N.C.O. and 2 men from "Z" Coy will remain behind if necessary to hand over KEMMEL CHATEAU.

2/Lieut F.M.F.West and 1 N.C.O. and 2 men from H.Q.Coy will remain if necessary to hand over DERRY CAMP.

7. Certificates of stores handed over and taken over will be rendered to Battalion H.Q. by 10.a.m. 19th inst.

8. Completions of relief will be reported to Battalion H.Q. in NEWPORT DUG-OUTS immediately in code by wire.

9. Transport Officer will arrange transport.

Sd/ C.H.Exham, Captain, A/Adjutant,
1st Royal Munster Fusiliers.

-2-17.

Appendix E.

O P E R A T I O N   O R D E R   No.11.   18-2-17.

By

Captain H.T.Goodland,Commanding, 1st Royal Munster Fusiliers,

---

Reference. WYTSCHAETE. Trench Map. 1/10000 edition 4.A.
and PLOEGSTEERT. -do- -do- 4. A.
and Brigade Trench Map D.N.27. Scale 1/10000.

---

1. A raid will be carried out by the 6th Battn Connaugth Rangers in accordance with 47th Infantry Brigade Operation Order No.96 on the enemy's Front.

Parties will enter the enemy's trenches at about the following points:- N.36.d.20.78., N.36.b.05.10., N.36.a.80.30.,

2. In accordance with para.4. of the above mentioned Operation Order O.C. Companies have already received notification in code that the O.C. 6th Connaught Rangers has decided on the operation taking place to-morrow morning 7-15.a.m. (19th inst)

If a postponement subsequent to this decision is absolutly necessary

O.C. Companies will be informed by a telegram from Battn H.Qrs in the pre-arranged code word.

3. In accordance with para.6. of the said Brigade Orders the following are the arrangements for transmitting the decision of O.C.Connaught Rangers as to the use of smoke or not.

An officer of "X" Company will be at the battle headquarters of the O.C. Connaught Rangers in the Front Line between N.36.5., and N.36.6., at 5.a.m. to-morrow morning the 19th inst, he will be handed the decision in writing by the O.C. Connaught Rangers. He will then immediately proceed with the message via the Front Line to the Right of "Y" Company there he will meet an officer of "Y" Company and hand over message. This Officer of "Y" Company will proceed at once via Front Line and REDAN AVENUE to the junction of LONG LANE & ULSTER ROAD, here he will meet an officer of "W" Company to whom he will hand the message. This officer of "W" Company will proceed at once via ULSTER ROAD & PICCADILLY to the Left of "W" Company one bay North of PICCADILLY in the Front Line and will hand over the message to an Officer of the 6th Royal Irish Regt who will be there, he will then go along his own front line and warn the men of his company.
These Officers will be detailed by the O.C.Companies concerned.

4. In accordance with the above mentioned Brigade Order the following are the arrangements for the distribution of"P.Smoke Bombs"and"Smoke Cases" in the Front Line. Stores of these are at present at SHAMUS DUGOUTS. The following parties will be sent to SHAMUS DUGOUTS by the O.C.Companies concerned on reciept of the message "SUPPER READY" from Battalion H.Qrs.
"Z" Company one party of 2 N.C.O's and 30 men to carry 25 boxes of 12 "P - Bombs " or 300 bombs in all., to O.C."W" Company.
Another party of 1 N.C.O. and 12 men to carry 30 "Smoke Cases" to O.C."W" Company, these will be carried 3 in sandbag, O.C.Company should arrange for sandbags.
"Y" Company 2 N.C.O. and 25 men to carry 21 boxes or 250 Bombs in all to O.C. "Y" Company.
Another party of 1 N.C.O. and 4 men to carry 10 "Smoke Cases" in sandbags to O.C. "Y" Company.
"X" Company on receipt of message will arrange for 50 "P.Bombs" to be carried to his remaining posts in Front Line also 10 "Smoke Cases" in sandbags.
The distribution of the above will be in accordance made at the conference with the Commanding Officer.
Care should be taken by the O.C. Companies concerned to see that the necessary lighting arrangements are brought by their parties.

5. The dispositions of men on the Comapny Fronts will be as arranged at the conference with the Commanding Officer.

6. SYNCHRONIZATION of Watches will take place in the following method. At the following times an officer from each company will ring up the Adjutant at Headquarters. They will merely ask for F.M.3 and the Adjutant will answer they must not ask for the Adjutant or Puce, on asking what is the time in as off-hand a way as possible they will be told either wait a sec, or wait a minute and when a "Dead Minute" comes round will be told the time. Times of ringing up will be as follows:-

"W" Company near 5.a.m. "X" Company near 5-25.am.
"Y" Company near 5-40.a.m. "Z" Company at 6-15.a.m.

7. If anything in these orders is not perfectly clear to every O.C.Company he will at once send a message to Battn H.Qrs asking for further explanation which will immediately be sent in as clear a manner as possible.

Cecil. H. De Law.
Captain, A/Adjutant,
1st Royal Munster Fusiliers.

SECRET. No.12. 21-2-17. Appendix "F"

OPERATION ORDER

By

Captain H.T.Goodland, Commanding 1st Battn.Royal Munster Fusiliers.

-------------------------oooooooooo-------------------

1. The 7/8th Royal Irish Fusiliers will relieve the 1st Royal Munster Fusiliers in the Right Subsection- SPANBROEK - MOLEN SECTOR on the 22nd instant.

2. "C" Coy 7/8th R.I.Fus will relieve "X" Coy 1st R.M.Fus with 2 platoons in the Front Line and 2 platoons at SHAMUS DUGOUTS.
"A" Coy 7/8th R.I.Fus will relieve "Y" Coy 1st R.M.Fus with 2 platoons in the Front Line and 2 platoons in S.P.6.
"B" Coy 7/8th R.I.Fus will relieve "W" Coy 1st R.M.Fus with 2 platoons in the Front Line and 2 platoons in ULSTER ROAD.
"D" Coy 7/8th R.I.Fus will relieve "Z" Coy 1st R.M.Fus with 2 platoons in S.P.7., 1 platoon in S.P.8., and 1 platoon in S.P.8 and PICCADILLY DUGOUTS.

3. 1 guide per platoon from "W" & "Z" Coys will be at LINDENHOEK CROSS ROADS at 5-30.p.m.
1 guide per platoon from "X" & "Y" Coys will be at DAYLIGHT CORNER at 5-30.p.m.
On relief companies will march to WAKEFIELD CAMP where the Battalion will be billeted.

4. Lewis Guns will be relieved in the morning., 1 guide per gun will be at DAYLIGHT CORNER at 11.a.m.

5. The Quartermaster will take over WAKEFIELD CAMP.
He will arrange for the 4 C.Q.M.Sgts and Sgt Gunnell for H.Q.Coy to attend.

6. Movements East of the LOCRE - DRANOUTRE ROAD will be by platoons at 300 yards interval.

7. Trench Store lists will be rendered to Battalion H.Q. by 10.a.m. the 23rd instant.
Great care should be taken in handing over these stores.

8. Any baggage to be removed from the trenches to WAKEFIELD CAMP will be piled by "W" & "Z" Coys and H.Q.Coy at FORT EDWARD., and by "X" & "Y" Coys at SHAMUS DUGOUTS.
Transport Officer will arrange transport.
Company horses will be at DAYLIGHT CORNER at 7.p.m.
H.Q.Coy horses will be at DAYLIGHT CORNER at 7-30.p.m.

9. Completion of reliefs will be immediately reported in code by wire to Battalion Headquarters.

Sd/ C.H.Exham,Captain,A/Adjutant.,
1st Battn Royal Munster Fusiliers.

W A R D I A R Y

FOR MONTH OF MARCH, 1917.

VOLUME ___

U N I T :- 1st Btn Royal Munster Fusiliers

Vol 13

Army Form C. 2118.

Instructions regarding War Diaries and Intelligence Summaries are contained in F. S. Regs., Part II. and the Staff Manual respectively. Title pages will be prepared in manuscript.

WAR DIARY
or
INTELLIGENCE SUMMARY.

(*Erase heading not required.*)

1st R Munster Fusiliers

Place	Date	Hour	Summary of Events and Information	Remarks and references to Appendices
Wakefield Camp	1/3/17		Battn. in camp. Enemy shelled Obtn. Balloon near camp. Shells (4.2) falling on LOCRE-DRANOUTRE road. Casualties occurred on road. Company training. Strength, O-42, OR 1031. To Hospital 6. Killed 1, Wounded 3. From Hospital 2.	
SPANBROEK SECTION.	2/3/17		Battn. moved into line relieving the 2nd R. Irish Regt. Relief complete 9 p.m. To Hospital 5, 1 to Base, Rejoined 5. Strength O 42: OR 1023.	Battn. Optn. order No 13.
Right Sub-Sector	3/3/17		Quiet day. CLOGHER VALLEY blown in in two places. Improved wire opposite CLOGHER VALLEY and DURHAM ROAD. Strength, O 42 OR. 1022. To Base 2, Wounded 1, Rejoined 1.	Bde order No. 99
"	4/3/17		Quiet night and forenoon. At 3 pm. our Artillery bombarded enemy back lines - duration 1½ hours. Enemy did not retaliate. Strength, O 42, OR 1020. To Hospital 4, Draft of 9 OR joined. Continued work, draining trenches, revetting breaks.	
"	5/3/17		Quiet night. Considerable trench mortaring by enemy during forenoon and up to 3.30 pm. He appears to be sending over a new variety with louder report. All fell in close vicinity of DEAD-HAIRS	

2353 Wt. W2544/1454 700,000 5/15 D. D. & L. A.D.S.S./Forms/C. 2118.

Instructions regarding War Diaries and Intelligence Summaries are contained in F. S. Regs., Part II. and the Staff Manual respectively. Title pages will be prepared in manuscript.

WAR DIARY
or
INTELLIGENCE SUMMARY.

(*Erase heading not required.*) 1. R. Muns. Fus.

(2)

Army Form C. 2118.

Place	Date	Hour	Summary of Events and Information	Remarks and references to Appendices
"			HOUSE and BULL RING. Snow fell in early morning. Large DUD	
			minenwerfer fell near DURHAM ROAD in patrol trench. 10in dia and	
			25in length with heavy brass driving band with lugs. If it exploded it	
			would have caused heavy casualties. Trenches in very wet condition.	
			Continued draining and rebuilding. Strength. O, 42 OR 1025.	
			To Hospital 1, Lieut COLFER died in hospital, from injuries re-	
			ceived by horse falling during frosty weather. Struck off strength.	
	6/3/17		Quiet night. Enemy Camouflet blown at about 5 a.m. Reported	
			opposite PECKHAM. 36 Div. Artillery on our right bombarded enemy	
			lines at 10 a.m. At 5.30 Battn was relieved by 7 Leinster Regt.	Battn. Optn
			Relief complete 8.30 pm. X Coy to COOKER FARM & GALWAY DUGOUTS.	orders
			W Coy. to FORT EDWARD & BEEHIVE DUGOUTS. Y Coy. to FORT REGINA &	No 14.
			YONGE STREET DUGOUTS, Z Coy to LA POLKA FARM & FORT SASKATCHE-	Bde order
			WAN. Battn. H.Q. at DOCTORS HOUSE. Battn goes into Bde Support.	No [illegible]
			Strength O-41, OR 1024. To Hospital 2, Killed 1, Rejoined 4.	
			Lieut FISHER struck off strength.	

Instructions regarding War Diaries and Intelligence Summaries are contained in F. S. Regs., Part II. and the Staff Manual respectively. Title pages will be prepared in manuscript.

WAR DIARY
or
INTELLIGENCE SUMMARY.
(Erase heading not required.)

Army Form C. 2118.

(3)

1 R. Muns. Fus.

Place	Date	Hour	Summary of Events and Information	Remarks and references to Appendices
DOCTORS HOUSE	7/3/17		Battn. in Bde. Support. Z Coy working on FORT SASKATCHEWAN rebuilding and draining. Y Coy working parties at KETCHEN AVE & ALBERTA. W Coy. working parties at ULSTER ROAD. X Coy working at SP 6 and DURHAM ROAD. Strength O. 40, OR. 1025. Rejoined 3.	
"	8/3/17		All Coys provided working parties. At 3·30 pm enemy started very intensive bombardment on front and support lines of whole section also right and left sections. SP 6 and SP 7 very heavily shelled. All Companies at once stood to and awaited orders. Enemy attacked on left sub-sector at 5 p.m. Batt. H.Q. shelled at DOCTORS HOUSE by 4·2 s. Direct hit obtained at about 4·30 pm on Battn. Water Cart which was demolished and wounding 7 men. Another direct hit on house at 9 pm was obtained with no casualties and little damage. Strength. O. 40, OR, 1028. Wounded 7, Killed 1,. Lieut CREGAN struck off strength.	
"	9/3/17		All Coys providing working parties. Enemy raided on Right Sub-sector at 5 am "S.O.S. attack" given and replied to promptly by our	

2353 Wt. W2544/1454 700,000 5/15 D. D. & L. A.D.S.S./Forms/C. 2118.

Instructions regarding War Diaries and Intelligence Summaries are contained in F. S. Regs., Part II. and the Staff Manual respectively. Title pages will be prepared in manuscript.

WAR DIARY
or
INTELLIGENCE SUMMARY.
(*Erase heading not required.*)

(4)

Army Form C. 2118.

1 R Muns. Fus.

Place	Date	Hour	Summary of Events and Information	Remarks and references to Appendices
			artillery. Coys at COOKER FARM, FORT EDWARD and BEEHIVE DUGOUTS stood to. Strength, O. 39. OR 1020. To Hospital 1, Rejoined 5. 2/Lieuts HARTLEY and McKEOWN to R.F.C.	
Right Sub-Section Spanbroek Molen Section	10/3/17		Battn ordered to relieve 7 Leinster Regt in SPANBROEK-MOLEN SECTOR instead of going into reserve. Relief began at 5.45 pm. Owing to intelligence of possible enemy attack the Leinster relief was stopped, and for some hours the Right Sub-section was doubly manned. At 2 am 11 inst, relief ordered to proceed. Relief complete at 4.30 am. Our patrol on right company front encountered an enemy patrol and a bombing affair ensued. Enemy withdrew. No casualties. 2 men who were left in a crater coming in afterwards. All front line and support trenches in very damaged condition from recent bombardment. Strength, O. 37. OR 1022. To Hospital 10, Rejoined 6. Draft of 5 joined. 3 Officers joined. 2nd Lieuts BORTHWHISTLE - LANG - O'BRIEN.	Battn Optn order No 15 (Cancelled) Optn order No 16. Bde order No 101. (Cancelled) Bde order 102.

2353 Wt. W2544/1454 700,000 5/15 D. D. & L. A.D.S.S./Forms/C. 2118.

Instructions regarding War Diaries and Intelligence Summaries are contained in F. S. Regs., Part II. and the Staff Manual respectively. Title pages will be prepared in manuscript.

WAR DIARY
or
INTELLIGENCE SUMMARY.
(Erase heading not required.)

1 R. Muns. Fus

5

Army Form C. 2118.

Place	Date	Hour	Summary of Events and Information	Remarks and references to Appendices
Spanbroek Section Right Sub-Sector.	11/3/17		All Coys in front line at work repairing breaks in line. Enemy very quiet. Sniper active opposite CLOGHER VALLEY and got one hit. Strength. O.40. OR 1023. Wounded 1, To hospital 6.	
	12/3/17		Quiet night. enemy holding their front line by small patrols only, who fire lights. Repairing work continuing. Enemy very quiet all day. Strength. O.40 OR 1016. To hospital 4. Rejoined 7. 2nd Lieut Lane struck off strength (R Dub F. attd)	
DERRY HUTS.	13/3/17		Quiet night, and enemy quiet all day. Relieved by the 15 R. Irish Rifles. Front line adjusted by Right Section (DURHAM ROAD) being taken over at noon by a Coy of 9 R Irish Fus. W Coy going to DERRY. Relief commenced at 5.45pm Complete at 10 pm. Coys marched as follows W & X to DERRY HUTS; Y & Z to KEMMEL CHATEAU. Strength O.39 OR 1019. To hospital 3, Rejoined 3.	Bttn. Opn. order No 17. Bde order No 103
	14/3/17		At DERRY HUTS & KEMMEL CHATEAU. Heavy bombardment on right at 1 am. Battery S of Camp shelled by 4.2s. during afternoon. Battalion moved to billets in BERTHON AREA, and relieved by 10 R Irish Rifles at 5 pm Companies marched to billets independently on relief. Relief complete at 7.50 pm. Battalion in billets at 12 midnight. Bde. H.Q. at THIERSHOEK. Strength. O.39. OR. 1020. To hospital 2, Rejoined 5.	Bttn Opn order No 18
BERTHON AREA.	15/3/17		Battalion commenced training. Strength. O.39. OR 1023. To hospital 2, Rejoined 1.	
	16/3		Battalion training. Strength O.39. OR 1022. To hospital 1, Rejoined 8, Draft joined 20	
"	17/3		do. Strength O.39. OR 1049. Rejoined 1. St PATRICKS DAY Church parade and sports.	
	18/3		Battalion training. Strength O.39. OR 1050. Rejoined 1.	

2353 Wt. W2544/1454 700,000 5/15 D. D. & L. A.D.S.S./Forms/C. 2118.

Instructions regarding War Diaries and Intelligence Summaries are contained in F. S. Regs., Part II. and the Staff Manual respectively. Title pages will be prepared in manuscript.

WAR DIARY
or
INTELLIGENCE SUMMARY.
(*Erase heading not required.*) 1. R. Muns. Fus.

Army Form C. 2118.

6

Place	Date	Hour	Summary of Events and Information	Remarks and references to Appendices
BERTHON AREA.	19/3/17		Battalion training. Strength, O.39 OR 1051. To Hospital 6.	
	20/3		do. Strength O 39 OR 1045 To Hospital 4	
	21/3		do Strength O.39. OR 1041 To Hospital 2, Draft of 19 joined.	
	22/3		do Strength O.39 OR 1058 To Hospital 3.	
	23/3		do Strength O.39 OR 1055 To Hospital 4. Rejoined 1, Draft of 15 joined	
	24/3		do Inspection of Battalion by Army Commander Lieut. Gen Sir H. Plumer, 12.30pm. Strength O.39 OR 1067 To Hospital 3, Rejoined 4	
	25/3		do Strength O.39 OR 1068	
	26/3		do Strength O.39 OR 1068	
	27/3		do Strength O.39 OR 1068 To Hospital 4.	
	28/3		do Strength O.39 OR 1064 To Hospital 3	
	29/3		do Field day in conjunction with 7 Leinster Regt and 6 Connaught Rangers and 53 Squadron R.F.C. Practising attack in new formation in waves and aeroplane contact scheme. Col. R. Monck Mason a/Bde for occasion. Successful operation but spoilt by rain! Strength O.39 OR 1060. To Hospital 5. Capt. Ferry to P.B. and struck off strength.	
	30/3		do Strength O.38, OR 1055. To Hospital 2. 2/Lt West to R.F.C.	
	31/3		Battalion marched to BIRR BARRACKS. Arrived noon. 2nd in Com and 4 Coy Comdrs to front line VIERSTRAET SECTION to reconnoitre. Lieut H.N. LAKE reported for duty. Posted to 2 Coy. Strength O.39 OR 1053.	

W. D. Goodland
Major
1 R Muns Fus.

2353 Wt. W2544/1454 700,000 5/15 D. D. & L. A.D.S.S./Forms/C. 2118.

S E C R E T.   1-3-17.

O P E R A T I O N   O R D E R S
By
Major H.T.Goodland, Commanding 1st Battn Royal Munster Fusiliers.   No.13.

%

1. 47th Infantry Brigade will relieve the 49th Infantry Brigade in the SPANBROEK SECTION on the 2nd of March 1917.

2. The 1st Royal Munster Fusiliers will relieve the 2nd Royal Irish Reg in the Right Sub-sector., SPANBROEK SECTION. Relief to commence at 5-45.
"Z" Coy 1st R.M.F. will relieve the Right Company 2nd R.I.Regt with 2 platoons in the front line and 2 platoons in SHAMUS DUGOUTS.
Company Headquarter's will be in SHAMUS DUGOUTS.
"X" Coy 1st R.M.F. will relieve the Centre Company 2nd R.I.Regt with 2 platoons in the front line and 2 platoons in S.P.6.
Company Headquarter's will be in S.P.6.
"Y" Company will relieve the Left Company 2nd R.I.Regt with 3 platoons in the front line and 1 platoon in ULSTER ROAD.
Company Headquarter's will be in ULSTER ROAD.
"W" Coy 1st R.M.F. will relieve the Support Company 2nd R.I.Regt with 2 platoons in S.P.7., 1 platoon in PICCADILLY DUGOUTS and 1 platoon in S.P.[illegible]

3. Companies will move off from their company parade grounds as follows
"Z" Company 4-30.p.m.   "Y" Company 4-45.p.m.   "X" Company 5-0.p.m.
"W" Company 5-15.p.m.   H.Q.Company 5-30.p.m.
All movements will be at 300 yards insterval between platoons
"Z" & "X" Companies will use KINGSWAY TRENCH.
"W" & "Y" also H.Q.Companies will use REGENT STREET.

4. Company Lewis Gun Teams under their respective Lewis Gun Officers will move off from WAKEFIELD CAMP at 10.a.m., to take over their respecti positions.

5. Advance parties of 1 Officer, 1 N.C.O. and 2 men from each company, and 1 N.C.O. and 2 men from H.Q.Company will proceed in the morning to take over trench stores.

6. The Signalling Officer will detail the necessary signallers to take over positions. They will leave WAKEFIELD CAMP at 10-30.a.m., an N.C.O., will take charge.

7. The 2nd in Command will hand over WAKEFIELD CAMP., the 4 C.Q.M.Sgts, will attend. Companies will detail 1 N.C.O. and 2men to remain behind to clean up company lines if necessary, each N.C.O., will report to the 2nd in Command before leaving camp.

8. Certificates of stores taken over will be rendered to Battn H.Q. by 10.a.m. 3rd inst. Great care should be taken in taking over these stores.

9. Completion of reliefs will immediately be reported to Battn.H.Q. NEWPORT DUGOUTS in code by wire.

10. Transport Officer will arrange the necessary transport.

11. 47th Infantry Brigade H.Q. will close at LOCRE at 7.p.m. and will open in LITTLE KEMMEL the same hour.

Sd/ C.H.Exham, Captain A/Adjutant.,
1st Royal Munster Fusiliers.

S E C R E T 1-3-17.

O P E R A T I O N O R D E R

By No.13.

Major H.T.Goodland,Commanding 1st Battn Royal Munster Fusiliers.

%

1.The 47th Infantry Brigade will relieve the 49th Infantry Brigade on the 2nd of March 1917.

2.1st Royal Munster Fusiliers will relieve the 2nd Royal Irish Regiment in the Right Sub-Sector., SPANBROEK SECTION.
"Z" Company will relieve the Right Company 2nd R.I.Regt with 2 platoons in the front line and 2 platoons in S.P.6.
Company H.Q. will be in S.P.6.
*

SECRET. NO.14

5-3-17.

OPERATION ORDER

By

Major H.T.Goodland., Commanding 1st Battn Royal Munster Fusiliers.

1. The 7th LEINSTER REGT will relieve the 1st ROYAL MUNSTER FUSILIERS IN THE Right Subsection - STANBROEK SECTOR on the 6th inst.

2. On completion of relief Companies will take over the following positions:-

"X" Company., COOKER FARM & GALWAY DUGOUTS.
With 3 platoons in COOKER FARM and 1 platoon in GALWAY DUGOUTS.
Company Headquarters will be at COOKER FARM.

"W" Company., FORT EDWARD & BEEHIVE DUGOUTS.
With 2 platoons in FORT EDWARD and 2 platoons in BEEHIVE DUGOUTS.
Company Headquarters will be at FORT EDWARD.

"Y" Company., FORT REGINA & YONGE STREET DUGOUTS.
With 1 platoon in FORT REGINA and 3 platoons in YONGE STREET DUGOUTS.
Company headquarters will be at YONGE STREET DUGOUTS.

"Z" Company., LA POLKA FARM & FORT SASKATCHEWAN.
With 3½ platoons in LA POLKA FARM and half a platoon and Lewis Gun team in FORT SASKATCHEWAN.
Company Headquarters will be at LA POLKA FARM.

Battalion Headquarters will be at ~~XXXXXXXXXXX~~, DOCTOR'S HOUSE.

3. Relief to commence at 5-30.p.m.

4. Each Company will detail an officer and 1 N.C.O., as an advance party to take over stores in their new positions.
These should be taken over in the morning.
When handing and taking over, stores must be carefully checked.
Both certificates to be rendered to Battalion Headquarters by 10.a.m. the 7th inst.

5. Transport Officer will arrange the necessary transport.
Any baggage for removal will be stacked at PILL ROAD & FORT EDWARD.

6. Completion of reliefs will be immediately reported in code to the Battalion Headquarters.

SD/ C.H.EXHAM., Captain A/Adjutant.
1st Royal Munster Fusiliers.

S E C R E T. **No.15.**

O P E R A T I O N   O R D E R

By **9-3-17.**

Lieut-Colonel R.H.Monck-Mason, Commanding 1st Royal Munster Fusiliers.

-o-o-o-o-o-o-o-o-o-o-o-o-o-o-o-o-o-o-o-o-o-o-o-o-o-o-o-o-o-

1. The 49th Infantry Brigade will relieve the 47th Infantry Brigade in the SPANBROEK SECTION on the 10th instant.

2. The 7/8th Royal Irish Fusiliers will relieve the 1st Royal Munster Fusiliers in Brigade Support.
Relief will commence at 2-30.p.m.
On relief the 1st Royal Munster Fusiliers will proceed to billets at WAKEFIELD CAMP.

3. The Quartermaster will take over WAKEFIELD CAMP., he will arrange for the four Company Quartermaster Sergeants' and Sergt Gunnell for H.Q. Company to attend.

4. Handing over certificates for trench stores will be rendered to Orderly Room by 10.a.m. the 11th inst., in handing over stores a careful check must be made.

5. Baggage for "W" & "X" Companies for removal to WAKEFIELD CAMP will be stacked at FORT EDWARD before 1.p.m. They will be removed after dusk.
Companies should detail a party to remain with their baggage until removal.
Any baggage of "Y" "Z" and Headquarter Companies will be stacked at N.21.d.1.5., on the main road for removal by the transport, at 2-30.p.m Transport Officer will arrange the necessary transport.

6. Completion of reliefs will immediately be reported in code to Battalion Headquarters, [illegible]'S HOUSE.
Arrival in camp will be immediately reported to Orderly Room, WAKEFIELD CAMP.

7. The following working parties will be found by the 1st Royal Munster Fusiliers., to-morrow the 10th inst.

"X" Company., Party "[illegible].F"- 8.a.m , and 12 noon reliefs, the 4.p.m. relief will be found by the incoming Battalion.

"W" Company., Party "A.4" at 8.a.m.

"Z" Company., Party "D" at 9.a.m.

All other working parties usually found by the Support Battalion will be found by the incoming Battalion.

Sd/ C.H.Saxham., Captain A/Adjutant.,
1st Royal Munster Fusiliers.

S E C R E T. 9-3-17.

O P E R A T I O N   O R D E R

No.16.

By

Lieut-Colonel R.H.Monck-Mason, Commanding 1st Royal Munster Fusiliers.

--oo--oo--oo--oo--oo--oo--oo--oo--oo--oo--oo--oo--oo--

1. The 1st Royal Munster Fusiliers will relieve the 7th Leinster Regt in the Right Subsection SPANBROEK SECTOR on the 10th inst. Relief will commence at 5-45.p.m.

2. "W" Company 1st Royal Munster Fusiliers will relieve the Right Company 7th Leinster Regt.
Company Headquarters will be in SHAMUS DUGOUTS.
"Z" Company 1st Royal Munster Fusiliers will relieve the Centre Company 7th Leinster Regt.
Company Headquarters will be in S.P.6.
"X" Company 1st Royal Munster Fusiliers will relieve the Left Company 7th Leinster Regt.
Company Headquarters will be in ULSTER ROAD.
"Y" Company 1st Royal Munster Fusiliers will relieve the Support Coy 7th Leinster Regt.
Company Headquarters will be in S.P.7.
Companies will move off from their present positions as follows:-
"W" Company will move off at 5-15.p.m. Route via KINGSWAY.
"Z" Company will move off at 5-0.p.m. Route via KINGSWAY.
"X" Company will move off at 5-15.p.m. Route via REGENT STREET.
"Y" Company will move off at 5-30.p.m. Route via REGENT STREET.

3. Company Lewis Gun teams under their respective Lewis Gun Officers will move off to take over their new positions at 2.p.m. Lewis Guns lent should be obtained before moving into the Line.

4. Advance parties of one officer and one N.C.O. and two men from each Company and one N.C.O. and two men from Headquarter Company will proceed at 2 p.m. to take over trench stores.

5. The Signalling Officer will detail the necessary signallers to take over their respective positions, they will take over as soon after dinners as possible.

6. Certificates of trench stores handed and taken over will be rendered to Battalion Headquarters by 10.a.m. the 11th inst. Great care should be taken in handing and taking over these stores.

7. Completion of reliefs will be immediately reported in code by wire to Battalion Headquarters NEWPORT DUGOUTS.

8. Baggage of "Y" "Z" and Headquarter Companies will be stacked outside the DOCTOR'S HOUSE for removal at dusk. The Transport Officer will arrange the necessary transport.

Sd/ G.E.[illegible]xham., Captain A/Adjutant.,
1st Royal Munster Fusiliers.

SECRET.

13-3-17.

OPERATION ORDER

By

No. 17.

Major H.T.Goodland., Commanding 1st Battn, Royal Munster Fusiliers.

-o-o-o-o-o-o-o-o-o-o-o-o-o-o-o-o-o-o-o-o-o-o-o-o-o-o-o-o-o-o-o-

Reference - FRANCE. Sheet 28.S.W. Edition 4 A. 1/20000.

1. 107th Inf.Bde., 36th Division will relieve the 47th Inf Bde. in the SPANBROEK-MOLEN SECTOR on the 13th inst.

2. The following adjustment of front will be made on the 13th March 1917 and is to be completed before noon.
(a) O.C. "W" Coy. 1st R.M.F. will hand over to the incoming company 9th Royal Irish Fusiliers, 108th Inf.Bde, that portion of the line from DURHAM ROAD to where the WULVERGHEM-WYTSCHAETE ROAD crosses our front trench at N.36.a.6.1.
SHAMUS DUGOUTS will also be handed over.
On relief "W" Coy.1st R.M.F. will proceed to West CampDERRY HUTS where they will be billeted.
(b) O.C. "W" Coy.1st R.M.F. will exercise the greatest care in seeing that the boundary id properly defined. Befoer he laeves for DERRY CAMP he should see the O.C. "Z" Coy. 1st R.M.F. and explain to him the actual boundary decided on.
O.C. "Z" Coy. 1st R.M.F. will then become responsible for the defence of the front up to that point.
(c) On completion of relief the code word "SATISFACTORY" will be wired to Battalion Headquarters.

3. 1st R.M.F. (less "W" Coy already relieved) will be relieved by the 15th Bn. Royal Irish Rifles in the Right Sub-section on the 13th inst.
Relief of companies will be as follows:-
"A" Coy 15th R.I.R. will relieve "Z" Coy.1st R.M.F., with 2 platoons in the front line from point N.36.a.6.1., on the Right exclusive, to REDAN AVENUE on the left inclusive, and 2 platoons in S.P.6.
Company Headquarters will be in S.P.6.
"B" Coy.15th R.I.R. will relieve "X" Coy. 1st R.M.F., with 3 platoons in the front line from REDAN AVENUE exclusive on the Right, to 1 bay North of PICCADILLY inclusive on the Left, and one platoon in ULSTER ROAD.
Company Headquarters will be in ULSTER ROAD.
"C" Coy.15th R.I.R. will relieve "Y" Coy.1st R.M.F., in Support, with 2 platoons in S.P.7., 1 platoon in PICCADILLY DUGOUTS and 1 platoon in S.P.8
Company Headquarters will be in S.P.7.
"D" Coy.15th R.I.R., will be billeted in East Camp DERRY HUTS.
Battalion Headquarters of 15th R.I.R. will be at NEWPORT DUGOUTS.

4. Guides will be sent as follows:-
"Z" Coy.1st R.M.F. one guide per platoon to DAYLIGHT CORNER at 5-40.p.m.
"X" Coy.1st R.M.F. " " " " "REGENT STREET at 5-40.p.m.
"Y" Coy 1st R.M.F. " " " " " REGENT STREET at 5-40.p.m.

5. Advance party and Lewis Guns of "A" Coy.15th R.I.R. will be at DAYLIGHT CORNER at 1.p.m.
Advance parties and Lewis Guns of "B" & "C" Companies 15th R.I.R. will be at entrance to REGENT STREET at 1.p.m.
O's.C. "X" "Y" & "Z" Companies 1st R.M.F. will have one guide for each gun position at the above mentioned rendezvous at the hours stated.
Signallers of 15th R.I.R. and advance party of H.Q.Coy, will be at DAYLIGHT CORNER at 1.p.m.
A guide will be arranged.

6. On completion of reliefs "Z" Coy.1st R.M.F. will be billeted at West Camp DERRY HUTS and "Y" & "Z" Companies at KEMMEL CHATEAU.
Battalion Headquarters will be at DERRY CAMP.

& ADVANCE PARTIES.

7. ADVANCE PARTIES.
Advance parties of one Officer, one N.C.O. and two men from "Z" Company 1st R.M.F. and one N.C.O. and 2 men from H.Q.Coy.will be at West Camp DERRY HUTS at 2.p.m.
One Officer, one N.C.O. and two men from "X" & "Y" Companies will be at KEMMEL CHATEAU at 2.p.m.
"W" Coy.1st R.M.F. will take over their billet as soon as convenient after arrival at West Camp DERRY HUTS.

8. Handing over certificates of Trench Stores will be renedered to O.R. by 9.a.m. sharp, the 14th inst.
In handing over, O'S.C.Companies must must be particularly careful about the accuracy of their returns.

9. Baggage for "W" and "Y" Companies will be stacked at SHAMUS DUGOUTS ready for removal after dusk.
Baggage for "X" and "Y" Companies should be stacked at FORT EDWARD.
Companies should each detail a party to remain with their baggage until removal.
The Transport Officer will arrange for necessary transport.
The Quartermaster will arrange for a second blanket per man to be brought to companies on the afternoon of the 13th inst at their billets.
Packs will not be brought up, but will be sent direct to BERTHEN AREA on the 13th inst.

10. Completion of reliefs will be immediately reported in code by wire to Battalion Headquarters at NEWPORT DUGOUTS.

SD/ C.H.Exham., Captain A/Adjutant.,
1st Royal Munster Fusiliers.

S E C R E T. 1-3-17.

O P E R A T I O N [illegible]

by [illegible]

Major [illegible] Woodland, Commanding, 1st Bn. Royal [illegible]

-0-0-0-0-0-0-0-0-0-0-0-0-0-0-0-0-0-0-0-0-0-0-0-0-

Reference - [illegible]-28. [illegible] Edition [illegible] 1/[illegible]

Reference [illegible] - S.W. Edition 2. 1/[illegible]

1. The [illegible] Inf. Bde. [illegible] Division will relieve the 47th Inf. Bde in the [illegible] Section [illegible], on the 14th inst.

2. The [illegible] Bn. Royal Irish Rifles will relieve the [illegible] in Brigade Reserve at [illegible] on the 14th [illegible] 1917. On relief the Battalion will be billeted in the [illegible] Edition 2. [illegible]

3. One guide per platoon and one guide for [illegible] will be at [illegible] at [illegible] to meet the [illegible] The guides from [illegible] will be marched to [illegible] The guides from [illegible] will report to [illegible] CORNER. Lieut [illegible] will be responsible for the correct distribution of guides to the various companies of the incoming Battalion. Lieut [illegible] will report at Orderly Room at 1.p.m. to receive further instructions.

4. On relief, companies will march to the new billeting area independently. All movements East of the [illegible] ROAD will be by platoons at 3[illegible] yards interval.

Companies will close up West of this line at a rendezvous chosen by the O.C Company.

The billeting [illegible] of each company who were sent in advance will meet his company on arrival at the bridge at the entrance to [illegible]

O's.C. Companies will be at Bn. [illegible] at 11.a.m. on the 14th inst to arrange the route.

5. Certificates of handing over camp stores will be obtained on relief and will be handed into Orderly Room by [illegible] p.m. the 14th inst. Certificates of cleanliness of billets on handing over, will also be handed in at the same time.

6. Lewis Guns.

Transport for Lewis Guns will be notified later.

7. The Signalling Officer will march H.Q. Coy. and Signallers, except the signallers at [illegible], who will march with the last company to move off.

8. The Transport Officer will arrange for blankets and all baggage required to be removed to the new area on the 14th inst.

Blankets must be stacked by 9.a.m., all baggage by 11.a.m.

9. Cookers will move off for the new area after dinners and will rendezvous at [illegible] CHURCH by [illegible] p.m. The Transport Officer will arrange to have an [illegible] at the rendezvous to act as guide.

The Quartermaster will arrange if possible for a hot meal on arrival of companies in billets

Sd/ [illegible], Captain & Adjutant.,

1st Royal Munster Fusiliers.

WAR DIARY FOR MONTH OF APRIL, 1917.

VOLUME:- ✓

UNIT:- 1st Ro. Munster Fus.

Vol #14

Instructions regarding War Diaries and Intelligence Summaries are contained in F. S. Regs., Part II. and the Staff Manual respectively. Title pages will be prepared in manuscript.

WAR DIARY or INTELLIGENCE SUMMARY.

(Erase heading not required.)

Army Form C. 2118.

1 R. Munster Fusiliers.

Place	Date 1917	Hour	Summary of Events and Information	Remarks and references to Appendices
BIRR BARRACKS, LOCRE	1/4		The Battalion billetted in BIRR BARRACKS for night 31/3–1/4 on return from training in BERTHEN AREA. Battalion moved into the line relieving the 8 Innis Killings. Relief commenced at 8 pm. Battn. began to march at 5 pm. Relief complete 10.30 pm. Strength O 38, OR 1051. To Hospital 5. Accidentally wounded 1. Lieuts. SHEA, HALDANE & HUSSEY joined.	1. Map of VIERSTRAAT SECTOR see Appendix A.
LEFT SUB SECTION VIERSTRAAT SECTOR.	2/4		Battalion Headquarters YORK HOUSE. Y Coy in front line, Z Coy in support WATLING ST. W Coy in S.P.13 and VAN KEEP. 1 Coy X Coy in SP13 and 3 Coys at BUTTERFLY FARM. 1 Platoon of LEINSTER Regt in FORT HALIFAX. Our Artillery fired on enemy line from 5 pm to 7 pm. Slight retaliation followed. Enemy swept our supports at night with M.G. fire. Strength O.41, OR 1045. To Hosp. 2, From Hosp. 2. 2/Lieut LAING died at BAILLEUL from Pneumonia.	
"	3/4		Front line trenches and supports slightly damaged from over night shell fire and repaired during night. Our Artillery fired again 5 to 7 pm, causing increased retaliation. Strength O.40, OR 1045. To Hosp. 4. Wounded 2. From Hosp. 2. Captain LEE joined and attached to Z Coy, taking command.	
"	4/4		Continued repair of trenches and started improving S.P.13 and VAN KEEP. Our Artillery again active 5 to 7 pm on enemy line. Enemy shelled intermittently all day. Battn. relieved by 7 Leinster Regt, going into Support. Strength O.41. OR 1041. Killed 2, Wounded 2, To Hosp. 2.	see Appendix B. H. Scott [illegible]

2353 Wt. W2544/1454 700,000 5/15 D. D. & L. A.D.S.S./Forms/C. 2118.

2.

WAR DIARY
or
INTELLIGENCE SUMMARY.
(Erase heading not required.)

1 R. Muns. Fus.

Army Form C. 2118.

Instructions regarding War Diaries and Intelligence Summaries are contained in F. S. Regs., Part II. and the Staff Manual respectively. Title pages will be prepared in manuscript.

Place	Date 1917	Hour	Summary of Events and Information	Remarks and references to Appendices
In Supports. RUSSIGNOL	5/4		Battalion disposed as follows in Support. Head Quarters, RUSSIGNOL ESTAMINET, and Z Coy. W Coy SAND BAG VILLA with 1 Plat. in SEIGE FM. Y Coy in SEIGE FARM. X Coy at LA POLKA and DOCTORS HO. Battn provided working parties for work on CHINESE LINES, Newwork all officers parties. 12 Parties in all daily. Successful raid at 8.45 pm by 6 R. Irish Regt. 21 Prisoners. Rocket firing parties and prisoners escorts were found by 1 R.M.F. Strength O.41. OR.1035 To Hosp. 1. Wounded 1.	
"	6/4		Battn working parties all day. Capt. BUTLER wounded at SEIGE FM. by shrapnel. Strength O.41. OR.1033 To Hosp 5. Wounded 2. From Hosp. 2.	
"	7/4		Battn working parties all day. Strength O.41. OR.1028. To Hosp. 3. Draft of 8 joined.	
"	8/4		Easter. All R C to mass. Working parties cancelled. Men cleaned up. Strength, O.41, OR.1033 To Hosp 3. From Hosp 4. Lieut PARROTT to Gen. List.	
	9/4		Relief cancelled. All working parties provided. Strength O.40, OR.1034 To Hosp 1. From Hosp 1. Col. MONCK-MASON went on leave. Major GOODLAND assumed command.	
[V]IERSTRAAT SECTOR. Left Sub Section.	10/4		Battn relieved in Support by 5 CONN. RGRS. Battn relieved 6 LEINSTER REGT in front line. W Coy in Front line, X Coy in support WATLING ST. (now called SHANNON TR.) Z Coy in S.P.13 and VAN KEEP. 1 Coy Y in S.P.13. 1 Coy Y in FORT HALIFAX. and 2 Coys Y in BUTTERFLY FM. Slight shelling at night. Strength. O.40. OR.1034 To Hosp. 1. Wounded 1. From Hosp. 1. Lieut O'Brien to U.K.	See Appendix C. [signature]

2353 Wt. W2544/1454 700,000 5/15 D. D. & L. A.D.S.S./Forms/C. 2118.

Instructions regarding War Diaries and Intelligence Summaries are contained in F. S. Regs., Part II. and the Staff Manual respectively. Title pages will be prepared in manuscript.

WAR DIARY
or
INTELLIGENCE SUMMARY.
(Erase heading not required.)

3

Army Form C. 2118.

1. R. Muns. Fus.

Place	Date 1917	Hour	Summary of Events and Information	Remarks and references to Appendices
VIERSTRAAT SECTOR Left Sub Section	11/4		Fairly quiet day. Work all night building up parapet. Work continued widening VAN HORN and VAN KEEP. NEW SUPPORT TR. renamed FERMOY TR. Some shelling of SP13. 2 Plats of Y Coy working on new dugouts at YORK HO. Battn HQ. Strength O. 39. OR 1033. To Hosp 1. Wounded 1.	
"	12/4		Snow fell making trenches very wet. Work on trenches continued but owing to weather little progress made. Our Artillery active. Some hostile sniping and more than usual shelling during day. Strength O. 39. OR 1031. To Hosp. 2. Wounded 1. From Hosp. 5. Draft of 4 joined. X Coy relieved W Coy in front line during night.	
"	13/4		Badly shelled during morning. Direct hit on CORK TR and in front line. 14 Casualties. Good work done on VAN KEEP. Work continued on dugouts at YORK HO. 2 new dugouts started in SHANNON TR. Strength O. 39. OR 1037. Wounded 11.	
"	14/4		All work continued & making good progress. Heavy shelling of SP13 and Ouvelane post. Sniping decreasing also MG fire. Enemy shelled Batteries rear of SEIGE FM with gas shells. They do not appear to have anything larger than 4.25 and bulk of shelling with field guns. Strength O. 39. OR 1026. To Hosp. 6. From Hosp 2.	
"	15/4		All work continued on VAN KEEP, VAN HORN and revetting front line parapet. Also continued Dugouts at YORK HOUSE and SHANNON TRENCH. Relieved in evening by 7 LEINSTER Regt. and Battalion moved into Div Reserve at BUTTERFLY FARM. N 19 A 6.2. Company met and ready. Strength O. 39. OR 1022. From Hosp 4. Draft of 4 joined. 2/Lieut DONNELLY joined	

2353 Wt. W2544/1454 700,000 5/15 D. D. & L. A.D.S.S./Forms/C. 2118.

Army Form C. 2118.

4

WAR DIARY
or
INTELLIGENCE SUMMARY.
(*Erase heading not required.*)

Instructions regarding War Diaries and Intelligence Summaries are contained in F. S. Regs., Part II. and the Staff Manual respectively. Title pages will be prepared in manuscript.

1 R. Muns. Fus.

Place	Date 1917	Hour	Summary of Events and Information	Remarks and references to Appendices
BUTTERFLY FARM. N19A.6.2.	16/4		Battn. in Div Reserve work on cleaning camp. Working parties sent up to work on CHINESE TRENCHES and R.E. pushing parties. Very rough & wet day. Strength, O. 40, OR 1030. From Hosp. 2.	
"	17/4		Working parties sent out. Farm building used as [illegible] caught fire [illegible] Successfully put out with little damage. Repaired by Battn. Pioneers. Strength. O. 40. OR 1032. From Hosp. 3. Draft of 4 joined. 2/Lieut HAND. S.R.M.F. joined.	
"	18/4		Working Parties sent out. W Coy moved to CLARE CAMP (M33 A. 8.4) to take over and pitch tents. Strength O. 41. OR 1039. To Hosp. 4. Rejoined 2.	
"	19/4		X Coy on working Parties. Y and Z Coys moved 2 pm to TALLYHO CAMP (approx X 5 A 5.2.) X Coy to DONCASTER CAMP M29A 2.3. Strength O. 41. OR. 1037. To Hosp. 1. From Hosp. 3.	[illegible]
TALLYHO CAMP X5A5.2.	20/4		Y, Z and W Coys cleaning up and drill. W Coy continuing work on CLARE camp. X Coy finding 100 men daily for working parties to RUSSIGNAC etc. Conference of C.Os at Bde H.Q. Bde H.Q. at MONT ROUGE M22 A. Strength O. 41. OR 1039. To Hosp. 1. From Hosp. 3.	
"	21/4		X Coy working Parties, W work on CLARE camp. Y & Z Coys drill and fitting clothing. All officers but 1 per Coy sent out to reconnoitre G.H.Q. line and the model of WYTSCHAETE at SCHERPENBERG. Strength O. 41 OR 1041	
"	22/4		X Coy continued working parties, W Coy on CLARE CAMP. — Brigadier inspected huts of Y & Z Coys — Strength O.41 OR 1050 To Hosp. 3 From Hosp. 2 — Lt ARCEDERNE-BUTLER and Capt BUTLER invalided.	
	23/4		X Coy on working parties, W. on CLARE CAMP and inspected by Brigadier. Y & Z Company training. Strength O. 39 OR 1049 To Hosp. 4 From Hosp. 2 2nd Lt HOLMES reported.	[illegible]

Instructions regarding War Diaries and Intelligence Summaries are contained in F. S. Regs., Part II. and the Staff Manual respectively. Title pages will be prepared in manuscript.

WAR DIARY
or
INTELLIGENCE SUMMARY.
(*Erase heading not required.*)

Army Form C. 2118.

Place	Date 1917	Hour	Summary of Events and Information	Remarks and references to Appendices
TALLY-HO CAMP X.5 a 5 2.	24/4		W and X Coys at same working parties, Y & Z on Company training. C.O. returned from leave. Strength O. 40 O.R. 1046. To Hosp. 5 From Hosp. 2	
KEMMEL SHELTERS N.19.c 8.2.	25/4		Battn. moved to KEMMEL SHELTERS, relieving 6th R. IRISH Regt. HQ at N.19.c.8.2 (sheet 28 S.W.) X Coy remained at DONCASTER HUTS. W, Y and Z Coys on working parties for 16th Div Sig. Coy. laying buried cable from SIEGE FM to S.P. 13. 2nd in Command went on leave. Strength O. 40 O.R. 1043. From Hosp. 3. To Hosp. 5 To Base 2	Appendix F.
	26/4		X Coy training (Company and Platoon training). The remainder of Battn on Signals' working parties. Strength O. 40. O.R. 1039 To Hosp 3 From Hosp. 3 Draft of 10 reported.	
	27/4		All companies on Bombing Ground, and working parties. 2nd Lts CARROLL and BAILY reported. Strength O. 40 O.R. 1049. To Hosp 1 From Hosp. 2 Same working parties for W, Y & Z Coys	
	28/4		Nil Strength O. 40 O.R. 1050 To Hosp 3 Strength O. 42 O.R. 1047. To Hosp. 7 From Hosp 4.	
	29/4 30/4		Strength O. 42. O.R. 1044. To Hosp. 3. From Hosp. 3 9 O.R. reported. The following officers reported - Capt KING, 2nd Lts FREEMAN, ENNIS, SHIEL and LOVE. Final Strength O. 47 O.R. 1054.	Appendix [illegible]

2353 Wt. W2544/1454 700,000 5/15 D. D. & L. A.D.S.S./Forms/C. 2118.

Appendix A.

SECRET. No.19/1.

OPERATION ORDERS

BY 31-3-17.

Lieut-Colonel R.H.Monck-Mason,Commanding,1st Royal Munster Fusiliers.

-0-0-0-0-0-0-0-0-0-0-0-0-0-0-0-0-0-0-0-0-0-0-0-0-0-0-0-

In continuation of Operation Orders No.19. Part 11. d/-29th inst.

(c) DISPOSITIONS.

"Y" Company will take over the Front Line.
"Z" Company will take over the Support Line in WATLING STREET.
"W" Company will take over S.P.13., and VAN KEEP.
"X" Company., disposition will be notified to-morrow.

(d) ORDER OF MARCH.
"Y" Company will move off from BIRR BARRACKS at 6-15.p.m.
"Z" Company will move off from BIRR BARRACKS at 6-30.p.m.
"W" Company will move off from BIRR BARRACKS at 6-45.p.m.
"X" Company will move off from BIRR BARRACKS at 7-00.p.m.
Headquarter Company will move off from BIRR BARRACKS at 7-15.p.m.
All movemants will be by Platoons at 200 yards interval.

(f) ADVANCE PARTIES.

The Signalling Sergeant will proceed with the Advance Party from Headquarter Company and take over Signalling Stations,Stores etc.

(g) BAGGAGE AND BLANKETS ETC.

Blankets, packs and baggage will be piled by Companies outside Orderly Room by 4.p.m.
Care must be taken to see that kits going to the Line and to Quartermaster's Stores are kept in seperate piles.
The Transport Officer will arrange for necessary Transport.

Lieut H.R.H.O'Reilly and 1 N.C.O. per Company will (if necessary) hand over Camp to the incoming Unit.

Sd/ C. H. EXHAM.,Captain A/Adjutant.,

1st Royal Munster Fusiliers.

Issued at ...8-45...p.m.

SECRET. No. 19

OPERATION ORDERS

BY

Lieut-Colonel R.H.Monck-Mason, Commanding 1st Royal Munster Fusiliers.

-0-0-0-0-0-0-0-0-0-0-0-0-0-0-0-0-0-0-0-0-0-0-0-0-0-0-0-0-

Reference.

(a) BELGIUM & FRANCE - Sheet 27. 2nd Edition. 1/40,000.
(b) FRANCE - Sheet 28.S.W. Edition 4.A. 1/20.000.

------------000------------

1. The 47th Inf.Bde. will relieve the 48th Inf.Bde. in Divisional Support, (LOCRE AREA) on the 31st instant.

(a) Relief. 1st Royal Munster Fusiliers will relieve the 8th Royal Dublin Fusiliers, in BIRR BARRACKS.

(b) Parade. The Battalion will parade on the road running from R.27. Central to the cross-roads at R.27.d.7.9., ready to move off at 9-45.a.m. Companies will fall in in line facing North, in the order, H.Q.Coy., "W" "X" "Y" & "Z" Companies, H.Q.Coy. on the Right flank at the cross-roads R.27.d.7.9.
Dress, full marching order.

(c) Transport. 1st Line transport will accompany the Battalion. Transport Officer will arrange to have 1st Line transport on the road running from BERTHEN to cross-roads R.28.d.90.60. (Head of the Column at the cross-roads R.28.d.90.60.) at 10.a.m.
When the Battalion has passed, transport will follow in rear of the Battalion.

(d) Cookers. Fires in cookers must be kept burning on the march. Dinners will be had on arrival at BIRR BARRACKS.

(e) Advance Party. An advance party of one N.C.O. from each Company and one N.C.O. from H.Q.Coy. will parade under Lieut E.R.H.O'Reilly, (The Billeting Officer) on the road outside Battalion H.Q. at 12-30pm. on the 30th instant, and will proceed to BIRR BARRACKS to take over Camp. Billets for the night will be provided by the 48th Inf.Bde.

(f) Quartermaster's Stores and Transport Lines. Quartermaster's Stores and Transport Lines will be taken over from the 2nd Royal Dublin Fusls. Quartermaster and Transport Officer will arrange to send advance parties to take over on or before the 31st instant.

(g) Stores, Baggage, Blankets, etc. S.A.A.; Grenades and tools will be taken with the Battalion.
Transport Officer will arrange for limbers accordingly.
Baggage and Blankets etc, will be stacked by 7.a.m. outside billets. Transport Officer will arrange for these to be collected and stacked at the cross-roads R.27.d.7.9., by 9.a.m.
Blankets will be rolled in bundles of ten, the Platoon, Company and Regiment will be put on a lable attached to each bundle. They will be moved by 16th Divisional Train A.S.C. to BIRR BARRACKS.
Each Company will detail a loading party of 1 N.C.O. and 4 men who will accompany the Wagons on the march and unload on arrival at BIRR BARRACKS. H.Q.Coy. will detail a similar party.

(h) All movements on the CANADA CORNER - LOCRE ROAD will be by Platoons at 200 yards interval.

(i) Companies will report to Orderly Room when all men and stores have arrived at BIRR BARRACKS.

PART.II.

The 47th Inf.Bde. will relieve the 49th Inf.Bde. in the VIERSTRAAT SECTION on the 1st of April 1917.

(a) 1st Royal Munster Fusiliers will relieve the 8th Bn.Royal Inns.Fusls. in the Left Sub-section.

(b) Major M.T.Goodland and the four Company Commanders will visit the new line on the 31st inst., and on completion of reconnaissance will rejoin the Battalion at BIRR BARRACKS.
A Bus will ~~xxxxx~~ be at SCHAEXKEN (R.36.c.5.9.) at 9-30.a.m. to take them to 49th Inf.Bde.H.Q., where they will be met by guides.

(c) Dispostions will be notified later.

(d) Order of march and times will be notified later.

(e) One guide.

(e). One guide per platoon and one Guide for H.Q. Company will be supplied by the 8th. Royal Inns. Fusiliers. They will be at the DRESSING STATION , KEMMEL. N.21.c. 80.55. at 7.30 p.m.

(f). Advance parties of one Officer per Company, one N.C.O. per platoon One Gas N.C.O., the numbers 1 of each Lewis Gun team and the necessary Signallers per Company will report at Headquarters 8th. Royal Inns. Fusiliers N.16.c. 90.25 at 3.30 p.m. to take over Stores etc., guides will be provided from there.
Sergeant Kenneally and the necessary Signallers will take over for H.Q. Company and will report at same time and place.
Parties will move under their own Officer.

(g). Arrangements as to blankets, baggage, etc., will be notified later.

(h). All movements will be by platoons at 200 yards interval.

(i). Completion of reliefs will be immediately reported in code by wire to Battalion Headquarters.

Sd/. C.H. [illegible]. Captain, A/Adjutant,

1st. Bn. Royal Munster Fusiliers.

(a). 1st. Royal Munster Fusiliers will relieve the 6th. Bn. Royal Inns. ~~xxxxxxr~~ Fusiliers in the left sub-section.
in the le

File

Appendix B.

SECRET. No.21.

OPERATION ORDERS 3rd April 1917.

BY

Lieut-Colonel R.H.Monck-Mason,Commanding 1st Royal Munster Fusiliers.

-o-o-o-o-o-o-o-o-o-o-o-o-o-o-o-o-o-o-o-o-o-o-o-o-o-o-

1. The 7th Leinster Regt will relieve the 1st Royal Munster Fusiliers in the Left Sub-section., VIERSTRAAT SECTOR on 4th April 1917.

2. RELIEFS.
"A" Company 7th Leinster Regt will relieve "Y" Company 1st Royal Munster Fusiliers in the Front Line.
"C" Company 7th Leinster Regt will relieve "Z" Company 1st Royal Munster Fusiliers in Support.
"B" Company 7th Leinster Regt will relieve "W" Company 1st Royal Munster Fusiliers in VAN KEMP and S.P.13. (New)
"D" Company 7th Leinster Regt will relieve "X" Company 1st Royal Munster Fusiliers with one Platoon in S.P.13., and 3 Platoons in BUTTERFLY FARM.

3. DISPOSITIONS ON RELIEF.
On relief 1st Royal Munster Fusiliers will move into Brigade Support and be disposed as follows;-
"Y" Company - SIEGE FARM. Company H. Q. will be at SIEGE FARM.
"Z" Company - FORT MOUNT ROYAL and ROSSIGNOL.
Company H. Q. ROSSIGNOL.
"X" Company - 3 Platoons - LA POLKA and 1 Platoon FORT SASKATCHEWAN.
Company H. Q. will be at DOCTOR'S HOUSE.
"W" Company - 3 Platoons - SANDBAG VILLA and 1 Platoon at FORT HALIFAX. Company H. Q. will be at SANDBAG VILLA.
Battalion Headquarters will be at ROSSIGNOL ESTAMINET.

4. GUIDES.
"W" "Y" & "Z" Companies and the 1 platoon of "X" Company now in S.P. 13., will have one guide per Platoon at Battalion H. Q. YORK HOUSE at 7-30.p.m.

5. ADVANCE PARTIES.
Advance parties of one Officer, one N. C. O. and two men and the necessary signallers and one N. C. O. and two men and signallers from H. Q. Company will take over the new positions and all stores etc, before 3.p.m. the 4th instant.

6. LEWIS GUNS.
Lewis Guns will be relieved at the same time as Companies and will move with their Companies to new positions.

7. Rations on the night of the 4th instant and the following nights, while the Battalion is in the Brigade Support will be disposed as follows:-
"W" Company - SANDBAG VILLA. - "Z" Company - ROSSIGNOL ESTAMINET.
"Y" Company - SIEGE FARM. - "X" Company - DOCTOR'S HOUSE.
Headquarters Company - ROSSIGNOL ESTAMINET.

8. Officers will arrange for the removal of their Company mess boxes etc., as no transport is being provided.

9. All movements in trenches (if in daylight) will be in parties of not more than 6 men. All movements after leaving trenches will be by Platoons at 200 yards interval.

10. Completion of reliefs will be immediately reported in code by wire to Battalion H. Q. YORK HOUSE.

SD/ G. H. MAHAN., Captain A/Adjutant.,

1st Royal Munster Fusiliers.

S E C R E T   No. ... Appendix "C"

O P E R A T I O N   O R D E R S

By

Lt. Colonel R. H. Monck-Mason Comdg. 1st. Bn. Royal Muns. Fusiliers.

In the Field 9. 4. 17

1. RELIEF. 1st. Royal Munster Fusiliers will relieve the 7th. Leinster Regt. in the left subsection VIERSTRAAT Sector on 10th. April 1917.

2. DISPOSITIONS. "W" Company will relieve Company 7th. Leinster Regt. in the front line. Coy. Hd. quarters in WATLING STREET.

"X" Coy. 1st. R.M.Fus. will relieve Coy. 7th. Leinster Regt. in Support in WATLING STREET & NEW SUPPORT TRENCH. Company Headquarters in WATLING STREET.
"Z" Company 1st. R.M.Fus. will relieve Coy. 7th. Leinster Regt. in VAN KEEP and S.P. 13 with one platoon in VAN KEEP and 3 platoons in S.P. 13. Company Headquarters S.P. 13.
"Y" Company 1st. R.M. Fus. will relieve Coy. 7th. Leinster Regt. in Battalion Reserve with 1 platoon in S.P. 13, 1 platoon in FORT HALIFAX and 2 in BUTTERFLY FARM.
The platoon in FORT HALIFAX is the Garrison of this S.P.
Battalion Headquarters will be at YORK HOUSE.

3. TIME OF RELIEF. The leading platoon of "W" Company will be at the entrance to WATLING STREET at 8 p.m.
The leading platoon of "X" Company will be at the entrance to WATLING STREET at 8.20 p.m.
The leading platoon of "Z" Company will be at the entrance to WATLING STREET at 8.40 p.m.
The platoon from "Y" Company for S.P. 13 will follow the last platoon of "Z" Company.
The platoon of "Y" Company for FORT HALIFAX will relieve after dusk by the overland route to FORT HALIFAX.

4. GUIDES. No guides will be supplied.

5. LEWIS GUNS. Lewis Guns will relieve with Companies in the evening. O.C. "W" and "Z" Companies will each be given a 5th. Gun from Battalion Headquarters. They will arrange as to the disposition of the 10 guns.

6. ADVANCE PARTIES. Each Company will send an advance party of 1 N.C.O., 2 men and No. 1's of Lewis Gun Team under Lewis Gun Officer to take over positions & stores before 3 p.m. 10th. inst.
A party will also be detailed from Headquarters Company.
The Signalling Sergeant will detail the necessary Signallers to go with each advance party.
O.C. "Y" Company will have to arrange a party for FORT HALIFAX as well as BUTTERFLY FARM.

7. TRANSPORT. O.C. Companies will make their own arrangements as to the removal of Kits, mess boxes etc., to the line. No Transport will be given. Transport Officer will arrange for the removal of baggage etc., of W, X and Z Companies to Quartermaster's Stores and of "Y" Company to BUTTERFLY FARM. Companies will leave Guards over Kits if necessary.

8. All movements in trenches will be in small parties of 6 at intervals. All movements on roads will be by platoons at 200 yards interval.

Completion of Reliefs will be immediately reported in code by wire to Battalion Headquarters.

G. H. EXHAM, Captain,

A/Adjutant, 1st. Royal Munster Fusiliers.

Appendix D

S E C R E T

No. 23

O P E R A T I O N   O R D E R S
By
Major H.T. Goodland Comdg. Royal Munster Fusiliers.
In the Field 14. 4.17

XXXXXXXXXXXXXXXXXXXXXXXXXXXXXX

Ref. Sheet 28 S.W. Edition 4a.

1. RELIEF. The Leinster Regiment will relieve the Royal Muns. Fusiliers in the left Subsection on the 15th. April 1917.

The Relief will commence at 8 p.m.

B. Coy. Leinster Regt. will relieve X Coy. R.M. Fus.
D. " " " " " W " "
C " " " " " Z " "
A " " " " " Y " "

2. DISPOSITION ON RELIEF. On relief the Royal Munster Fusiliers will move into Bde. Reserve at BUTTERFLY FARM N.19.a.6.9. Companies will move independently.

3. LEWIS GUNS. Lewis Gun Teams will be relieved at the same time as Coys. No's 1 of the Leinster Teams will be up during the day to reconnoitre Gun positions.

4. ADVANCE PARTIES. The Quartermaster will arrange to take over BUTTERFLY FARM Camp. He will arrange for the 4 Coy. Q.M. Sergts. and Sgt. Mc.Cann for Headquarter Coy to attend.

5. MOVEMENT. All movement in trenches (If in daylight) will be in parties of not more than 6. All movements after leaving trenches will be by platoons at 200 yards interval.

6. TRENCH STORES. Certificates of handing over Trench Stores and Certificate for taking over BUTTERFLY FARM Camp will be handed in to Orderly Room by 11 a.m. the 16th. inst.

7. TRANSPORT. All Company Officers Mess Boxes etc., will be piled at YORK HOUSE by 8 p.m.. Transport Officer will arrange for the removal of all baggage, stores etc., from YORK HOUSE.

He will also arrange for baggage from Quartermaster's Stores being brought to BUTTERFLY FARM Camp.

8. Completion of Relief will be immediately reported in B.A.B. Code by wire to Battalion Headquarters at YORK HOUSE.

9. Acknowledge.

(Sd.) C.H. Exham, Captain, A/Adjutant
Royal Munster Fusiliers.

14. 4. 17

Issued at 5 P.M.

Copy No. 1 to W Coy.
" " 2 " X Coy.
" " 3 " Y Coy.
" " 4 " Z Coy.
" " 5 " Bde. Hd.Qrs.
" " 6 " Comdg. Offr.
" " 7 " 2nd. in Comd.
Copy No. 8 O.C. Ft. Halifax
" " 9 Tpt. Officer
" " 10 Qr. Master
" " 11 R. S. M.
" " 12 Signal Sergeant.
" " 13 Leinster Regt.

(2 Copies retained).

Appendix E

SECRET No. 25

OPERATION ORDERS

By

Major H. T. Goodland Comdg. Royal Munster Fusiliers

In the Field 18. 4. 17

Reference Sheet
28 S.W. Edition 4a.

The 48th. Infantry Brigade will relieve the 47th. Infantry Brigade in the VIERSTRAAT SECTOR on the 19th. April 1917.
On relief 47th. Brigade will move into Divisional Reserve.

1. RELIEF
The 2nd. Royal Dublin Fusiliers will relieve the Royal Munster Fusiliers in BUTTERFLY CAMP
The relief will commence at 2 p.m.

2. DISPOSITIONS ON RELIEF.
On relief the Battalion will be disposed as follows:-

"W" Company CLARE CAMP M.35 A 8.6
"X" Company DONCASTER HUTS

"Y" Company)
"Z" Company) TULLY HOE CAMP X 5 C 5.5.
Battn. Hdqrs.)

3. ADVANCE PARTIES.
An advance party of 1 Officer, 1 N.C.O. and 4 men from "X" Company will leave BUTTERFLY FARM at 1.30 p.m. .
Advance Parties of 1 Officer, 1 N.C.O. and 4 men each from "Y" and "Z" Coys. and 1 N.C.O. and 2 men from Hdqr. Coy. will move off from BUTTERFLY CAMP at 10 a.m. and proceed to TULLYHOE CAMP.
Parade outside Orderly Room, the senior Officer will take the party.
Haversack rations will be carried.

4. TAKING & HANDING OVER.
The Second in Command will take over TULLYHOE CAMP. The Camp will be ready by 12 noon. The officer from "X" Company who goes with the advance party will take over the portion of DONCASTER HUTS allotted to "X" Company. He will arrange with the representative of the Leinster Regiment.
Lieutenant H.R.H. O'Reilly will arrange to take over CLARE CAMP. The Quartermaster will hand over BUTTERFLY CAMP to the incoming Unit, the 2nd. Royal Dublin Fusiliers at 12 noon.
All handing over and taking over Certificates will be rendered to Orderly Room by 11 a.m. the 20 th. inst.

5. ORDER OF MARCH .
Companies will move off from BUTTERFLY FARM in the following order at the time stated
"Y" 2 p.m.)
"Z" 2.30 p.m.) Route to TULLYHOE CAMP via LOCRE S.3.d.2.6.,
Hdqrs. 3.0 p.m.) M.32.b.6.4. & M.31.d.8.5. . or via MONT-VIDAIGNE, MONTNOIR, M.26.c.45.40

"X" Company 3.30 p.m. Packs will be carried

6. MOVEMENT.
All movements will be by platoons at 200 yds. interval.

7. WORKING PARTIES.

Parties B.1 (a) and B.1(b) will be found by O.C. "X" Company on the 19th. inst.. Packs, equipment and Great coats (if not worn) of party B.1(b) will be taken to DONCASTER HUTS by Transport. O.C. "X" Company will detail a party to unload at DONCASTER HUTS and remain in charge of the above.

8. LEWIS GUNS.

Transport will be provided for Lewis Guns. Lewis Gun hand Carts will be sent to transport lines.

9. BAGGAGE.

All baggage and blankets will be stacked in Company Lines by 10 a.m. ready for removal. Officers mess kit will be taken on the Company GENERAL PURPOSE CARRIER.

10. WATERCARTS.

1 Watercart will be sent to TULLYHOE CAMP and 1 to CLARE CAMP

11. TRANSPORT

The Transport Officer will arrange for transport for the following :-

(1). Blankets and baggage
(2). Packs, equipment and Great coats of 47 O.R. on Working party B.1.(b).
(3). Lewis Guns and ammunition.
(4). 14 tents to be taken from BUTTERFLY CAMP to CLARE CAMP. These will be struck by 9.30 a.m., O.C. Detachment Leinster Regt. BUTTERFLY CAMP will arrange.
1 Motor Lorry will report at BUTTERFLY FARM at 10 a.m.

12. Companies will report by wire to Battalion Headquarters TULLYHOE CAMP when all the Companies are in New Billets.

13. Acknowledge.

Issued at 8.15 pm. Copy No. 14

(Sd.) . C. H. EXHAM, Captain, A/Adjt.,

Royal Munster Fusiliers.

Copy No. 1 to O.C. "W" Coy.
Copy No. 2 to O.C. "X" Coy.
Copy No. 3 to O.C. "Y" Coy.
Copy No. 4 to O.C. "Z" Coy.
Copy No. 5 to 47th. Brigade.
Copy No. 6 to Comdg. Offr.
Copy No. 7 2nd. in Command
Copy No. 8 to Transport Officer
Copy No. 9 to Quartermaster
Copy No. 10 to R. S. M.
Copy No. 11 to 7th. Leinster Regt.
Copy No. 12 to "A" Royal Dublin Fuslrs.
Copy No. 13 to O.C. Detachment Leinster Regt.

Copy No 14) File.
Copy No. 15)

SECRET   No. 2[illegible]

OPERATION ORDERS

By

Major R. T. Goodland Comdg. Royal Munster Fusiliers.

In the Field 17. 4. 17

Reference 28 S.W. 4 a

1. "D" Company will parade on the road outside Orderly Room at 10 a.m. to-morrow morning the 18th. inst., and will move off at 10.5 a.m. to CLARE CAMP M. 33.a.8.6.
   They will be accomodated there until joined by the remainder of the Battalion on the 19th. inst..

2. All movements to the New Camp will be by platoons at 200 yds. interval.

3. The O.C. "D" Company will get the camp prepared for occupation by the Battalion on the 19th. inst.. The Quartermaster will take the camp over on the 19th. inst..

4. "D" Company's Cooker will accompany the Company on the March. Dinners will be had on arrival at CLARE CAMP.

5. Officers' baggage and the men's blankets will be piled ready for removal by 9 a.m.

6. Packs will be carried.

7. The Transport Officer will arrange for the removal of baggage and blankets to CLARE CAMP.

8. Arrival at CLARE CAMP will be reported by wire to Battalion Headquarters.

9. Acknowledge.

Issued at ...10:40 pm....   Copy No...7.......

Copy No. 1	O.C. "D" Company
" " 2	Transport Officer
" " 3	Quartermaster
" " 4	47th. Brigade
" " 5	Comdg. Officer.
" " 6	R. S. M.
" " 7 }	File
" " 8 }	

Captain, A/Adjutant,

Royal Munster Fusiliers.

Appendix F.

SECRET No. 26

OPERATION ORDERS
By
Major H. T. Goodland Comdg. Royal Munster Fusiliers.
In the Field 24. 4. 17

1 RELIEF

Royal Munster Fusiliers will move from their present billets on 25th. April 1917 and will be disposed as follows in new billets.:-

"W" "Y" "Z" and Headquarters Coys. KEMMEL SHELTERS

"X2 Company DONCASTER HUTS.

2. ORDER OF MARCH
"X" Company will remain as at present.
"Y" Company will leave TALLYHO CAMP at 9.30 a.m.
"Z" Company will leave TALLYHO CAMP at 10.0 a.m.
"W" Company will leave CLARE CAMP at 11.15 a.m.
Headquarter Coy. will leave TALLYHO CAMP at 10.30 a.m.
Dress - Full marching Order. Steel Helmets will be worn.

3. TAKING AND HANDING OVER

The Quartermaster will take over KEMMEL SHELTERS. He will arrange for the Company Quarter master Sergeants of "W" "Y" and "Z" and Sgt. Mc.Cann for Headquarters Coy. to attend.
O.C. "W" Company will detail 1 Officer to hand over CLARE CAMP
2nd. In Command will hand over TALLYHO CAMP.

4. MOVEMENT.
Movements East of a line drawn North and South through WESTOUTRE will be by platoons at 300 yards interval.

5. WATERCARTS.
1 watercart will be sent to KEMMEL SHELTERS.

6. BAGGAGE.
All baggage, kits, blankets etc., of "Y" and "Z" Companies will be stacked outside Orderly Room by 9 a.m.
"W" Company's baggage, kits, blankets etc., will be stacked by 10 a.m. at CLARE CAMP.
Officers mess boxes, etc., will be taken on the General Purpose Carrier.

7. TRANSPORT.

Transport Officer will arrange for the necessary Transport for the removal of Stores from TALLYHO CAMP and from CLARE CAMP.

8. SANITATION

Great care will be taken to see that TALLYHO CAMP and CLARE CAMP are left in a clean and Sanitary condition.

9. O.C. Companies will report to Battalion Headquarters at KEMMEL SHELTERS when their Companies get in their new positions.

(Signed). C.H. EXHAM, Captain,

A/Adjutant, Royal Munster Fusiliers

SECRET

Appendix G

OPERATION ORDERS No. 27
By
Lt. Colonel R. H. Monck-Mason Comdg. 1st. Royal Muns. Fuslrs.
In the Field 28. 4. 17

xxxxxxxxxxxxxxxxxxxxxxxxxxxxxxxxxxxx

Ref. Sheet 28 S.W. 4 A 1/20,000
and Sheet 27 S.E. 1/20,000

---

1. RELIEF.
The 1st. Royal Munster Fusiliers will be relieved in their present billets and march to new Billets in the CAESTRE AREA on the 30th. April 1917.

2. ADVANCE PARTY.
An advance party of one N.C.O. per Company and 1 N.C.O. from Headquarter Company will be at LOCRE CHURCH at 5 p.m. on the 29th. inst., where a bus will meet them to convey them to the new Area.
The unexpended portion of the day's rations and rations for the 30th. will be taken, also one blanket per N.C.O..
This party will remain in the New Billets on the night of the 29th.
Lt. H. H. Lake, the billeting Officer, will ride over to the new area on the morning of the 29th. inst., and reconnoitre the area.
The area allotted to the Battalion is Squares W.3.d., W.4., W.9, W.10.W.16.
Suggested Transport Site is at W. 3. d. 10.05.
He will arrange for his servant and kit to travel on the bus with advance party.
The Brigade Interpreter will meet the Billeting Officer at ROUGE CROIX at 4 p.m. on the 29th. inst..

3. HANDING OVER.
2nd. Lt. F. A. HALDANE and 1 N.C.O. and three men from "W" "Y" and "Z" Companies and 1 N.C.O. and three men from Headquarter Company will remain at KEMMEL SHELTERS to load Lorries and clean the Camp.
1 man from each Company will be detailed to ride on one of the Lorries On completion of duty they will join the Battalion in the new Area.
The Quartermaster will hand over the Camp.
Route - Via - BAILLEUL - METEREN - FLETRE.
O. C. "X" Company will arrange with O.C. 7th. Leinster Regiment to hand over the portion of DONCASTER HUTS occupied by "X" Company to the Representative of the 7th. Leinster Regiment, on the morning of the 30th. before moving off.

4. ORDER OF MARCH
The Battalion will move off on the 30th. inst., in the order and at the time stated.
Headquarter Company 7 - 8 a.m. (in two platoons).
"W" Company 7.15 a.m. "Y" Company 7.32 a.m. "Z" Company 7.48 a.m.
"X" Company will follow "W" Company as a Company as soon as the last Platoon of "W" Company has passed DONCASTER HUTS.
Movements East Of LOCRE will be by platoons at 300 yards interval.
The Battalion will close up on the head of the Column at M.34.a.80.90., and will move off from there as a Battalion.
All movements will be in threes.
Pack mules will be in rear of each Company. Limbers and Lewis Gun Hand carts in rear of the Battalion. O's C. Companies will detail one man to call at Transport Lines and lead Company Pack mules.
O's C. Companies will detail two Lewis Gunners per Limber to march in rear of Limbers.
Sergeant Murphy will take charge of Lewis Gun Limbers.

5. BAGGAGE ETC.
All baggage, blankets, kits, etc., will be stacked by 6 a.m. the 30th. inst., ready for removal.
"W" "Y" "Z" and Headquarter Companies' Kits will be stacked outside Company Lines near the road.
"X" Company on the parade Ground at DONCASTER HUTS.

6. TRANSPORT

Transport - less pack animals, Lewis Gun Limbers and Lewis Gun Handcarts (which will accompany the Battalion) will move under Brigade Transport Officer in order of Units.
2 Motor Lorries will be at LOCRE CHURCH at 8 a.m. on the 30th. inst., for use of the Transport Officer.
The Quartermaster will arrange for a guide to be there to take over Lorries from a representative of 47th. Brigade.
"W" "Y" and "Z" Companies are allotted one Limber each for Lewis Guns.
"X" Company will draw the 6 Lewis Gun Handcarts from Transport Lines, at 9 a.m. 29th. inst....

7. WORKING PARTIES

No working parties will be found on the 30th. inst.

8. BREAKFASTS

Breakfasts will be had at 6 a.m.

9. DRESS Marching Order, with helmets carried on the pack.

10. CERTIFICATE

The usual certificates as to handing over will be obtained and handed in to Orderly Room by 12 noon on the 1st. proximo.

11. O.C. Companies will report in writing by runner when their Companies are in Billets.

(Signed) C. H. EXHAM, Captain,

A/Adjutant, 1st. Royal Munster Fusiliers.

Issued at ....11 pm........ Cop No. ...14.......

Copy No1 to Commanding Officer
Copy No. 2 to Adjutant.
Copy No. 3 to R. S. M.
Copy No. 4 to Battalion Signalling Officer
Copy No. 5 to Battalion Intelligence Officer
Copy No. 6 O. C. "W" Company
Copy No. 7 O.C. "Y" Company
Copy No. 8 O.C. "Z" Company
Copy No. 9 O.C. "X" Company
Copy No. 10 to O.C. 7th. Leinsters
Copy No. 11 to 47th. Bde. H.Q.
Copy No. 12 to Transport Officer
Copy No. 13 to Quartermaster

Copies 14 & 15) File.

W A R D I A R Y :

-----------oOo----------

VOLUME:-

FOR MONTH OF MAY, 1917.

UNIT:- 1st Royal Munster Fusiliers

Vol. 15

Instructions regarding War Diaries and Intelligence Summaries are contained in F. S. Regs., Part II. and the Staff Manual respectively. Title pages will be prepared in manuscript.

WAR DIARY
or
INTELLIGENCE SUMMARY.
(*Erase heading not required.*)

Army Form C. 2118.

1st Bn R. Munster Fusiliers.

Place	Date	Hour	Summary of Events and Information	Remarks and references to Appendices
KEMMEL SHELTERS	1.5.17	10 am	The 1st Royal Munster Fusiliers were relieved by the 7th Leinster Regt (less one company) and proceeded to DONCASTER HUTS. 5 Officers reported for duty. Captain L. S. KING took over command of Z Coy from Capt. I.C.C. LEE. 2Lt G.J. FREEMAN posted to Z Coy. 2Lt J R LOVE to Y Coy, 2Lt C.F. ENNIS to X Coy and 2Lt C. SHEIL to W Coy. Strength 47 Officers and 1054 Other ranks. Hospital 1 man.	See App: A.
DONCASTER HUTS.	2.5.17		Training carried on in Bomb throwing - Lewis Gun - and wiring - Working parties found. Strength 47 Officers and 1059 other ranks. 4 men rejoined + 6 to hospital.	
DONCASTER HUTS.	3.5.17		Captain O'Brien and Capt Pearce struck off. Training carried on in Bomb throwing - and rapid wiring - working parties found. Strength 45 Officers and 1051 Other ranks. Hospital 1 - Rejoined 1.	
DONCASTER HUTS.	4.5.17.	8/10 am	Lieut Maher attached to Trench Mortar Battery. Divine Service for R.C. at LOCRE CHURCH. Strength 44 Officers and 1051 Other ranks. Hospital 10 - Rejoined 1.	
DONCASTER HUTS.	5.5.17.	8.45 pm	The 1st Royal Munster Fusiliers commenced to relieve "A" Royal ~~[illegible]~~ in the left sub section of the VIERSTRAAT SECTOR. Z Coy - Front line. Coy HQ WATLING Street. Y Coy 3 platoons in WATLING Street and one in VAN KEEP. X Coy in SP 13 - and W 1 platoon in CHINESE WALL N. one platoon CHINESE WALL S. 1 in FORT HALLIFAX and 1 in YORK HOUSE. BATT HQ YORK HOUSE. Strength 44 Officers and 1042 Other ranks. Hospital 8. Rejoined 3.	See app: B.

2353 Wt. W2544/1454 700,000 5/15 D. D. & L. A.D.S.S./Forms/C. 2118.

Instructions regarding War Diaries and Intelligence Summaries are contained in F. S. Regs., Part II. and the Staff Manual respectively. Title pages will be prepared in manuscript.

WAR DIARY

or

~~INTELLIGENCE SUMMARY.~~ 1st Bn R Munster Fusiliers.

(Erase heading not required.)

Army Form C. 2118.

Place	Date	Hour	Summary of Events and Information	Remarks and references to Appendices
Left Sub-Section. VIERSTRAAT SECTOR	6.5.17.		Nothing of importance occurred. The line was quiet in our sector. Strength 44 officers and 1037 other ranks. Hospital 1 rejoined 3. 2 Lieutenants O'Sullivan, O'Reilly and Williams reported for duty. 2 Lts O'Sullivan & Williams to [illegible] Coy. 2 Lt O'Reilly to [illegible] Coy. H.N.L.	
Do.	7.5.17.	10.15 pm	~~Nothing of importance occurred~~ – H.N.L. Strength 47 officers and 1039 other ranks. 2 men to [illegible]. 3 wounded and 1 to Hospital. Draft of 36 other ranks arrived. At 10.15 pm YORK HOUSE was shelled for 40 minutes with 200 odd rounds of 150 mm 105 and 77 mms. Two men were wounded, no damage was done. H.N.L.	
Do.	8.5.17		Nothing of importance occurred – Strength 47 officers and 1070 other ranks. Hospital 5 – rejoined 3. H.N.L. –	
Do	9.5.17	11 pm	Nothing of importance occurred – A patrol went out and reported on state of enemy's wire opposite N18.7. Returned at 12.30 am. 9/10th. Strength 47 officers and 1065 other ranks. Hospital 2 wounded 1. rejoined 5. H. N. Lake Lt. –	

2353 Wt. W2544/1454 700,000 5/15 D. D. & L. A.D.S.S./Forms/C. 2118.

Instructions regarding War Diaries and Intelligence Summaries are contained in F. S. Regs., Part II. and the Staff Manual respectively. Title pages will be prepared in manuscript.

WAR DIARY

~~or INTELLIGENCE SUMMARY~~. 2nd Bn. R. Munster Fusiliers.

(Erase heading not required.)

Army Form C. 2118.

Place	Date	Hour	Summary of Events and Information	Remarks and references to Appendices
Left Sub Sector VIERSTRAAT SECTOR	10.5.17	9 pm	The 2nd Bn R. Munster Fusiliers were relieved by the 8th R. Inniskilling Fusiliers and proceeded to CURRAGH Camp. Strength 47 officers and 1070 other ranks. Hospital 5. Rejoined 3. H.N.L.	App: C.
CURRAGH CAMP	11.5.17	10.55 am	Battalion marched to ROUGE CROIX. CAESTRE. Strength 47 officers and 1070 other ranks. Hospl. Rejoined 1. H.N.L.	App: D.
ROUGE CROIX. CAESTRE	12.5.17	9.30 am	Mass at CAESTRE. Strength 47 officers and 1073 other ranks. 1 to U.K. Hospl. Rejoined 1. Draft of 28. H.N.L.	
Do	13.5.17		Training carried out in Bombing, bayonet fighting, the attack & rifle range. Captain L. S. King took over command of X Company from Lt F. S. Woodley. Captain LAWLOR on rejoining took over Z Company from Capt KING. Strength 47 officers and 1100 other ranks. Hosp. 4. H.N.L.	
Do	14.5.17		Training in Bombing, bayonet fighting, the attack and rifle range. Strength 47 officers and 1073 other ranks. Hospital 2. Draft of 5 joined. H.N. Lake Lt.	

2353 Wt. W2544/1454 700,000 5/15 D. D. & L. A.D.S.S./Forms/C. 2118.

Army Form C. 2118.

WAR DIARY
or
~~INTELLIGENCE~~ SUMMARY. 1st Bn R. Munster Fusiliers.
(Erase heading not required.)

Instructions regarding War Diaries and Intelligence Summaries are contained in F. S. Regs., Part II. and the Staff Manual respectively. Title pages will be prepared in manuscript.

Place	Date	Hour	Summary of Events and Information	Remarks and references to Appendices
ROUGE CROIX CAESTRE	15.5.17		Strength - 47 officers and 1099 other ranks. Hospital 7 - rejoined 3. H.H.L.	~~App~~ HHL
DO.	16.5.17	10.15 am	Battalion moved to training area - three days march - 1st day half at WALLON CAPPEL. Strength 47 officers and 1095 other ranks. Hospital 3. H.H.L.	App: E.
WALLON CAPPEL	17.5.17	10 am	Moved to LONGUENESSE via ARQUES. Strength 47 officers 1092 other ranks. Hosp 2 - Base 1 - rejoined 1. H.H.L.	
LONGUENESSE.	18.5.17	10 am	Moved to BAYENGHEM les SENINGHEM. Strength 47 officers 1090 other ranks - Hosp 1 HHL.	
BAYENGHEM les SENINGHEM.	19.5.17		Strength 47 officers and 1088 other ranks. Hosp 1. Draft 8 ? H.H.L.	
DO.	20.5.17		Divine Service at 8.30 am. Strength 47 officers and 1096 other ranks. Hosp. 2 rejoined 7. H.H.L.	

H. H. Lake Lt.

2353 Wt. W2544/1454 700,000 5/15 D. D. & L. A.D.S.S./Forms/C. 2118.

Army Form C. 2118.

WAR DIARY
or
~~INTELLIGENCE SUMMARY~~. 1st Bn R. Munster Fusiliers.

(Erase heading not required.)

Instructions regarding War Diaries and Intelligence Summaries are contained in F. S. Regs., Part II. and the Staff Manual respectively. Title pages will be prepared in manuscript.

Place	Date	Hour	Summary of Events and Information	Remarks and references to Appendices
BAYENGHEM LES SENINGHEM	21.5.17		Training carried out on specially selected and modelled ground for a possible attack to be made. Strength 47 Officers and 1111 other ranks – Hospital 4, rejoined 7. H.H.L.	
Do.	22.5.17		Strength 47 Officers and 1115 other ranks. Transferred 2. Base 3. Hosp 2. From Hosp 4. H.H.L.	
Do.	23.5.17		Strength 47 Officers and 1112 other ranks – Capt Bolton to U.K. Hosp 4 – from Hosp 1. H.H.L.	
Do.	24.5.17		Strength 46 Officers and 1110 other ranks. From Hosp 2 – to Hosp 6 – Draft of 3 joined. H.H.L.	
Do.	25.5.17		Strength 46 Officers and 1109 other ranks Hosp 3. rejoined 1. H.H.L	
Do	26.5.17		Strength 46 Officers and 1107 other ranks. 2nd Lieut Harris to MGC. Hosp 6 Draft of 6 joined. H.H.L.	
Do.	27.5.17		Strength 45 Officers and 1107 other ranks. From Hosp: 2 H.H.L.	
Do	28.5.17		Strength 45 Officers and 1109 other ranks. Hosp 3. H.H.L.	
Do	29.5.17	7am	Strength 45 Officers and 1106 other ranks. Hosp 4 – from Hosp: 1. The Battalion marched to ARQUES. H.H.L.	
ARQUES	30.5.17	8am	The Battalion marched to WALLON CAPPEL area. Strength 45 Officers and 1103 other ranks. Hosp 5 H.H.L.	Appendix F.
WALLON CAPPEL.	31.5.17	7.30am	The Battalion marched 12 miles to CLARE CAMP. Strength 45 Officers and 1098 other ranks. Hosp 9.	

H. H. Lake. Lt
1st Bn R. Munster Fusiliers

2353 Wt. W2544/1454 700,000 5/15 D. D. & L. A.D.S.S./Forms/C. 2118.

SECRET.

WAR DIARY.

FOR MONTH OF JUNE, 1917.

VOLUME :-

UNIT:- 1st Battn Royal Munster Fusrs

Vol 16

Instructions regarding War Diaries and Intelligence Summaries are contained in F. S. Regs., Part II. and the Staff Manual respectively. Title pages will be prepared in manuscript.

WAR DIARY or INTELLIGENCE SUMMARY.

(Erase heading not required.)

Army Form C. 2118.

(1)

1st R. Munster Fusiliers.

Place	Date	Hour	Summary of Events and Information	Remarks and references to Appendices
	1917			
CLARE CAMP.	JUNE 1st		Battalion under canvas. Companies bathed and fitted clothes and boots. Owing to hostile long distance shelling during early hours of morning, the Brigadier ordered all ranks to sleep in fields adjacent to Camp for safety. Strength, O 45 OR. 1084 To Hosp. 3 From Hosp 2 Lt Poindestre struck off.	
	2.		Continued bathing and fitting boots and clothing. Overland routes to front line reconnoitred by Coy. officers and trenches in the VIERSTRAET SWITCH visited. Strength, O 44 OR. 1083 To Hosp. 7 Killed 1. Wd 4 From Hosp 2. (Capt Eshaw to G.H.Q. School)	
VIERSTRAET SWITCH TRENCH SYSTEM.	3		Battalion marched at 9.45 pm via overland routes to new position in the VIERSTRAET SWITCH, in battle order. Some casualties caused by shelling around ROSSIGNOL ESTAMINET. Many tear gas shells fired. Strength, O. 43 OR. 1070 To Hosp. 1 From Hosp 2 Kd 1	Bde. Order BATTN. ORDER.
	4		Companies distributed as follows:- W Coy in ROOK TRENCH, with H.Q. in DOCTORS HD. X Coy in RAVEN TRENCH with H.Q. in DOCTORS HD.	J Edwards 7/05 for C.R.M.F.

T2134. Wt. W708—776. 500000. 4/15. Sir J. C. & S.

Instructions regarding War Diaries and Intelligence Summaries are contained in F. S. Regs., Part II. and the Staff Manual respectively. Title pages will be prepared in manuscript.

WAR DIARY
or
INTELLIGENCE SUMMARY.
(Erase heading not required.)

(2)

Army Form C. 2118.

1st R. Muns. Fus.

Place	Date	Hour	Summary of Events and Information	Remarks and references to Appendices
	JUNE.		Contd.	
VIERSTRAET SWITCH.	4		Y Coy. in STORK TRENCH RIGHT, and Z Coy in STORK TRENCH LEFT. Battalion H.Q. in KNOLL DUGOUTS, ROSSIGNOL ROAD. Pack mule transport only used for bringing rations. Considerable hostile shelling with H.V. and LACHRYMATORY shells. Strength O. [illegible] OR 1070 To Hosp. Killed nil Wounded From Hosp 3	
	5		Battalion being equipped with battle stores and S.A.A. and Grenades etc. Water cans being concentrated and carrying parties being organized. Strength. O. 43 OR 1069 To Hosp.	
	6		Battalion finally equipped with all battle stores and equipment. From Hosp 4 To Base 1 Battalion moved into their assembly positions and completely posted by 2 a.m. 7th. Position was along CHINESE WALL between SPs 11 & 12. Jumping off trenches were dug along front of CHINESE WALL. 100 OR and 2 officers of 6th CONNAUGHT RANGERS, as moppers up accompanied Battn. and were posted 50 yds E of CHINESE WALL. Battalion H.Q. were in IRISH HOUSE DUGOUTS. Strength O. 43 OR. 1060 To Hosp. 2 From Hosp 1	J. E. [illegible] R. Mun. Fus.

T2134. Wt. W708—776. 500000. 4/15. Sir J. C. & S.

Instructions regarding War Diaries and Intelligence Summaries are contained in F. S. Regs., Part II. and the Staff Manual respectively. Title pages will be prepared in manuscript.

WAR DIARY or INTELLIGENCE SUMMARY.

(Erase heading not required.)

Army Form C. 2118.

(3)

1st Royal Munster Fusiliers

Place	Date	Hour	Summary of Events and Information	Remarks and references to Appendices
Kemmel [illegible]	June 7		Report on operations leading to the capture of Wytschaete attached. Strength O. 43 O.R. 1059. To Hosp. 1 Off. killed (2/Lt. T. Hursey) 52 OR killed. 2 Offs Wod. (2/Lt Sheil & Lt Marshall) 106 OR wounded	Report on Wytschaete A. Letter to Bn from [illegible] B. Maps showing [illegible] C. Operation order D. Report on operations by [illegible] E.
"	8.		At 7 am. the Battalion was relieved by the 7th R. I. Rifles and came back to the Alberta Dugouts. Strength O. 40 O.R. 948. To Hosp 2. 1 Accdt wounded. From Hosp 2	
Butterfly Farm	9		The Battalion marched off by Platoons at intervals at 1 p.m. for Butterfly Farm. Clothing, Boots and equipment inspections carried out. Strength O 40 O.R. 947	
"	10		Companies bathed and fitted clothes + Boots. Strength O 40 O.R. 951. 3 from Hosp. To Hosp 4	
"	11		Continued Inspections. Bathing Parades. Strength O 40 O.R. 946. To Hosp 6	
	12		Companies at the disposal of Coy Comm. for parades & inspection. Strength O 40 O.R. 940	
Meteren Area	13		Battalion moved to the Meteren Area. Strength O 40 O.R. 940. To Hosp. 3 From Hosp. 2	J. Ewart? Lt for OC RMF

T2134. Wt. W708—776. 500000. 4/15. Sir J. C. & S.

Instructions regarding War Diaries and Intelligence Summaries are contained in F. S. Regs., Part II. and the Staff Manual respectively. Title pages will be prepared in manuscript.

WAR DIARY
or
INTELLIGENCE SUMMARY.
(*Erase heading not required.*)

(H) 1st Royal Munster Fusiliers

Army Form C. 2118.

Place	Date	Hour	Summary of Events and Information	Remarks and references to Appendices
	June			
Metteren AREA	14		Lewis Gun Class under Capt Lee + Sec Lt Love started Bombing, Bayonet Fighting + Musketry exercises carried on from 9 A.M to 12.30 p.m. Company + Platoon Drill 2 to 3 p.m. Strength O. 40. O.R. 938. To Hosp. 2. From Hosp. 1.	
	15		Above Parades continued Strength O 40. O.R 937. To Hosp. 8. From Hosp. 1.	
	16		Divine Service Parades Strength O 40. O.R. 930 To Hosp. 3 From Hosp. 3 Draft 3 joined [illegible] to R.F.C. [illegible]	[illegible]
BUTTERFLY FARM	17.		Battalion moved to Butterfly Farm Strength O 36. O.R. 933 To Hosp. 6. From Hosp. 1	
METTEREN AREA	18		From 1 AM to 3.40 AM Butterfly Farm was under Shell Fire from the enemy. During the bombardment the troops took cover in trenches behind the Farm. There were two casualties At 8 AM the Battalion moved off for the Metteren area Strength O 36 O.R 928 From Hosp 1.	J E [illegible]

T2134. Wt. W708—776. 500000. 4/15. Sir J. C. & S.

WAR DIARY
or
INTELLIGENCE SUMMARY.
(Erase heading not required.)

Army Form C. 2118.

Instructions regarding War Diaries and Intelligence Summaries are contained in F. S. Regs., Part II. and the Staff Manual respectively. Title pages will be prepared in manuscript.

(5) 1st Royal Munster Fusiliers

Place	Date	Hour	Summary of Events and Information	Remarks and references to Appendices
	June			
Metteren	19		Companies bathed & fitted boots & clothing	
			Strength O 36 OR. 927 To Hosp 11. From Hosp 3	
ECKE AREA.	20		Battalion moved off for Godewaersvelde (Ecke Area) arriving at 7.10 A.M	
			Strength O. 36 OR. 919.	
	21		Companies at disposal of Company Commrs. for various inspections	
			Strength O. 26 OR. 919 To Hosp 3. From Hosp 1.	
Esquelbecq AREA.	22		Battalion moved to LEGGERS-CAPPEL (ESQUELBECQ AREA)	
			Strength O. 26. OR. 917 To Hosp 3 From Hosp 1.	
	23		Companies at the disposal of Coy. Commds for inspection of Clothing Rifles, Ammunition & Feet.	
			Strength O 26 OR. 915. To Cadet School 1. To Hosp 2 From Hosp: 7. Ptes Cahill & Bateman joined Draft 23/6/[illegible]	
	24		Divine Services held at LEGGERS-CAPPEL	
			Strength O 38 OR. 929. To Hosp 4 From Hosp 1. Draft of 7 joined.	

[illegible signature] for OC 1st R.M.F.

T2134. Wt. W708—776. 500000. 4/15. Sir J. C. & S.

Instructions regarding War Diaries and Intelligence Summaries are contained in F. S. Regs., Part II. and the Staff Manual respectively. Title pages will be prepared in manuscript.

WAR DIARY
or
INTELLIGENCE SUMMARY.

(6)

(Erase heading not required.)

1st ROYAL MUNSTER FUSILIERS.

Army Form C. 2118.

Place	Date	Hour	Summary of Events and Information	Remarks and references to Appendices
ZEGERS CAPPEL.	June	25.	NIL. Strength Off 38 Other Ranks 939. To Hosp. 4 From Hosp. 1 Draft of 7 joined.	
	"	26	NIL. Instructions regarding parade for rehearsal for inspection by G.O.C. 19th Corps. Strength Off 38. O Ranks 943.	Hosp.
	"	27.	Inspection by G.O.C. 19th Corps. Strength Off 38 Other Ranks 942. To Hosp. 6. From Hosp 2	
	"	28.	NIL. Off 38. O Ranks 938. To Hosp. 4 From Hosp 2	
	"	29.	NIL. Off 38 O Ranks 936 To Hosp. 3. From Hosp. 1. Draft of 11 joined	
	"	30.	NIL. Off 38. O Ranks 945.	

J Edwards 2/Lt
for O.C. 1 R.M.F.

T2134. Wt. W708—776. 500000. 4/15. Sir J. C. & S.

S E C R E T

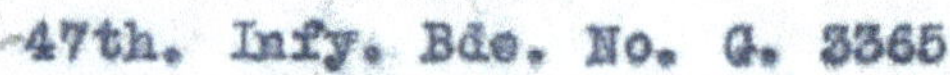

47th. Infy. Bde. No. G. 3365

Report on the WYTSCHAETE Operations June 1917.

1. Preliminary dispositions. On the night of the 2/3 June The 47th. Infantry Brigade welieved the 48th. Brigade in the right subsection of the VIERSTRAAT, the front extending from N.24.c.2.2. to N.24.a.45.78, a distance of 800 yards in a straight line. The line was unsuitable for a Jumping Off ground owing to the pronounced ASH POINT Salient, whilst the Northern 50 or 60 Yards with SNIPE TRENCH and LARK LANE had been so persistently destroyed by the enemy that thy were untenable. The Support Line was made up of PARK AVENUE and FARMER TRENCH some 200 Yards in rear with a Reserve Line along the CHINESE WALL about 600 Yards in rear of the front line, behind this was the VIERSTRAAT SWITCH , the second line of defence, about a mile from the front line.

The main communications were VIA GELLIA this was in a good state except for the last 150 Yards to the East which was constantly being destroyed by the enemy. ROSSIGNOL ROAD was very good from YORK ROAD to the CHINESE WALL, but it was blown in for the next 200 yards during the last two orthree days before the attack. Thecommunication along OAK TRENCH has always been a poor trench, and it had the additional disadvantage of running at an angle to the front line . ASH LANE had been improved and remained good to the finish.

Owing to the danger of giving away the projected attack I decided that of the two alternatives it would be better to jump off from the front Line instead of constructing an Assembly trenchat the back to cut off the salient. Another difficulty was the large amount of wire which had been put down without method and at every sort of angle in front of our trenches. This was cut through with great method and very gradually for the last three or four nights.

The 6th. Connaught Rangers occupied the front Trenches from 2nd. to 5th. June with the 1st. Munsters in Support in the VIERSTRAAT SWITCH The form r carried out a very successful raid on the PETIT BOIS Salient on the night of the 4th. June penetrating as far as the NANCY SUPPORT.

On the night of the 5/6th June the front Battalion was relieved by 2 Companies of the 6th. Royal Irish Regt. on the right, and by 2 Companies of the Leinsters on the left. The dividing line betweenx Battalions being ASH POINT. On the night of the 6/7th. June the remaining Companies of these two Battalions moved up from LOCRE whilst the Munsters and Connaught Rangers occupied CHINESE WALL as far North as S.P. 12 inclusive with the hedges on the West. Two rows of Assembly Trenches were also cut about 100 yards to the East of the CHINESE WALL. By 2 a.m. all Units were in position.

2. DISPOSITIONS FOR ATTACK. Two Companies from both the 6th. Royal Irish Regt. and the 7th. Leinsters were in the front Trench and furnished the first two waves, the remainder of these battalions were in the PARK LINE and formed the 3rd. and 4th. Waves.

m The 1st. Munsters around the CHINESE WALL , with 100 men of the 6th. Connaught Rangers as moppers up, were in Reserve.

The remainder of the Connaught Rangers furnished carrying parties Viz:- 100 for the R.E. 90 for Bde. carrying party, 50 for Stokes 40 for 10 M.G's, besides 60 men to furnish Garrisons and labout for 3 strong posts.

A Section of 2 T.M's (Stokes) was attached to each of the 3 attacking Battalions with the 4th. Section in reserve at th ammunition dumps. 2 M.G's were also attached to each attacking Battalion whilst the remaining 10 gunswere under the orders of the D.M.G.O. and were employed in making a barrage, in conjunction with the Artillery. from TIT ROAD.

3. PREPARATIONS ETC.

3. PREPARATIONS BEFORE THE ATTACK.

(a). Each man carried 170 rounds S.A.A. 2 Mills Bombs, current day's ration, 2 sandbags, a waterproof sheet and 2 green flares.

As a second water bottle could not be obtained from Ordnance only one was carried.

Each platoon took one or two yellow and black flags to mark their forward positions, and each Company 30 S.O.S. red lights.

A shovel, behind the pack and pointing upwards, was carried by every alternate man of the first two attacking Battalions and by 5 or 6 men of each platoon in the reserve Battalion.

All available wire cutters and wire breakers were taken.

All brasses on equipment were dulled, as they show up in the sunlight, and bayonets were to be dulled if time permitted, Officers were warned about giving themselves away by showing up their maps, and warned to dirty them. I consider that Khaki coloured maps should be issued.

About 20 Bridges were put down over OAK TRENCH on the last night, as also some across BROADWAY. In the front trench the trench boards, with rungs knocked out were utilized as ladders.

(b). The following points in training were especially practised viz:- The men to kneel at all halts and never lie down. The first line of the first wave to fire when advancing. Lewis Gun to cross fire with each other instead of shooting straight to the front.

Waves not to be more than 50 Yards apart when crossing NO MAN'S LAND. The first line to advance as close as possible to the barrage and not pay too much attention to dressing whilst waves in rear were to be very particular about keeping touch and not losing direction.

The necessity of waves being on the objective hafx 5 minutes before the time of departure so as to start straight and have their boundaries clearly pointed out.

and to leave the Objective punctually to time.

The absolute necessity for correctness in synchronization of watches

Liaison with flank Battalions practised and Officers told off to accompany them.

The importance of keeping up Rifle fire.

Gaps in the wire to be marked with tape, to prevent Units in rear missing them. The importance of avoiding any noise, striking matches or smoking cigarettes when going into or waiting in the Assembly Trenches.

4. Zero was at 3.10 a.m. on the 7th. June. On our front the mines at MAEDELSTEDE and PETIT BOIS went up, the former some four seconds late. At the same time every gun opened fire. The Infantry after waiting 20 seconds for the debris to settle went over the parapet 2 Companies of the Royal Irish on the right and 2 of the Leinsters on the left. They advanced in 2 waves. The light was very bad and the glare from the mines with the dust and falling debris caused the leading waves to lose considerable direction. In addition the MAEDELSTEDE Mine blocked the front of the right Battalion which had to move round either flank. The smoke drifted towards our lines and increased the difficulty. However the moral effect of the mines on the enemy far outweighed all these disadvantages.

Whilst smoke can't be avoided if mines are blown I am against its use in the shape of smoke shells for helping the attack. A decision has to be arrived at some hours before and if the wind changes shortly before Zero the disadvantages to the attackers are far more serious than any advantages that could have been gained if the wind had been favourable.

The barrage was splendid but difficult for advancing troops to follow owing to the effects of the mine explosions, As the waves advance the fumes partially gassed many men, and made them violently sick. The danger was that th enemy might put down a heavy barrage along NO MAN'S LAND which could not be cleared in the deep reentrant 350 yards wide opposite ASH POINT for 12 minutes owing to our own barrage, but to reduce the chance of being caught by the enemy's fire waves closed up to within 30 yards of each other.

The waves were practically into the enemy's front line before any hostile fire was brought to bear on NO MAN'S LAND though a few stray shots unfortunately caused the deaths of Major W. REDMOND and 2nd. Lieut.

2nd. Lieut. HEWETT.
On the right the firs opposition occurred just east of the HAMDELSTEDE crater, where a M.G. and a few Germans offered some resistance , which was soon disposed of, and 12 to 14 of the enemy surrendered. The light increasing, the various waves straightened out and men got into their proper positions as the flank boundaries became visible. The Red Line was secured without further opposition punctually to time (3.30 a.m. by "A" and "B" companies of the Royal Irish Regt. who immediately started consolidating. Up to then the enemy had been shelling our support Line (PARK AVENUE) and the neighbourhood of CHINESE WALL , chiefly with 5.9 and 4.2., and lines of shellx holes about 200 yards to the east of the latter showed the accuracy of his shooting. He now brought back his fire to NO MAN'S LAND and his old front line.
On the left the Leinsters found the front line empty . One prisoner stated he was occupying the front teench when a mine went up within 100 metres of him, half burying him, and he did not know what had happened to his comrades.
NANCY SWITCH was held by the enemy, but they were quickly bayonetted. Great difficulty was experienced going on towards NANCY SUPPORT as the enemy had dug himself into numerous shell holes and owing to smoke it was difficult to see him. Firing from the hip here proved very success--ful and some prisoners were taken.
On reaching the RED LINE there was some confusion owing to Units having been mixed up by loss of direction.
This was however, put right and the Leinster Regiment rested on its proper flank(NANCY AVENUE) It was not however in touch with the ROYAL IRISH the reason probably being that the Leinsters were late in reaching their objective on the right, and the Royal Irish finding their left in the air, had thrown it back to form a defensive flank. A direct hit about 3.30 a.m. on the Leinsters H.Q. in PARK AVENUE seriously wounded Major STANNUS , acting C.O. and Captain ACTON the Adjutant, killed Captain ROCHE of the 47th. T.M. Battery and killed 2nd. Lt. PICKERING and 1 N.C.O. of the 113th. R.F.A. Army Brigade, besides wounding 6 men of the same Brigade.

5. ATTACK ON THE BLUE LINE (SECOND OBJECTIVE).

On the right the Royal Irish advanced at 4.15 a.m. according to Schedu "D" Company on the left immediately found resistance in the BOIS DE WYTSCHAETE , the enemy having taken cover in concrete dugouts etc. unti untilthe barrage passed over them, One Machine Gun held up the right o the Company near N.24.d.5.7. but No. 1 Stokes Section was brought up and fired about 85 rounds whilst the bombers worked roundand soon overcame the opposition. Finding the left od D Company was held up Capta O'BRIEN-BUTLER put himself attheir head and rushed the opposition. He was unfortunately killed by a sniperat a distance of 5 yards, but the men excited by his death swept down all opposition and bayonetted the hostile party. The rest of the advance consisted of tree to tree fighting. C and part of D Company reached the BLUE LINE punctually at 4.30 a.m. The remainder of D had gone too much to their left and got mixed up with the Leinsters.
On the left the 2 Companies of Leinsters were late in coming up. Capt. W. FARRELL of the Leinsters at once decided to push up some of his own men from the RED LINE and about 20 men under 2/nd. Lt. ROBB were pushed on, and secured connection with the 49th. Brigade. in the HOSPICE . The two companies arriving shortly after, the left one met with little opposition, but the right Company came in for a good deal of Machine Gun Fire. and ahad to call on assistance from the Support Company in the RED LINE. After a stiff fight they reached the BLUE LINE about 6.50 a.m. Connection was established all along the BLUE LINE and with the flanks, and a deep traversed trench dug. By the afternoon it had also been protected by wire entanglement. The abnormal heat and very difficult nature of the ground were very trying to the troops.
The tanks moved up on the right of the woods past the BLUE LINE at 6.15 a.m. and drew considerable M.G. Fire The Royal Irish moved forward to their advanced Battalion H.Q. at N.24.c.4.7. at 8.10 a.m. The enemy was then shelling our old support and reserve lines. On arrival at the H.Q. at the RED LINE it was still being shelled with 4.2's

About 9.30 a.m. the shelling practically ceased on it, until 2.30 p.m. when the red and blue lines were again heavily shelled. The Leinster advanced H.Q. were at N.24.b.0.4. When the two Battalions went forward our old front line was held by 6 Lewis Guns of the 6th. Connaught Rangers.

6. NATURE OF THE GROUND.

Whilst our Trenches suffered very little those of the enemy were everywhere battered and his wire knocked about, so that it was no longer an obstacle. It seemed as if hardly a square foot of the enemy's ground had escpaed been hit either by a shell or a T.M. bomb. The ground the Brigade had to traverse included the whole of the PETIT BOIS and the BOIS DE WYTSCHAETE except two or three corners on the North . The main defences of the enemy in the way of M.G. emplacements had been organized in the BOIS DE WYTSCHAETE , whilst the trees (some of which had fallen) gave cover to his snipers . The advance was rendered mor difficult by the WYTSCHAETEBEEK , which rises in a deep pond near the E end of the wood and runs down the centre of the wood forming other deep ponds and bogs, which can only be crossed in places On either side there is a steep rise to the North and South sides of the wood. The interior of the wood was one huge mass of shell holes mixed up with some very deep ones made by our T.M's. East of the wood there is a very steep rise to the Village of WYTSCHAETE . The village itself was a heap of ruins and some of the old wroads were unrecognizable. The main portion of the village lay in our section extending up to the STEINYZER CABARET , which marked our right flank.
The Brigade Boundaries are shown on attached map.

7. ATTACK ON THE GREEN AND BLACK LINES (3rd. & 4th. Objectives).

At 5.50 a.m. the 1st. Munsters left the Assembly trenches , in front of the CHINESE WALL which they had dug in the night of the 6/7th. June. They moved in Artillery Formation "W" and "Y" Coys. leading on the right and left respectively followed by 4 Officers and 100 O.R. of the 6th. Conn. Rgrs. attached as moppers up. These in turn were followed by "X" Company on the right and "Z" Company on the left.
This advance across awful country has been reported by all who saw it as a sight never to be forgotten. A captured German Officer stated they moved as if on parade. A wounded officer stated that as they passed him the men were full of spirits and some were smoking cigarretes.
Notwithstanding the difficulties of the BOIS DE WYTSCHAETE they never lost direction or formation and arrived punctually in time just short of the BLUE LINE where the two leading Companies and the moppers up deployed the 1st. wave consisting of four platoons of "W" and "Y" Company, the 2nd. of the moppers up , and the third , the remaining 4 platoons of "W" and "Y" Coys.
30 Yards separated the waves. Notwithstanding the difficulty of the ground the deployment was well carried out.
The leading Companies crossed the BLUE LINE at 6.50 a.m. according to Schedule, without casualties, Prisoners then began to come in in large numbers, A good deal of opposition, however, was encountered chiefly from enemy snipersand M.G's firing from concrete emplacements. These were quickly silenced without checking the advanceby means of rapid rifle fire and bombing parties on the flanks.
On reaching the WYTSCHAETE -OOSTTAVERNE Road many prisoners were captured in dug-outs, someyimes 25 to 30 at one place. Before reaching a line running N and S through WYTSCHAETE Church several more M.G's were overcome. Here 2nd. Lt. HUSSEY was killed. The two leading Companies reached the GREEN LINE at 7.20 a.m.
Punctually at 7.30 "X" and "Z" Companies crossed the Green Line. Along the srnken road here many prisoners were captured or killed in dugouts.
At 7.50 a.m. the BLACK LINE was taken and consolidation commenced.
The Line

The 48th. Brigade passed through the patrols about 1.40 p.m. when both patrols were withdrawn.
The line selected was actually 150 yards in rear of the position laid down as it had a better field of fire and a ditch in front. These Companies only lost a dozen men in taking their objectives. Owing to shelling the O.C. "X" Company pushed his Company forward about 150 yards in front of the consolidated line. Requirements for digging in were found in the big enemy dump close by, full of engineering stores of all kinds, and covering between 40,000 and 50,000 Square Yards.
Captured dugouts were so well mopped up by the Rangers that not a single enemy appeared after we had passed. They took 1 Officer and 97 O.R. prisoners and 2 M.G's which they handed over to the Munsters.
Great ~~difficulties~~ difficulty was experienced in getting back messages owing to the heavy barrage put on the Village by the enemy.
Soon after reaching the BLACK LINE a big wiring party of the 48th. Brigade came up and wired the position under R.E. supervision. It was not necessary to call on the Stokes for assistance. Captain SCOTT the senior Munster Officer present reports that when first crossing the VIERSTRAAT-OOSTTAVERNE road he noticed several dugouts West of the Church. Some hours later he found they no longer existed, this shows they had been mined by the enemy.
As soon as the GREEN LINE was reported taken carrying parties were sent up to Battalion H.Q. with Bombs, S.A.A. picks and shovels and water in petrol tins. The quantity supplied was more than adequate especially as regards water as 5000 bottles of soda water were discovered in a house near the BLACK LINE.
Captain LAWLOR Commanding "Z" Company states he was continuously in touch with troops on his left and with "X" Company on his right up to the BLACK LINE.

8. ADVANCE TO THE MAUVE LINE.

Owing to the casualties in "Y" Company the left patrol of about 50 men was found by "Z" Company. This patrol and a similar one from "W" Company pushed forward after reaching the BLACK LINE, as far as OIL TRENCH, where they were in touch with each other and a patrol of the WORCESTERS on the left. 2nd. Lt. MOLONEY commanding left patrol, states a number of the enemy were driven out of OOSTTAVERNE wood and hedge rows by our searching barrage. He sent back 17 prisoners and took 5 limbers with dead horses and harness. Two tanks took up a position in rear waiting to see if all was correct before withdrawing. Our right patrol went out at 8.40 a.m. and met a party of Worcesters between SOMMER FARM and LEG COPSE.
The 48th. Brigade passed through the patrols about 1.40 p.m. when both patrols were withdrawn.
When at LEG COPSE the patrol also saw some 77 mm guns about 900 yards to the S.E. These were apparently removed by our cavalry patrols later.

9. 47th. M.Gun Company.
The 10 Guns along TIT ROAD opened barrage fire at 3.11 a.m. At 6.19 a.m. No. 27 gun was temporarily knocked out, and No. 21 Gun at 7.30 a.m. The remaining guns continued firing till 7.50 a.m. when all guns changed their barrels. The teams then quickly cleaned and refilled them with oil and water etc., and moved forward to O.19.d.50.35 where they dug themselves in. By this time 4 guns had consolidated on the BLUE LINE and 2 guns had reached the BLACK LINE, where they dug in. S.A.A. was immediately rushed up by carrying parties and pack mules and very soon over 100,000 rounds were available for all guns, besides 3400 rounds with each gun. Carrying parties consisting of 40 men for the 10 guns and 8 men detailed from each of the three attacking Battalions continued to carry up S.A.A. and water all day. Numerous German Machine Gun Bolts were found, which were immediately filled with our ammunition and were found to work quite well in our guns. The forward 8 guns were withdrawn on relief and after completing the guns on the BLUE LINE to 8, the remainder were withdrawn to the CHINESE WALL.

10. SIGNALLING
The arrangements made by Lieut. FERGUSON, Bde. Signalling Officer, were most excellent and he deserves the greatest credit for his work.
The Brigade Forward Party under Lieut. JOURDAIN of 6th. Conn. Rangers ~~wer~~ were

were in position in the shaft running to LUNETTE dugouts and were in -ed to pass over with the last wave of the leading Battalions. Owing to heavy shelling at the top of the shaft, it was only with great difficulty that the party with its full equipment were safely led out and finally established in the neighbourhood of the junction of NANCY SUPPORT and NANCY AVENUE. Communication was established with the Battalion Forward parties at about 4.10 a.m. thanks to the determination and skilful handling of his men by Lieutenant JOURDAIN. Visual signalling by both leading Battalions was established with KEMMEL HILL and wires run out from the head of the buried cable.
On the advance of the Royal Munster Fusiliers the Brigade forward Station was established at WYTSCHAETE CHURCH and the telephone lines maintained in spite of continual breaks through shell fire.

11. All Battalions agree that the artillery barrage was magnificent. The C.O. 1st. Munsters states, the troops were able to hug it so closely that they were on the enemy before he could offer any very sever resistance. Those who endeavourded to do so were killed and the rest surrendered with eagerness. I consider our small number of 374 casualties was due to the wonderful shooting of the artillery. Every M.G. emplacementI saw had been knocked out and rendered useless before the advance whilst the trenches were everywhere battered almost beyond recognition. The result was that the enemy was completely demoralized before Zero, and his fighting spirit was almost Nil. A German Officer commenting on the opposing artilleries stated " You have only to look on your side all green, on ours, all brown and devastation.

12. An appendix giving our casualties is attached the fact of only 12 men being missing is most satisfactory and reflects great credit on the arrangements for evacuating the woundedand the excellence of Battalion arrangements.
A sketch showing the objectives is also attached.
The Leinsters claim to have captured about 60 prisoners, and to have killed from 80 to 100 of the enemy. The also took 4 machine guns and mountings, 2 Trench Mortars (which were too heavy to remove) 1 M.G. Tripod, (apparently British), some hundreds of rifles and bayonets many thousand rounds of S.A.A. huge quantities of bombs and equipment, and a few hand mines, besides a very fine dynamo in a dugout which could not be moved.
The Royal Irish Regt. took 3 M.G's, 2 medium Minenwerfer and 2 Stick Bomb throwers, but brought noe of them away.
The Munsters took 7 Machine Guns(2 by Conn. Rgs. Mopping up party)
2 Light T.M's and 2 Heavy T.M's
The behaviour of all ranks was splendid, all displayed the same keenness and eagerness and, as is usual with the Irish, the difficulty was in restraining the men.
The result has filled all ranks with the greatest delight, and has raised the morale of the men to the highest pitch.

13. <u>STRONG POINTS.</u>
Three strong points NAG POINT (N.24.d.58.70), WOOD POST (O.19.c.28.95), and CHURCH POST (O.19.b.20.05) were made by the Conn. Rgrs under supervision of the 156th. Field Coy. R.E. They were all completed and wired the same night, and the work reflects great credit on Major MARSDEN and the Royal Engineers. Machine Guns were eventually put into them and the garrisons of 20 men each from the Connaught Rangers were relieved by similar numbers from the Royal Irish the same evening, with the exception of CHURCH POST.

14. The Royal Irish Regt. took over the section occupied by the Leinsters in support at 8 p.m. on the 7th. June, the latter withdrawing to our Old Support line. The former were relieved by 2 Companies of the 7th. Royal Irish Rifles of the 48th. Brigade at 4.30 a.m. on the 8th. whilst the Munsters were relieved by two Companies of the same Regt. at 7.45 a.m. on the samedate. The Brigade was then withdrawn to our Old 1 lines and on the 9th. marched back to back billets.

Tanks.

15. TANKS
The tanks advanced on the right and left of WYTSCHAETE WOOD and advanced towards OOSTTAVERNE WOOD after the BLACK LINE had been taken. The names of the Tanks were "One eyed Riley" and "Riley's Daughter".
On one occasion a tank came up to a dug out just to the South of WYTSCHAETE WOOD and halted, immediately about 20 prisoners came out and surrendered.
The Tanks were out in front while patrols were out
There was not much for them to do owing to want of targets, and most of the M.Gun emplacements etc., had already been demolished by shell fire fire, but the fact of their being there gave great moral support. One of the Tanks came into action about 200 yds. west of WYTSCHAETE CHURCH on the KEMMEL -WYTSCHAETE Road for a short time. They were up to time and in the right place to assist us had an opportunity occurred.

16. I should like to add a special word of praise to Captain PRIESTMAN, Brigade Major, who worked unceasingly day and night, and left nothing forgotten. He was greatly helped by Captain LAMBERT Bde. Intelligence Officer, . Captain HARRISON the Staff Captain was invaluable in arranging about Stores and supplies and everything worked without a hitch. He was well assisted by Captain HALL of the 1st. Munsters and Captain SHAW Bde. Bombing Officer, who worked indefatigably.
It is difficulty to pick out special names when all worked so well, but the four Commanding Officers - Lieut. Colonel ROCHE-KELLY, 6th Royal Irish Regt., Lieut. Colonel FEILDING 6th. Connaught RANGERS, Major STANNUS 7th. Leinsters and Lt. Colonel MONCK-MASON 1st. Munsters, are deserving of special mention for the way in which they trained their men beforehand and handled them during the fight. Captain J. FARRELL took command of the Leinsters when Major STANNUS was wounded, and Lt. WICKHAM of the 47th. T.M. Battery, when Captain ROCHE WAS killed, and both did most excellent work. Captain CLAPHAM of t the 47th. M.G. Coy. again proved his excellence as a Commanding Officer.

(Signed) E. PEREIRA, Brigadier General.

Comdg. 47th. Infantry Brigade.

12. 6. 17

OFFICERS

	Killed	Wounded	Missing
6th. Royal Irish Regt.	4	6	-
6th. Connaught Rgrs.	-	2	-
7th Leinster Regt.	-	8	-
1st. Royal Munster Fus.	1	2	-
47th. T. M. Battery	1	-	-
47th. M. G. Company.	1	-	-
TOTAL	7	18	0

OTHER RANKS

	Killed	Wounded	Missing
6th. Royal Irish Regt.	12	74	4
6th. Connaught Rangers	4	32	2
7th. Leinster Regt.	13	85	5
1st. Royal Munster Fus.rs.	6	94	-
47th. T. M. Battery	1	8	1
47th. M. G. Company	-	8	-
TOTAL	36	301	12

SUMMARY

	Killed	Wounded	Missing
Officers	7	18	-
Men	36	301	12
	43	319	12

GRAND TOTAL 374 Casualties.

HEADQUARTERS.
1st BATTALION
No. 300
Date 15/6/17

REPORT ON OPERATIONS LEADING TO THE CAPTURE OF WYTSCHAETE

------- : BY :-------------

The 1st. Royal Munster Fusiliers

At 5 .50 a.m. on June 7th. 1917 The Battalion left the Assembly Trenches in front of CHINESE WALL which had been prepared on the night of the 6/7th. in Artillery formation, the following being disposition of Companies:

W Company and Y Company led on the right and left respectively. followed by 4 Officers and 100 other Ranks of the 6th. Connaught Rangers attached as moppers up to the Battalion; These were followed in their turn by X Company on the right and Z Company on the left.

The Battalion advanced in good order in the above formation until the leading Companies had arrived at a point just short of the BLUE LINE already captured and held by the 6th. Royal Irish Regiment and the 7th. Leinsters. Here the two Leading Companies and the Moppers up deployed into extended Order forming three waves of which the first consisted of 4 Platoons of "W" and "Y" Company , the second of the Moppers up and the third of the 4 remaining platoons of "W" and "Y" Company. Thirty yards separated the waves. The deployment was well carried out in spite of the wooded and broken nature of the Ground.

The Leading Companies crossed the BLUE LINE at 6.50 a.m. without a casualties. Prisoners then began to come in, in large numbers . A good deal of opposition however, was encountered, chiefly from enemy snipers and Machine Guns, firing from Concrete emplacements. These were quickly silenced without checking the advance by means of rapid rifle fire and bombing parties on the flanks.

On arrival at the WYTSCHAETE-OOSTTAVERNE Road numbers ~~of Prisoners~~ of Prisoners were captured in the Dug-outs there in batches sometimes as large as 25 and 30 men. Before reaching a line running North and South ~~and South~~ through WYTSCHAETE CHURCH several more Machine Guns were overcome. It was here that Lt. HUSSEY was killed ~~and was killed~~ and 2nd. Lt. MARSHALL was wounded both Officers belonging to "Y" Company The two leading Companies reached the GREEN LINE at 7.20 a.m. .

At 7.30 a.m. the 2 rear Companies (X and Z) crossed the GREEN LINE . Along the sunken road ~~road~~ here a large number of prisoners were captured or killed in dug-outs at 7.50 a.m. the BLACK LINE was taken and consolidation at once commenced. The Line consolidated is actually ~~some~~ 30 yards in rear of the position laid down owing to the fact that there was a ditch in front and that a better field of fire could be obtained from the line selected by the Officers Commanding X and Z Company. These Coys. took their objective with a loss of not more than a dozen men between them while they were passing through WYTSCHAETE , however, and during the consolidation the Town was heavily shelled by the enemy especially on the right so that the Officer Commanding W Company thought it advisable to push his Company forward in front of the BLACK LINE as a temporary measure .

A good temporary trench was constructed and firestep, Lewis Gun positions positions were selected and manned 150 yards in front. The organization of the BLACK LINE for defence was facilitated by the presence in the vicinity of a large enemy dump containing engineering stores of all kinds and covering between 40,000 and 50,000 Square Yards.

ARTILLERY

The barrage maintained by our guns was magnificent . The troops were able to hug it so closely that they were on the enemy before he could offer any very severe resistance. . Those who endeavoured to do so were killed and the rest surrendered with eagerness.

MOPPERS UP

Captured dug-outs were so well mopped up during the advance that there is not a single case to record of the enemy appearing from one after our men had passed it by.

COMMUNICATIONS

Great difficulties was experienced in getting messages back after WYTSCHAETE had been taken and much delay was caused in the transmission of messages by the Heavy barrage put upon the Town by the enemy during consolidation of the BLACK LINE

WIRING

Soon after the BLACK LINE was reached a wiring party of the 48th. Infy. Brigade came up and wired the position

MACHINE GUNS AND STOKES

Excellent work was done by the Section of the 47th. Machine Gun Company attached to the Battalion . Great assistance was also rendered by Lt. ~~G. F. MAHER~~
G. F. MAHER and the men of his Section of the 47th. Trench Mortar Battery although the advance was so successful that at no time was it necessary to call upon his guns.

SUPPLIES

As soon as the GREEN LINE was reported taken carrying parties were sent up to Battalion Headquarters with Bombs , S.A.A. Picks and shovels and water in petrol tinsthe quantity supplied in each case was more than adequate especially as regards water as several large cases o f soda water were discovered at the dump in the vicinity of the BLACK LINE .

RELIEF.

The Battalion was relieved by two Companies of the 7th. Royal Irish Rifles at 7.45 a.m. the 8th. inst. :

CASUALTIES

	Officers	Other Ranks	
Killed	1	5	
Wounded	2	63	Total 114.
Missing	-	43	

MINED DUGOUTS.

I should like to point out that Captain SCOTT reports that in Crossing the VIERSTRAAT OOSTTAVERNE Road west of the Church he noticed ~~these~~ severalvdug-outs existing there. On returning to the same place some hours later he found the whole line of dug-outs had ceased to exist . This points to the fact that they had been mined by the enemy.

PATROLS.

Patrols were sent out from the BLACK LINE as directed by B and C Company. They proceed as far as OIL TRENCH No enemy was seen. An Abandoned 77 M.M. Battery was found. The guns which were in good condition were removed by our Cavalry.

CONCLUSION

The success of the Operation was due to the excellent handling ogf the men by Company and Platton Commanders and Sergeants and to the fine discipline, keenness and gallantry displayed by the men themselves. The close touch kept with the Barrage and the promptitude with whichany obstacles encountered were treated.

I cannot speak too highly of the conduct of all Ranks . I am submitting as soon as possible a list of recommendations for immediate reward.

I should like to mention the following remarks made by a captured German Officer .

He stated that he had heard of the fighting capacity of the Irish Soldier but had never met him personally before . He said that my Battalion advanced to the attack as though they were on parade

Appendix 1 Rough Sketch Shewing Boundaries Objectives etc.
Appendix 2. List of Officers who took part in the Offensive.

R Monck Mason Lt. Colonel,

Commanding 1st. Royal Munster Fusiliers.

3. 6. 17

APPENDIX 2

Nominal Roll of Officers who took part in the Offensive

HEADQUARTER COMPANY

Lt. Colonel R. H. Monck-Mason D. S. O.
Captain L. B. King (to remain at Bn. Headquarters)
Lt. & A/Adjutant H. H. Lake
2nd. Lt. GJ. Freeman (ntelligence Officer)
2nd. Lt. D. F. Hartigan (Signalling Officer)

W Company

Captain J. E Scott
2nd. Lt. C. Sheil
2nd. Lt. R. C. Williams
2nd. Lt. S. B. Holmes

Y Company

2nd. Lt. E. T. Hussey
2nd. Lt. R. W. Marshall
2nd. Lt. G Donnolly
2nd. Lt. J. R. Love

X Company

Lt. F. S. Woodley M.C.
2nd. Lt. M.C. Conley
2nd. Lt. C. P. Ennis
2nd. Lt. J. J. Carroll

Z Company

Captain J. H. Lawlor
Lt. E. J. Mahony
2nd. Lt. W. Moloney
2nd. Lt. P. A. Haldane

x x x x x x x x x x x x x x

To/ Headquarters,
47th. Infantry Brigade.

REPORT ON "TANKS" SUPPORTING 1ST. R. M. FUS.
in the Action on 7th. June.

There is really very little comment concerning the co-operation of tanks, as there was so little scope for them . The Tanks advanced on the right and left of WYTSCHAETE woodand advanced towards OOSTTAVERNE Wood after the black Line had been taken. The names of the tanks were "One eyed RILEY" and "RILEY'S DAUGHTER"
On one occasion a Tank cam up to a dug-out just to the South of WYTSCHAETE Wood and halted , immediately about 20 prisoners came out and surrendered.
The Tanks were out in front while the patrols were out.
There was not much for them to do owing to want of targets, and most off the Machine Gun emplacements etc. had already been demolished by shell fire, but the fact of their being there gave great moral support . One of the Tanks came into action about 200 Yards WEST of WYTSCHAETE CHURCH on the KEMMEL -WUTSCHAETE road for a short time . All that could be done was done by them. They were up to time and in the right place to assist us had an opportunity occurred.

R Markham Lt. Colonel,

Comdg. 1st. Royal Munster Fusiliers.

11. 5. 17

C
Sandbag Villa
YORK ROAD
Parrot Fm.
Fort Calgary
Beaver Hall
Via Gellia
Welchen Avenue
V.C. ROAD
Rossignol Line
Turner Road
Fort Saskatchewan

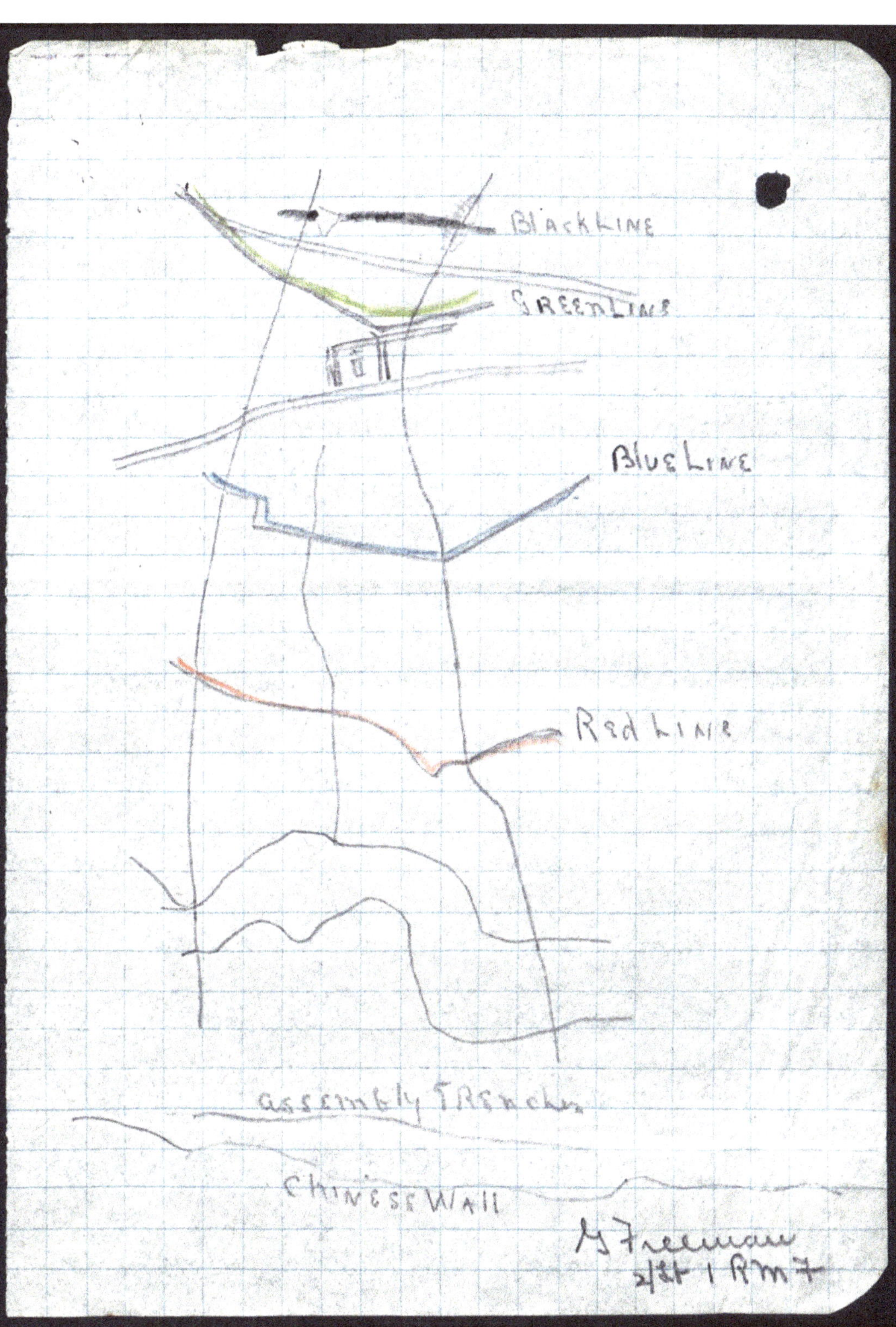

Black Line
Green Line
Blue Line
Red Line
assembly Trenches
Chinese Wall
G Freeman
2/Lt 1 RM7

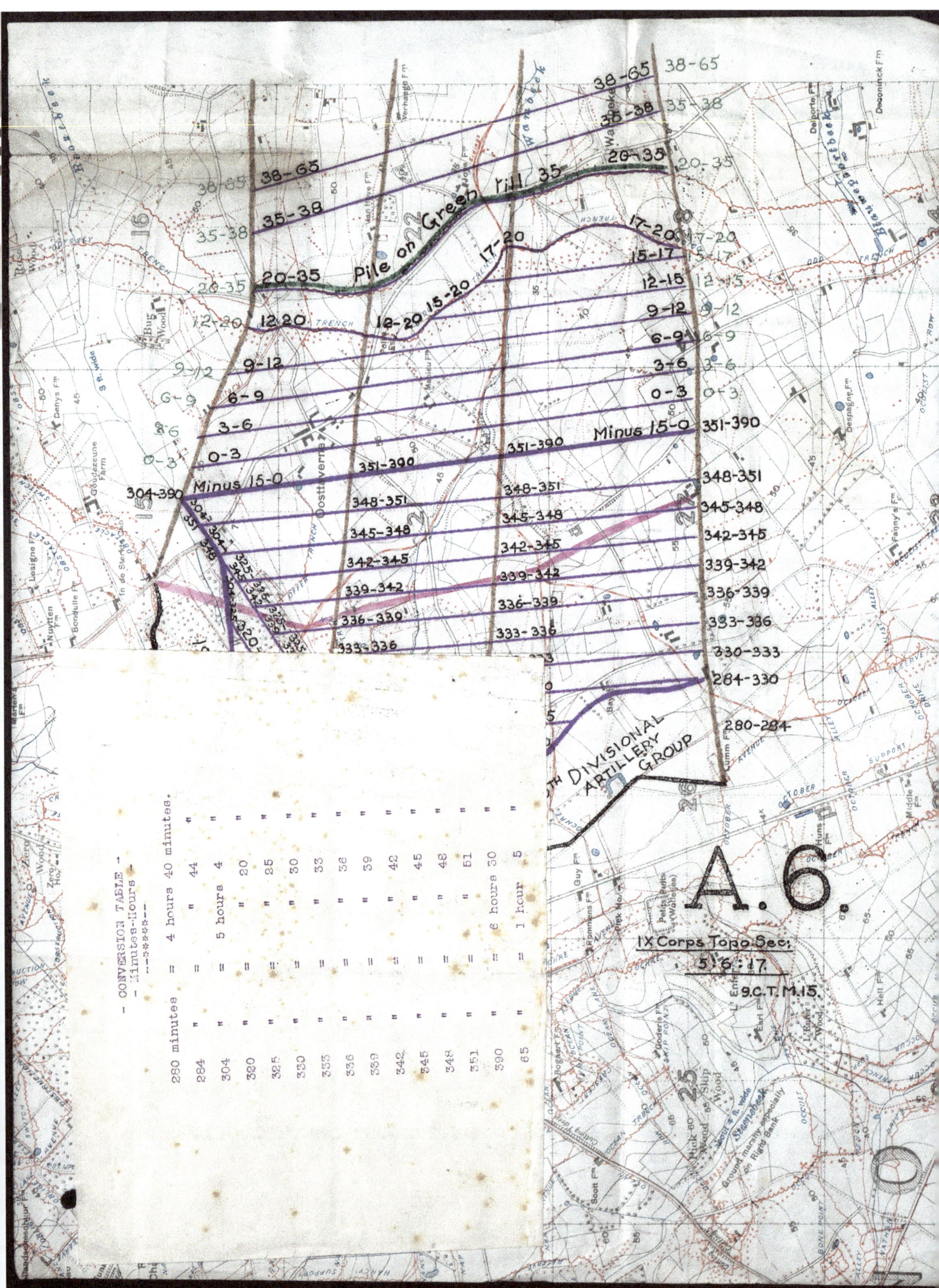

- CONVERSION TABLE -
- Minutes-Hours -
--*****--

280 minutes	=	4 hours 40 minutes.
284 "	=	" 44 "
304 "	=	5 hours 4 "
320 "	=	" 20 "
325 "	=	" 25 "
330 "	=	" 30 "
333 "	=	" 33 "
336 "	=	" 36 "
339 "	=	" 39 "
342 "	=	" 42 "
345 "	=	" 45 "
348 "	=	" 48 "
351 "	=	" 51 "
390 "	=	6 hours 30 "
65 "	=	1 hour 5 "

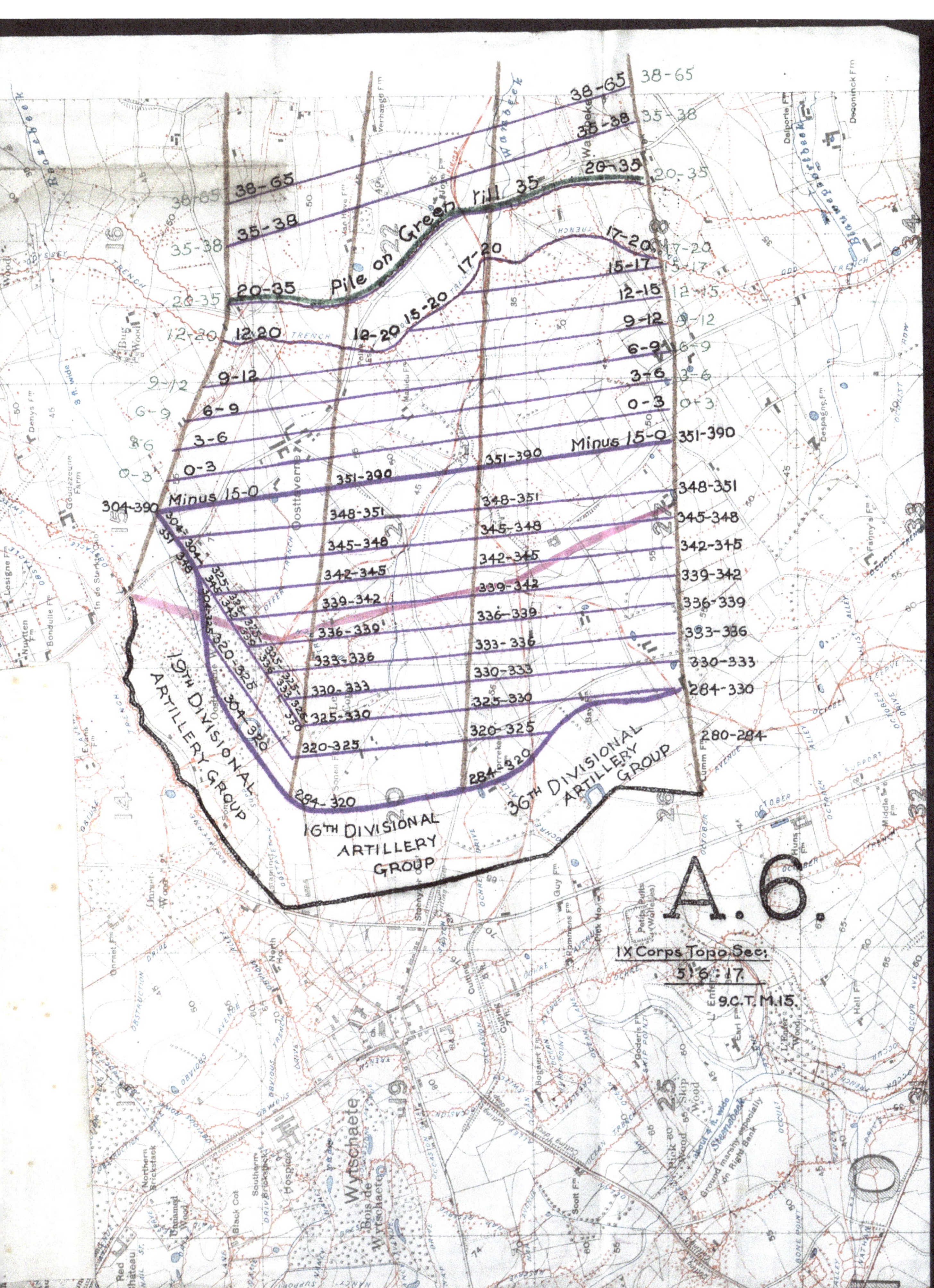

A.6.
IX Corps Topo Sec:
5·6·17.
9.C.T.M.15.
Pile on Green Hill 35
Minus 15-0
19th DIVISIONAL ARTILLERY GROUP
16th DIVISIONAL ARTILLERY GROUP
36th DIVISIONAL ARTILLERY GROUP
38-65
35-38
20-35
17-20
15-17
12-15
9-12
6-9
3-6
0-3
12-20
15-20
304-390
351-390
348-351
345-348
342-345
339-342
336-339
333-336
330-333
325-330
320-325
284-320
284-330
280-284
Wambeek
Oosttaverne
Wytschaete
Bois de Wytschaete
Goudezeune Farm
Denys Fm
Bug Wood
Despagne Fm
Fanny's Fm
Delporte Fm
Hospice
Northern Brickstack
Southern Brickstack
Red Château
Black Cot
Guy Fm
Earl Fm
Skip Wood
Hell Fm
Middle Fm
Lumm Fm
Verhaege Fm
Onraet Wood
Onraet Fm
Steenebeek
Ground marshy especially on Right Bank

WAR DIARY.

FOR MONTH OF JULY, 1917.

VOLUME :- 20

UNIT :- 1st R. Munster Fuslrs.

Vol 17

Instruc[illegible] regarding War Diaries and Intelligence Sum[illegible] are contained in F. S. Regs., Part II. and the Staff Manual respectively. Title pages will be prepared in manuscript.

WAR DIARY
or
~~INTELLIGENCE SUMMARY.~~
(Erase heading not required.)

1/R L. MUNS. FUS.

Army Form C. 2118.

Place	Date	Hour	Summary of Events and Information	Remarks and references to Appendices
	1917			
ZEGGERS CAPPEL	1 July		O. 38. O.R. 945. Draft of 13 joined. [illegible] from Hosp. 2 to Hosp. 1 to Base. [illegible]	
	2 "		O. 38. O.R. 942. 2Lt J.P. [illegible] joined for duty. 3 to Hosp. 6 to Base. [illegible]	
	3 "		O. 39. O.R. 933. Draft of 12 joined. 1 to Hosp. 1 from Hosp.	
	4		O. 39. O.R. 941. 1 to Hosp. 2 from Hosp.	
	5		O. 39. O.R. 948. Draft of 8 joined. 1 to Hosp. 1 from Hosp.	
	6		O. 39. O.R. 953. 5 to Hosp. 1 to Base. 6 from Hosp.	
	7		O. 39. O.R. 952. 1 to Hosp. and from Hosp.	
	8		O. 39. O.R. 953. 1 to Hosp.	
	9		O. 39. O.R. 951. 2 to Hosp.	
	10		O. 39. O.R. 950. 1 posted to 47 T.M.B.	
	11		O. 39. O.R. 943. 3 to Hosp. 1 from Hosp. Draft of 7 joined.	
	12		O. 39. O.R. 949. 1 to Hosp.	
	13		O. 39. O.R. 948. 2 to Hosp. 1 from Hosp.	
	14		O. 39. O.R. 952. 4 to Hosp. 2 from Hosp.	
	15		O. 39. O.R. 950. 1 to Hosp. 1 from Hosp. Draft of 11 joined.	
	16		O. 39. O.R. 961. 1 to Hosp. 1 from Hosp. 2Lt Wilkinson reported for duty. Battalion moved to the TATINGHEM area via BROXEELE - S NOMELIN - St OMER - St MARTIN - AU LAERT.	App.

T2134. Wt. W708—776. 500000. 4/15. Sir J. C. & S.

Instructions regarding War Diaries and Intelligence Summaries are contained in F. S. Regs., Part II. and the Staff Manual respectively. Title pages will be prepared in manuscript.

WAR DIARY
or
INTELLIGENCE SUMMARY.
(Erase heading not required.)

Army Form C. 2118.

Place	Date	Hour	Summary of Events and Information	Remarks and references to Appendices
	1917			
TATINGHEM	17 July		0.40 ORs 961 2 to Hosp 2 to Base.	
"	18		0.40 ORs 953 2 to Hosp 2 from Hosp.	
	19		0.40 ORs 953 1 to Hosp. Tactical exercise carried out	
	20		0.40 ORs 952 5 to Hosp 2 from Hosp. Tactical exercise carried out	
	21		0.40 ORs 949 3 to Hosp 1 from Hosp	
	22		0.40 ORs 947 4 to Hosp 2 from Hosp.	
	23		0.40 ORs 945 2 from Hosp. Battalion moved to WINNEZEELE No 2 area by rail.	App. B
WINNEZEELE	24		0.40 ORs 947 3 to Hosp.	
"	25		0.40 ORs 944. Draft of 16 joined. Battalion moved to WATOU No 3 area	App. C
WATOU	26		[illegible]	
	27		[illegible] Tactical exercise carried out	
	28		[illegible] Draft [illegible]	
	29		[illegible]	
	30		[illegible]	
			0 40 ORs 967 1 to Hosp 1 [illegible]	
	31		[illegible]	
			0 40 ORs 966 5 [illegible]	

T2134. Wt. W708—776. 500000. 4/15. Sir J. C. & S.

O P E R A T I O N   O R D E R S   No. 43.

By

Lt.Col. R.H.Monck-Mason.D.S.O., Comdg,1st Royal Munster Fusiliers.
In-the-Field 15th July,1917.

-o-o-o-o-o-o-o-o-o-o-o-o-o-o-o-o-o-o-o-o-o-o-o-o-o-o-

1. The Battalion will move to-morrow the 16th instant to the TATINGHEM area via BROXEELE - ST. MOMELIN - ST. OMER - ST. MARTIN AU LAERT in accordance with attached march table, and will be suceeded in present billets by a Battalion of the 47th Inf. Bde.

2. The Battalion will/ fall in in threes facing S.W., on the main ERKELBS - BRUGGE - ZEGERS RAOD in the following order:-

Scouts - Drums - "X" - "H.Q." - "Y" - "Z" - "W"., ready to march off at 4,45a.m.
Head of the column will ~~be at Headquarter~~ Mess.
Dress, Battle order, steel helmet will be attached to haversack.

3. Transport will accompany the Battalion.

Furber Purpose Carriers will travel in rear of the Battalion.

4. Packs Officers Valises, etc will be stacked at Company Headquarters in vicinity of main road and left in charge of one storeman per Company for collection by Quartermaster.
No pack with steel helmet attached will be accepted for conveyence.

Company Mess boxes for conveyence in H.Q. Mess cart to be sent to H.Q. Mess by 4.30.a.m.

5. O.C. "W" Company will detail an Officer for O.C. Stragglers,who will report to the Adjutant ten minutes before the Battalion moves off.

6. The greatest care will be taken to leave billets and their surroundings in a clean and sanitary condition.

SD/ M.H. FITZGERALD, Lieut A/Adjutant.,

1st Royal Munster Fusiliers.

Issued at...6.P.M...... Copy No...14....

Copy No.1. Commanding Officer.
Copy No.2. 2nd-in-Command.
Copy No.3. Adjutant.
Copy No.4. Transport Officer.
Copy No.5. Quartermaster.
Copy No.6. Signalling Officer.
Copy No.7. O.C. "W" Company.
Copy No.8. O.C."X" Company.
Copy No. 9 O.C. "Y" Company.
Copy No.10 O.C. "Z" Company.
Copy No.11 47th Inf. Bde.
Copy No.12 R. S. M.
Copies No. 13 and 14 Filed.

March Table to accompany [illegible] 1st R.M.F. O.O. No. 43.

Units in order of march.	Hour of passing Starting Point, Cross Roads G.12.a.95.75.	Billeting Area.	Now occupied by.	Remarks.
47th T.M. Battery.	5.40.a.m.	TATINGHEM.	48th T.M.Battery.	1. Leading Unit not to cross PONT TOURNANT -ST. MOMELIN before 8.a.m.
6/Royal Irish Regt,	5.45.a.m.	LEULINE ETREHEM	9/Royal Dublin Fus.	
6/Connaught Rangers.	6.5.a.m.	CORMETTE AU. DENTHUN	7/R.Irish Rifles.	2. Guides will meet Units at ST. MARTIN AU LAERT.
1/Rl.Munster Fus.	6.15.a.m.	TATINGHEM	2/Royal Dublin Fus.	
7/Leinster Regt..	6.25.a.m.	Camp at TATINGHEM	8/Royal Dublin Fus.	
Brigade H.Q.	6.35.a.m.	TATINGHEM	H.Q. 48th InfBde.	
143 Coy. A.S.C.	6.40.a.m.	TATINGHEM (X.7.b.3.3.)	145 Coy. A.S.C.	

SECRET. OPERATION ORDERS. No. 44.

by

Lt.Colonel R. H. Monck-Mason D.S.O. Comdg.1st.Royal Muns.Fuslrs.

In the Field 21-7-1917.

xxxxxxxxxxxxxxxxxxxxxxxxxxxxxxxx

1. The Battalion will proceed to WINNEZEELE No.2 area by rail on July 23rd.1917. Transport less those portions otherwise ordered will proceed by road on July 22nd.& 23rd.
Parade in Sections of Threes, in Main Road TATINGHEM facing N.E.
Head of Column at Road Junction X.2.c½2.[illegible]. in the following order:-
Drums. Headquarters. W. X.Y. & Z Coys.,
ready to march off at 8 a.m.
DRESS:- Full Marching Order. Caps will be worn.

2. Movement by Rail will be made as follows:-
1 Omnibus Train .. Depart 9 a.m. by which will travel the following:-
4 Cookers with Horses & Drivers.
2 Watercarts " "
1 Mess Cart
4 Chargers with Grooms.
Medical Officer.
Maltese Cart with Horse & 2 O.R.Medical Personnel.

1 Personnel Train ... Departing at 10-30 a.m.
Entrainment ....St.OMER.
Detrainment ....ABEELE.

3. Transport Details travelling in Omnibus train will arrive at St.OMER Station on July 23rd.at 5-50 a.m.

4. There is accomodation in each Personnel Train for 2 Battalions with Lewis Guns & such handcarts as may be in Possession.
No Transport may travel by Personnel Train. Accomodation per Coach:-
40 Men in Marching Order.
Men will be told off into Travelling parties of this numberebefore the Battalion moves off. 1 Guide per Company will beselected to report to Battalion Entraining Officer directly on Arrival at St.OMER. Battn. will arrive at St.OMER station at 9-15 a.m.

5. Capt.R.T.BAXTER & 2/Lt.C.F.ENNIS will superintend the entrainment of the Battalion & will report to Captain D.E.Shaw half an hour before the arrival of the Battalion. They will be provided with a marching out state of the Battalion which they will hand to this Officer.
A Marching Out State will be rendered by all Companies to Orderly Room tomorrow by 6 p.m.

6. ADVANCE PARTIES.
1 N.C.O.per Coy., 1 N.C.O.for H.Q.Coy. & a representative for Transport & Quartermaster's Stores will report with Bycicles to Captain MOLONY at Battn.Headqrs.at 2 p.m.July 22nd. Theywill report to the Area Commandant at WYNNEZEELE for Billets & provide guides for the Battn. & for Transport by Omnibus Train at ABEELE Station on July 23rd.

7. Battalion immediately after detraining will march to Billets by Route to be notified later; 500 yards in rear of the Leinster Regt.

8. Transport under Brigade Transport Officer will move by Road as Follows, carrying Rations for 23rd.July inclusive :-
(a) July 22nd. Pass Starting Point Cross Roads St.MARTIN AU LAERT:-
143 Coy. A.S.C. .... 10 a.m.
Transport Leinster Regt..........10-5 a.m.
" Royal Munster Fus.......10-10 a.m.
" Connaught Rngrs.........10-15 a.m.
" Royal Irish Regt........10-20 a.m.
" Brigade H.Qrs...........10-25 a.m.
and March via St.OMER 7 CLAIRMARAIS to NOORDPEENE reportingtn in Advance to Area Commandant NOORDPEENE for Billets.

(b) July 23rd. Inthe same Order as in (a).
To march via HARDIFORT to WINNEZEELE No.2 Area at such an hour as to Complete the March by 10 a.m. To report in advance to Area Commandant WINNEZEELE for Billets.

OPERATION ORDERS. No. 44. 21/7/1917.(Contd.)

9. SUPPLY ARRANGEMENTS.
(a) There will be two distributions of rations on the 21st.inst;i.e. for consumption on the 22nd.& 23rd.instants.Rations for Consumption by Train Portion on 23rd.inst.will be delivered to Quartermasters on 21st.instant,the proportion of Rations required for Road Portions being retained on Supply Wagons.
(b)On July 23rd.rations for consumption on 24th.instant.will be dumped in 47th.Brigade Area,WINNEZEELE & delivered to Units.

10. TRANSPORT.
1 Lorry is being provided for the Battalion & will report at 47th.Inf. Bde.H.Qrs.at 6 p.m.on 22nd.instant,where a Guide from the Quartermaster should report to the Staff Captain to Guide it to Battalion Headqrs. This lorry will make one Journey only, transport has not been provided for Packs.

11. BILLETING ARRANGEMENTS.
The Battalion will be Billetted in Camp "C"J.4.b.6.6.,15 Tents for Officers,57 Tents for Other Ranks. H.Q.Mess in Farm at J.4.b.666. Barn for 50 o.r.in Farm,Transport in Field adjoining Farm.

12. MEDICAL ARRANGEMENTS.
On arrival in the new area Sick will be collected daily from Units H.Q.by 111th.F.A.

13. Acknowledge.

(Signed.) M. E. FitzGerald. Lieutenant;

A/Adjt.1st. Bn. Royal Munster Fusiliers.

The following Orders for travelling are to be strictly adhered to:-
(1) No.man to be outside or on top of Trucks.or Carriages.
(2) No man to be allowed to Get out at any station without leave.
(3) Officers will look out on either side of the train at all halts to see these orders carried out.
(4) On reaching Platform men will be told off by Parties to each Coach. Rifles will be first handed in & on a whistle being blown, the men will entrain.
(5)On Reaching Destination men will not detrain until the signal is given by whistle,Rifles will then be handed out.
(6) Detraining Point must be cleared with utmost despatch.Men will be marched out of the Station as quickly as possible,halted when clear & allowed to fall out.
(7) Each carriage Party will be under the charge of an N.C.O.who will give the order to dress 10 Minutes before the train arrives at its Destination.The men will then put on their equipment.

S E C R E T.

O P E R A T I O N   O R D E R S   No. 45
By
Lt. Colonel R. H. Monck-Mason Comdg. 1st. Royal Muns. Fus.
In the Field 24. 7. 17

1. The Battalion will move to-morrow July 25th. to WATOU, Area No. 3 and will fall in in column of threes on road outside Camp facing South, head of Column 200 Yards South of Entrance to Camp ready to march off at 7.15 p.m. .

2. Order of March :- Scouts, drums, W X Y Z and H.Q. Coys.
Movement will be in accordance with attached table.
Dress - Battle Order, Caps will be worn .

3. ADVANCE PARTIES.
1 N.C. O per company and 1 from H.Q. Company and representatives from Transport and Quartermaster Stores with bicycles will report to Lieutenant E. J. MAHONY at 9 a.m. to proceed to take over Billets in the new area.
Guides will meet the Battalion at E.38.d.40.30.

4. BILLETING ARRANGEMENTS
The Following billets will be occupied by the Battalion:-

K.5.d.8.8.	Officers 9	O.R. 120	Mess Hut and Stores.
K.5.d.4.4	Officers 2	O.R. 150	and Mess
K.12.a.3.3.	Officers Nil	O.R. 80	Office and Transport
K.12.a. 1.3.	Officers 3	O.R. 90	and Mess
K.17.a.2.10.	Officers Nil	O.R. 50	
K.12.a.4.4.	7 Tents for Officers	20 tents (SCOTS CAMP) for O.R.	

5. TRANSPORT.
1 Lorry is allotted to the Battalion and will report at 47th. Brigade Headquarters at 4 p.m. on the 25th. inst.. The Quartermaster will arrange to send a guide to report to the Staff Captain at 3.30 p.m. to guide Lorry to Battalion Headquarters.
This Lorry is to be dismissed in time to report to 49th. Brigade WINNEZEELE at 10 p.m. on the 25th. inst.

6. MEDICAL ARRANGEMENTS.
111th. Field Ambulance will move on 26th. July to L.20 b.7.7..
The Sick will be collected daily from Battalion Headquarters by 111th. F.A. for admission to 113th. F.A. at L.9.b.1.3. while in the WATOU AREA

7. ACKNOWLEDGE.

(Signed) M.H. FitzGerald, Lieutenant,
A/Adjutant. 1st. Royal Munster Fusiliers.

Copy No...........   Issued at ....

Copy No. 1 47th. Infy. Bde.
Copy No. 2 Commdg. Officer
Copy No. 3 2nd. In Command.
Copy No. 4 Adjutant
Copy No. 5 Quartermaster
Copy No. 6 Transport Officer
Copy No. 7 Signalling Officer
Copy No. 8 R. S. M.
Copy No. 9 "W" Company
Coyp No. 10 "X" Company
Copy No. 11 "Y" Company
Copy No. 12 "Z" Company
Copy No. 13 Medical Officer
Copy Nos. 14 and 15 File

March Table to accompany Operation Order No. 45

Serial No.	Date	Unit	From	To-	Route	Starting point	Head will pass at	Tail will clear at	Remarks
1	25.7.17	Bde. H.Q. T. M. B.	WINNEZEELE Area No..2	WATOU Area No. 3	WINNEZEELE DROGLANDT WATOU	Rd. Junction at J.17.b.00.70	6.50 pm.	6.55 pm	500 Yds distance will be maintained Between Battns.
2	do	6th. R.Ir.Reg.	do	do	do	do	7.0 p.m.	7.10 p.m	WATOU No. 3 area will not be entered before 9 p.m.
3	do	6th. Conn. Rgrs.	do	do	do	do	7.15 pm.	7.25 pm.	Bde. H.Q. will move straight to Bde. H. Qrs. WATOU
4.	do	7th. Lein. Regt.	do	do	do	do	7.30 pm.	7.40pm.	
5	do	1/R.Muns.Fus.	do	do	do	do	7.45pm.	7.55 pm.	

App D

secret

OPERATION ORDERS No. 46
By
Lt. Colonel R. H. Monck-Mason D.S.O. Comdg. 1st. Royal Muns. F[illegible].
In the Field 29..7. 17.

Ref. Map Sheet 27 N.E. 1/20,000

1. The Battalion will move to-morrow 30th. inst. to the BRANDHOEK area. Movement will be in accordance with attached March Table.

2. Battalion will fall in in column of threes on road outside "W" Company's Billets facing South East ready to march off at 7.15 a.m. Order. of March Scouts, Drums, "Y" "Z" H.Q" "W" and "X" Coys Transport will accompany the Battalion. Furbur carriers will march in rear of Battalion.
Dress - Full Marching Order. Caps will be worn.

3. O.C. "X" Company will detail an O.C. Stragglers who should report to the Adjutant ten minutes before the Battalion moves off.

4. All Baggage, Officers' Kits etc.,will be stacked at Company Billets ready for removal by Transport Officer at 5 a.m.

6. O's C Companies will satisfy themselves that tents and Billets occupied by them in the present area are left in a thoroughly clean and sanitary condition.

(Signed M. H. FitzGerald, Lieutenant,
A/Adjutant, 1st. Bn. Royal Munster Fusiliers.

Issued at .... Copy No........

Copy No. 1 47th. Inf. Brigade.
Copy No. 2 Commanding Officer
Copy No. 3 2nd. In Command
Copy No. 4 Adjutant
Copy No. 5 O.C. H.Q. Company
Copy No. 6 "W" Company
Copy No. 7 "X" Company
Copy No. 8 "Y" Company
Copy No. 9 "Z" Company
Copy No. 10 Quartermaster
Cop No. 11 Transport Officer
Copy No 13 R. S. M.
Copies Nos. 14 and 15 File.

App E

S E C R E T

O P E R A T I O N   O R D E R S   No. 47

By

Lt. Colonel R. H. Monck-Mason D.S.O. Comdg. 1st. Royal Muns. Fus.
In the Field 30. 7. 17.

xxxxxxxxxxxxxxxxxxxxxxxxxxxxxxxx

1. A Working Party will be provided from the Battalion for work on Burying Cables forward from MILL COTTAGES towards FREZENBERG in conjunction with 600 Other Ranks of the 7th. Leinster Regt. under the direction of A.D. Signals 19th. Corps.
This party will be under the orders of Lt. Colonel BUCKLEY D.S.O.

2. The party will be required to be at GOLDFISH CHATEAU on Z day at Zero plus 1 Hour and 30 minutes where they will be met by an Officer and guides of A.D. Signals 19th. Corps.
The party will parade for entrainment at POPERINGHE Railway Station RUE DE YPRES at Zero plus 15 minutes.

3. Bivouac Grounds at L.4 and DURHAM REDOUBT in H.11 and 12 are allotted to the party during the period the work is in progress. Packs and surplus equipment will be deposited on the Bivouac Ground and placed under a Guard prior to the party moving forward.
Tools will be drawn at GOLDFISH CHATEAU under arrangements to be made by A.D. Signals.
The party will probably have to be accomodated in the forward area for at least two nights.

4. This party will be composed as follows:- W X Y and Z Coys. 150 other ranks each, H.Q. Company 100 other ranks.

5. Transport will march to Bivouac Ground on Z day. Head to pass cross roads G.4.d.30.40 at Zero plus 10 hours, Route Via BRANDHOEK and VLAMERTINGHE surplus of the Battalion will move by march route with the transport. Water Carts will march with the first line transport to the Bivouac Ground and petrol tins will be carried.

6. SUPPLIES.
(a) Rations for Consumption on 31st. July will be delivered to Battn. at 7.a.m. 30th. instant at WATOU.
(b) Rations for Consumption on 1st.& 2nd. August will be delivered by Lorry & dumped at GOLDFISH CHATEAU, Sheet 28. H.11.a.8.1. at 9 p.m. July 30th. Regimental Quartermaster Sgt.& a small unloading Party from the Q.M. Stores Personnel will report at Brigde.H.Q.No.16 RUE de BOESCHAPE, POPERINGHE, at 8 p.m. on 30th. July to proceed with Lorries carrying Rations. Unload at GOLDFISH CHATEAU & remain there until the arrival of the Battn.

(c) 1 day's Ration will be a preserved ration.

7. Zero Hour together with time, place & order of Parade will be notified later.

(Signed) M. H. FitzGerald. Lieutenant;

A/Adjt. 1st. Battn. Royal Munster Fusrs.

Issued at .... Copy No.........

Copy No.1 47th. Inf.Bde.
" 2. Commanding Officer.
" 3. 2nd.in Command.
" 4. Adjutant.
" 5. O.C. H.Q.Coy.
" 6. O.C."W" Coy.
" 7. O.C."X" "
" 8. O.C. "Y" "
Copy No.9. O.C. "Z" Coy.
" 10. Quartermaster.
" 11. Transport Officer.
" 12. R.S.M.
" 14 & 15. File.

S E C R E T

March Table to accompany Operation Order No. 46 dated 29. 7. 17.

Unit	Date	From WATOU No. 3	To BRANDHOEK	STARTING POINT Cross Roads K.12.c.60.30 Head will pass	Tail will clear	Route	Remarks.
1st. Royal Muns. Fus.	Y day	do	Camp G.9.a.20.40	7.15 a.m.	7.25 a.m.	L.1.d.10.25 L.9.c.10.90 L.11.b.80.80. L.6.c.90.40 GRANDE PLACE POPERINGHE [illegible].	Move to be completed by 10 a.m.

47/16

W A R   D I A R Y .

FOR   MONTH   OF   AUGUST,   1917.

VOLUME..........

U N I T   1st Royal Munster Fusiliers

Vol 18

Instructions regarding War Diaries and Intelligence Summaries are contained in F. S. Regs., Part II. and the Staff Manual respectively. Title pages will be prepared in manuscript.

WAR DIARY
or
INTELLIGENCE SUMMARY.
(Erase heading not required.)

Army Form C. 2118.

August — 1st Royal Munster Fusiliers

Place	Date	Hour	Summary of Events and Information	Remarks and references to Appendices
DURHAM REDOUBT (H.11. central)	1.8.17		The Battalion relieved 8th R. Dublin Fus. in trenches just East of ST. JEAN – POTIJZE line & came under orders of 164th BDE. 55th DIV. Casualties: wounded 3 O.R. Hospital: 2 O.R. Strength: 40 officers. 927 O.R.	Appendix A
CAMBRIDGE TRENCH. I.5.a.10.70	2.8.17		The Battalion was relieved by 164th BDE. & proceeded to CAMBRIDGE TRENCH on completion of relief, coming under orders of 47th INF. BDE. Casualties: wounded 6 O.R. To Hospital 4 O.R. from Hospital 3 O.R. Strength 40 officers, 922 O.R.	Appendix B
RIGHT SUPPORT. (YPRES–ROULERS RLY – D.25.c.65.70)	3.8.17		The Battalion relieved 7 Leinster in Right Support. H.Q. Western Edge of WILDE WOOD. Casualties: Wounded 2nd Lt. W.F. TREACY & 21 O.R. To hospital 52 O.R. from Hospital 2 O.R. Strength 40 officers & 915 O.R.	Appendix C
" "	4.8.17		Casualties: Killed 2 O.R. D. of W. 1 O.R. Wounded: 32 O.R. To Hospital 84 O.R. from Hospital 1 O.R. Strength 39 officers & 864 O.R.	

D. D. & L., London, E.C.
(A7883) Wt. W809/M1672 350,000 4/17 Sch. 52a Forms/C/2118/14

Instructions regarding War Diaries and Intelligence Summaries are contained in F. S. Regs., Part II. and the Staff Manual respectively. Title pages will be prepared in manuscript.

WAR DIARY
or
INTELLIGENCE SUMMARY.
(*Erase heading not required.*)

Army Form C. 2118.

August — 1st Royal Munster Fusiliers

Place	Date	Hour	Summary of Events and Information	Remarks and references to Appendices
RIGHT SUPPORT. (YPRES-ROULERS RLY — D.25.c (6.1))	5.8.17		The Battalion was relieved in Right Support by 8th R. Dub. Fusiliers & proceeded to BRANDHOEK No. 2 area on completion of Relief, entraining at ASYLUM (YPRES) H.12.d.50.90. Casualties Killed 6 OR. Wounded 2Lts. G.J. FREEMAN & O.H. BAILY. & 18 OR. To Hospital 20. O.R. Strength: 39 officers & 745 O.R.	Appendix D
BRANDHOEK No. 2. Area	6.8.17		In Camp at EYRIE HUTMENTS. Casualties: Wounded: 1 OR. To Hospital 2 OR. From Hospital: 4 O.R. Strength: 37 officers & 701 OR.	
" "	7.8.17		Casualties: ~~to~~ To Hospitals 12 O.R. From Hospital ~~4~~ 17 OR. Strength: 37 officers & 702 O.R.	
" "	8.8.17		Casualties: Wounded 1 OR. To Hospital: 1 OR. From Hospital: 17 OR. Major J. STACKPOOLE, Lts. C. B. CALLANDER M.C. & W.F. SUGRUE, & 2Lts. L.T. DENSON & T.G. CAHILL joined the Battalion. Strength: 37 officers & 707 OR.	

D. D. & L., London, E.C. (A7883) Wt. W809/M1672 350,000 4/17 Sch. 52a Forms/C/2118/14

Instructions regarding War Diaries and Intelligence Summaries are contained in F. S. Regs., Part II. and the Staff Manual respectively. Title pages will be prepared in manuscript.

WAR DIARY
or
INTELLIGENCE SUMMARY.
(Erase heading not required.)

Army Form C. 2118.

August 1st Royal Munster Fusiliers

Place	Date	Hour	Summary of Events and Information	Remarks and references to Appendices
BRANDHOEK No. 2 Area.	9.8.17		Lt. F.S. WOODLEY M.C. posted to 8th Royal Irish Rifles to Command a coy. Casualties: To Hospital 4 O.R. from Hospital 9 O.R. Strength 42 officers + 722 O.R.	
" " "	10.8.17		Casualties: Wounded 3 O.R. To Hospital 5 O.R. from Hospital 3 O.R. Draft of 20 O.R. joined the Battalion. Strength 41 officers + 727 O.R.	
FREZENBERG. (D.25.C.4.7)	11.8.17		Battalion relieved 8th Royl. Dublin Fusiliers in Front Line following being Disposition of Coys: Front Line: Right Y coy. Left W coy. Support Right X coy. Left Z Coy. Casualties: Wounded 5 O.R. Missing 4 O.R. To Hospital 7 O.R. from Hospital 11 O.R. Strength 41 officers + 712 O.R. Headquarters at FREZENBERG REDOUBT (about D.25.C.4.7. vide Map: FREZENBERG 1/10,000) under orders 48th INF. BDE.	Appendix E. Appendix E.
" " "	12.8.17		Heavy hostile Shelling continued all day & during the night. Casualties: Killed 6 O.R. Missing 3 O.R. Wounded 17 O.R. To Base 1 O.R. To Hospital 4 O.R. from Hospital 8 O.R. Strength 41 officers 707 O.R.	

D. D. & L., London, E.C.
(A7883) Wt. W809/M1672 350,000 4/17 Sch. 52a Forms/C/2118/14

Instructions regarding War Diaries and Intelligence Summaries are contained in F. S. Regs., Part II. and the Staff Manual respectively. Title pages will be prepared in manuscript.

WAR DIARY
or
INTELLIGENCE SUMMARY.
(Erase heading not required.)

Army Form C. 2118.

August   1st Royal Munster Fusiliers.

Place	Date	Hour	Summary of Events and Information	Remarks and references to Appendices
FREZENBERG (D.25.C.4.7)	13.8.17		Severe Hostile Shelling throughout the day. Casualties: Wounded: Capt. L.S. KING & 10 OR. Missing 1 OR. To Hospital: 2 OR. From Hospital 9 OR. Strength: 41 officers & 684 OR.	
ÉCOLE (YPRES)	14.8.17		Severe Hostile Shelling throughout the day. Casualties: Wounded 13 OR. Missing 1 OR. To Hospital 8 OR. From Hospital 7 OR. Strength 40 officers & 680 OR. The Battalion was relieved by 2nd Royal Dublin Fusiliers & proceeded to ÉCOLE, YPRES on completion of relief.	Appendix F.
OLD GERMAN LINE (Ridge 56)	15.8.17		Casualties: wounded 11 OR. Missing 4 OR. To Hospital 7 OR. From Hospital 6 OR. Strength: 40 officers & 665 OR. The Battalion moved to assembly positions in OLD GERMAN LINE, & reported in occupation at 2.20 AM.	Appendix G.
" "	16.8.17		Battalion in Support to 48th INF. BDE. during operation E. of FREZENBERG RIDGE. Zero hour 5.45 AM. Dispositions Y & Z Coys. IBEX RESERVE. W Coy. ICE TRENCH & SUPPT. X Coy. IBEX TRENCH & SUPPT. H.Q. IBERIA TRENCH.	Appendix H.

D. D. & L., London, E.C.
(A7883) Wt. W809/M1672 350,000 4/17 Sch. 52a Forms/C/2118/14

Instructions regarding War Diaries and Intelligence Summaries are contained in F. S. Regs., Part II. and the Staff Manual respectively. Title pages will be prepared in manuscript.

Army Form C. 2118.

WAR DIARY
or
INTELLIGENCE SUMMARY.
(*Erase heading not required.*)

August. 1st Royal Munster Fusiliers

Place	Date	Hour	Summary of Events and Information	Remarks and references to Appendices
OLD GERMAN LINE (Ref [illegible])	16.8.17 [contd]	7.23 AM	X coy. moved forward to DOUGLAS TRENCH to support 2nd Ryl. Dublin Fusiliers.	Appendex H.
		9.20 AM	" moved forward beyond DOUGLAS TRENCH. Z coy. moved forward to DOUGLAS TR.	
		5 pm.	W coy followed by X coy. moved forward to close support in IBEX RESERVE. Y coy moved forward to BLACK LINE. Severe hostile Shelling. Casualties: Killed 1 OR wounded 15 OR. Missing 1 OR. To Hospital 2 OR. From Hospital 10 OR. Strength 40 officers 640 OR.	
VLAMERTINGHE No. 3 Area	17.8.17		Casualties: Killed. 3 OR. Missing: 2Lt J. R. LOVE. Wounded Lt. C. B. CALLANDER. M.C. & 2Lt. J. CARROLL + 7 OR. From Hospital 3 OR. Strength 40 officers + 640 OR. The Battalion was relieved by different units of 15th Division. Proceeded to Camps at VLAMERTINGHE. No. 3 Area on completion of relief.	Appendix I
" "	18.8.17		Casualties: Wounded 1 OR. To Hospital 1 OR. From Hospital 1 OR. Lt. T. H. PEN-DESIRE dispatched the Battalion. Strength: 37 officers & 633 OR.	

D. D. & L., London, E.C. (A7883) Wt. W809/M1672 350,000 4/17 Sch. 52a Forms/C/2118/14

Instructions regarding War Diaries and Intelligence Summaries are contained in F. S. Regs., Part II. and the Staff Manual respectively. Title pages will be prepared in manuscript.

WAR DIARY
or
INTELLIGENCE SUMMARY.
(Erase heading not required.)

Army Form C. 2118.

August. 1st Royal Munster Fusiliers

Place	Date	Hour	Summary of Events and Information	Remarks and references to Appendices
WATOU B area	19.8.17		The Battalion moved to WATOU "B" area. Casualties 2Lt. G.F. HAND wounded. To hospital: 1 OR. From hospital 3 OR. Draft of 53 OR. joined the Battalion. Strength: 38 officers + 632 OR.	Appendix J
EECKE.	20.8.17		The Battalion moved to EECKE. Casualties: To Hospital 3 OR. From Hospital 1 OR. 2Lt. SHAW struck off Establishment. Commanding Officer went on leave to U.K. Strength: 36 officers. 757 OR.	Appendix K
GOMIECOURT.	21.8.17		The Battalion moved to GOMIECOURT via CAESTRE + BAPAUME. Strength: 36 officers + 785 OR.	Appendix L
" " "	22.8.17		In Camp at GOMIECOURT. Casualties. From Hospital 3 OR. Draft of 28 OR. joined the Battalion. Strength: 36 officers + 785 OR.	
" "	23.8.17		In Camp at GOMIECOURT. Casualties: To Hospital 1 OR. From Hospital 2 OR. Strength 36 officers + 816 OR.	

D. D. & L., London, E.C. (A7883) Wt. W809/M1672 350,000 4/17 Sch. 52a Forms/C/2118/14

Instructions regarding War Diaries and Intelligence Summaries are contained in F. S. Regs., Part II. and the Staff Manual respectively. Title pages will be prepared in manuscript.

WAR DIARY
or
INTELLIGENCE SUMMARY.
(Erase heading not required.)

Army Form C. 2118.

August — 1st Royal Munster Fusiliers

Place	Date	Hour	Summary of Events and Information	Remarks and references to Appendices
GOMIECOURT	24.8.17		In Camp. Casualties: To Hospital 7 OR. From Hospital 5 OR. Strength: 36 officers + 817 OR.	~~Appendix~~ M
MOYENNEVILLE [A.5.a.8.8]	25.8.17		The Battalion relieved 7th Leicesters in Southern Camp MOYENNEVILLE. Casualties To Hospital 1 OR. Strength: 36 officers + 815 OR.	Appendix M
SUPPORT-N. of BULLECOURT	26.8.17		The Battalion relieved 9th K.O.Y.L.I. in Support N. of BULLECOURT. Casualties: To Hospital 2 OR. from Hospital 3 OR. Strength. 36 officers + 813 OR.	Appendix N
" " "	27.8.17		Casualties: To Hospital 2 OR. From Hospital 4 OR. Draft of 15 OR. joined the Battalion. Strength: 36 officers + 814 OR.	
" "	28.8.17		Strength: 35 officers + 831 OR. Draft of 25 OR. joined the Battalion. Casualties. To Hospital 1 OR. from Hospital 1 OR.	

D. D. & L., London, E.C. (A7883) Wt. W809/M1672 350,000 4/17 Sch. 52a Forms/C/2118/14

Instructions regarding War Diaries and Intelligence Summaries are contained in F. S. Regs., Part II. and the Staff Manual respectively. Title pages will be prepared in manuscript.

WAR DIARY
or
INTELLIGENCE SUMMARY.
(Erase heading not required.)

Army Form C. 2118.

August. 1st Royal Munster Fusiliers

Place	Date	Hour	Summary of Events and Information	Remarks and references to Appendices
SUPPORT. N. of BULLECOURT.	29.8.17		Strength: 35 officers + 856 O.R. Draft of 26 O.R. joined the Battalion.	
	30.8.17		Strength: 35 officers + 882 O.R. 2 O.R. rejoined from Hospital.	
	31.8.17		Strength: 35 officers + 884 O.R. Casualties: 2 O.R. wounded.	

J.W. [illegible] Major.
Commdg. 1st Royal Munster Fus.

D. D. & L., London, E.C.
(A7883) Wt. W809/M1672 350,000 4/17 Sch. 52a Forms/C/2118/14

Appendix A

S E C R E T. 47th Inf. Bde. No. G 3760

7th Leinster Regt.
6th Connaught Rangers.
6th Royal Irish Regt.
1st R Muns. Fusrs.
47th T.M.Battery.
Bde. Signals.
Staff Captain.
16th Division (for information).

ADVANCE WARNING.

1. The 47th Inf. Bde. will relieve the 48th Inf. Bde. on the night of the 1st/2nd August, 1917.

2. Reliefs will be as follows:-
(a) 7th Leinster Regt. will relieve A Battalion in CAMBRIDGE ROAD
(b) 1st R.Muns. Fusrs relieve B Battalion in ~~OXFORD ROAD~~.
(c) 6th Royal Irish Regt. relieve C Battalion in HALF MOON STREET.
(d) 6th Conn. Rangers relieve D Battalion holding a trench believed to be just East of the line SAINT JEAN - POTIJZE.

3. Commands:-
The 7th Leinster Regt and the 6th Royal Irish Regt. will come under the orders of the 15th Division.
The 6th Connaught Rangers and 1st R.Muns. Fus, under the order of the 55th Division.

4. Movements:-
(a) The 7th Leinster Regt and 1st R.Muns. Fus. will move by march route.
(b) The 6th Connaught Rangers and 6th Royal Irish Regt. and Bde. H.Q. it is hoped to move by train - leaving at 6 p.m. also 47th T.M.Battery.

5. The 47th T.M.Battery will relieve the 48th T.M.Battery at GOLDFISH CHATEAU.

6. Bde. H.Q. will be at GOLDFISH CHATEAU.

[signature]
Major,
1-8-17. Brigade Major, 47th Infantry Brigade.

413
415
408
409
410
411

Appendix B

SECRET. Copy No. 7

IMBUE ORDER NO. P.1.

2nd. August 1917.

1. IMBUE and two attached Battalions - JAUNT and JABBER - will be relieved in the early morning of the 2nd. by a Brigade of UNBOLT.

2. The following guides will meet Capt. WALKER at junct-ion of CONGREVE WALK and ST JEAN-WIELTJE ROAD at 8 a.m. 2nd. inst:-

IMPUTE	...	1 N.C.O. & 4 O.R.
IMPOSE	...	1 " 4 "
IMPART	...	2 O.R.
IMMORAL	...	2 O.R.
IMAGE	...	2 "
JAUNT	...	1 N.C.O. & 4 O.R.
JABBER	...	1 " " "

3. The destination and detailed orders for move of Units will follow later.

4. ACKNOWLEDGE.

ackd

E Walker

Captain.
Brigade Major.
IMBUE.

Issued at
7 a.m.

Copy No. 1. IMPART.
2. IMPOSE.
3. IMPUTE.
4. IMPEL.
5. IMMORAL.
6. IMAGE.
7. JAUNT.
8. JABBER
9. IGNITE.
10. IRON.
11. INANE.
War DIARY.
13. FILE.

5 Move to be made in absolute silence
necessity for absence of lights must be
impressed on all ranks

6 ACKNOWLEDGE

M. H. FitzGerald
Lt. a/adjt.

15.8.17

Appendix I

1st Royal Munster Fusiliers
MH. 137

1. The Battalion will be relieved by various Battalions of 15th Division in present sector on night of 17th/18th. Reliefs will be carried out as follows:–

1 Coy K.O.S.B. will relieve Z Coy in DOUGLAS TRENCH
2 Coys. H.L.I " " W & X Coys in IBEX RESERVE
1 Coy. H.L.I " " Y Coy in IBEX TRENCH
1 Coy H.L.I " take over trenches at BILL COTT.
HQ. H.L.I " relieve H.Q. R.M.F. in LIBERIA TRENCH

Coys will report completion of relief personally to Battalion Signalling officer who will meet them at junction of TRENCH BOARD TRACK with OLD GERMAN FRONT LINE.

2. The following guides will be sent to report to the Adjutant at 5pm. Only intelligent men will be chosen for this:–

17

Appendix C

SECRET.

Copy No. 10

47th Inf. Bde. Warning Order No. 145.

2nd August, 1917.

1. The 16th Division is to relieve the 15th Division in the Right Sector of the XIX Corps front on the night 3/4th August.

2. Subject to further development, it is the intention of the Divisional Commander to hold the line with three Brigades in depth, 47th Inf. Bde. holding the front system. 49th Inf. Bde. will be Bde. in Support, 48th Inf. Bde. will be Bde. in Reserve.

3. The 47th Inf. Bde. will hold the front system with 3 Bns. in front line and one in reserve. The latter Battn. to occupy the area between the BLUE LINE and the OLD GERMAN FRONT LINE.

4. The line will be divided approximately as follows:-

7th Leinster Regt. from about 100 yards South of the YPRES - ROULERS Railway (Right Boundary of XIX Corps) on the right to about 100 yards South of the Cross Rds. at D.25 central, on the left.

1st Royal Munster Fusrs. from about 100 yards South of the Cross Rds. at D.25 central on the right to about D.25.b.00.90 on the left.

6th Royal Irish Regt. from about D.25.b.00.90 on the right to about D.19.c.85.75. (Left Boundary of ~~XIX Corps~~ Right Div. XIX Corps) on the left.

6th Connaught Rangers will be Battalion in reserve.

5. Commanding Officers will arrange to thoroughly reconnoitre their respective positions and all approaches.

6. Hours of relief will be notified later.

7. On completion of relief the whole of the 47th Inf. Bde. will come under the orders of the Brigadier General, Commanding 47th Infantry Brigade. His Hd.Qrs. will be at MILL COTT (I.5.a.0.6).

8. ACKNOWLEDGE.

Ackd

[signature]
Capt. for Major,
Brigade Major, 47th Infantry Brigade.

Issued through Signals.

Copy No. 1. B.G.C.
2. Bde. Major.
3. Staff Captain.
4. 15th Division.
5. 16th Division "G"
6. 16th Division "Q"
7. 6th Royal Irish Regt.
8. 6th Connaught Rangers.
9. 7th Leinster Regt.
10. 1st R.Munster Fusrs.
11. 47th M.Gun Company.
12. 47th T.M.Battery.
13. 49th Inf. Bde.
14. 48th Inf. Bde.
15. [illegible]th Inf. Bde.
16. 4[illegible]th Inf. Bde.
16. Bde. Signals.
17. Bde. Bombing Officer.
18. Bde. T'port Of'cr.
19. 143 Coy. A.S.C.
20. Bde. Supply Officer.
21. 111th Fd.Amb.
22. 156 Coy. R.E.
23. C.R.E.
24. A.D.M.S.
25. War Diary.
26, 27 retained.

Appendix E

S E C R E T. O P E R A T I O N O R D E R S. No.150.

by

Lt-Col.R.H.Monck-Mason D.S.O. Comdg. 1st.Bn.Roy.Muns.Fus.

In the Field 10/8/1917.

XXXXXXXXXXXXXXXXXXXXXXX

1. The Battalion will be placed at the Disposal of the G.O.C. 48th.Infantry Brigade from the evening of the 11th.instant.

2. "W" "X" & "Y" Coys.will relieve 8th.Royal Dublin Fusiliers in Front Line System & will be met by Guide from R.D.F. at MENIN GATE at 8 p.m. arrangements as to transport for those Companies will be notified when received.

3. "Z" Coy.will relieve 2 Companies of 6th.Connaught Rangers in Support & be met by Guide at MENIN GATE at 4 p.m. This Coy. will be conveyed by Lorry from G.11.c.6.3. to MENIN GATE. Time of Departure of Lorry will be 2-30 p.m.

4. The following Stores will be carried:- 10 Watson Fans. Instructions as to drawing these will be issued later.

170 Rounds S.A.A. }
2 Mills Bombs. }
Rations & Water for 2 days } On the Man.
Iron Rations. }
2 Sandbags. }

5. All movement will be by platoons at 200 yds.intervals.

6. ACKNOWLEDGE.

(Sd.) M.H.Fitzgerald. Lieutenant;

A/Adjutant. 1st. Bn. Royal Munster Fusrs.

Copy No. __________. Issued at 11 p.m.

Copy No.1 Commanding Officer.
Copy No.2 Second in Command.
Copy No.3 Adjutant.
Copy No.4 Sigs.Officer.
Copy No.5 Intelligence Offr.
Copy No.6. O.C."W" Coy.
Copy No.7 O.C."X" Coy.
Copy No.8 O.C."Y" Coy.
Copy No.9 O.C."Z" Coy.
Copy No.10. Transport Officer.
Copy No.11 Quartermaster.
Copy No.12 47th. Inf.Brigade.
Copy No.13 R.S.M.
Copy No. 14 & 15 Filed.

SECRET. Appendix F.

Operation Order MH 195

1. The Battalion will be relieved by 2nd Royl Dublin Fus. on evening of 14th inst. & will proceed to ECOLE YPRES on completion of relief.

2. Guides. 1 reliable guide per Coy. & 1 N.C.O. per Coy. to take over billets at ECOLE will report to Lt. CALLANDER at Bn. H.Q. at 4 p.m. It is important that only reliable men be chosen to act as guides in order to accelerate relief.

3. Completion of relief will be notified at once by runner to Bn. H.Q.

4. All trench stores including S.O.S. Very Flares will be handed over to relieving Coys. & receipts obtained. These will be sent to Bn. H.Q. by 3 p.m. 15th inst. (This includes Bombs & Sandbags in possession).

5. All movement to be by platoons at 200x distance.

6. ACKNOWLEDGE.

14.8.17 [illegible signature]

Appendix G

1st Royal Munster Fusiliers
Order MH 203

1. The Battalion will move tonight 15th inst to assembly positions in Old German Trench System W of BLUE LINE in following order Y coy, Z coy, W coy, X coy.
Movement to be by platoons at 200x distance
Time of marching off of first platoon 11 pm.
Battalion to be in position by 2·30 AM. 16th inst

2. Dispositions on arrival at assembly position will be as follows Y coy — IBEX RESERVE (Right)
Z coy — " " - (Left)
W coy — ICE TRENCH + SUPPT.
X coy — IBEX " " " "
H.Q. — I 5.b.9.1

3 Before marching off following stores will be drawn + distributed
2 bombs per man
Extra Water bottle " "
1 days Ration " " (in addition to Iron Ration)
6 Shovels per platoon
170 rds S.A.A. per man (i.e. 50 extra)

4 Coys will notify Bn H.Q. at once when in position

W Coy — 2 guides
X coy — 2 guides
Y — 1 guide
Z — 1 guide

3. On completion of relief coys will proceed to No. 3 Area VLAMERTINGHE & will report to STAFF CAPTAIN at GOLD FISH CHATEAU for guides. All movement to be by platoons at 200x distance. Tracks to be used as far as possible up to MENIN GATE

4. Probable hour of commencement of relief 7.30 pm.

5. ACKNOWLEDGE.

[illegible]
Lt & Adjt

17.8.17

appendix. J.

S E C R E T   O P E R A T I O N   O R D E R S   No. 151

By

Lt. Colonel R. H. Monck-Mason D.S.O. Comdg. 1st. Royal Muns. Fus.
In the Field 18. 8. 17

xxxxxxxxxxxxxxxxxx

The Battalion will move to the WATOU "B" area in accordance with attached March Table

2. Entraining Point VLAMENTINGHE. Detraining Point POPERINGHE

3. Transport will move in accordance with table attached

4. Lt. T. H. POINGDESTRE and 2nd. Lt. G. DONNELLY and a party of 50 other Ranks as already detailed will march with the Transport. All movemmnts eastoff VLAMENTINGHE Wwill be by Plateons at 200 yds. interval Attention will be paid to March discipline

5 W and X Coys. unders of Major J. W. STACKPOOLE will proceed by 1st. Train entraining at 8.30 a.m. will march off from camp at 7 a.m. 2nd. Lt. D. J. O'SULLIVAN will act as entrainment Officer for this party
Y and Z Coys. will proceed by the 2nd. Train entraining at 10 a.m. will leave camp at 8 a.m. 2nd. Lt. F. A. HALDANE will act as entrainment Officer for this party
Headquarter Company will be divided into four sections and attached to Companies for purpose of entrainment Coys. will be told off in carriage parties of three sections of three and 1 N.C.O. before marching off PiPipers will be allotted to Companies

6. O's C Y and Z Coys. will ensure that all Tents and bivouac shelters at present occupied by the Battalion are in a thoroughly clean and sanitary condition before moving off and will detail the necessary parties to effect this. The Quartermaster will hand over the Camp to the area Commandant and obtain receipt for all tents and bivouac shelters none of which are to be removed from the area
Dress Battle Order Caps will be worn.
2 Lorries have been allotted to the Battalion and will report at H.16.d.1.6. at 7 a.m. 19th. Inst.
Quartermaster will arrange to have guides to meet them.

8. Supply railhead will be at WIPPENHOEK ~~xx~~ from the 18th. inst.

9. ACKNOWLEDGE.

(Signed) M. H. FitzGerald, Lieutenant,

A/Adjutant. 1st. Bn. Royal Munster Fusilierw.

March Table to accompany Battalion Order No. 181

Date	Unit	From	To	Route	Time of Strating	Time of entraining
19.8.17	1st. R.M.Fus. W & X Coys.	Present Camp	VLAMERTINGHE	Direct	7 a.m.	8.30 a.m.
do	Y & Z Coys.	do	do	do	8 a.m.	10 a.m.

MARCH TABLE FOR TRANSPORT 1ST. R. M. FUSILIERS.

Unit	From present position	To	Starting time	Route, Starting Point H.16.a.4.9.
1st. R. M. Fus.	do	L.14.b.3.4.	6.30 a.m.	H.9.a.73.52 - - H.8.a.66.32 - H.8.a.50.28. - BUSSEBOOM / POPERINGHE - L.6.c.9.1. - Road through L.9.b. and thence to respecyive camp

File

Appendix K

No 52

SECRET OPERATION ORDERS
By
Lt. Colonel R. H. Monck-Mason D.S.O. Comdg. 1st. Royal M...
In the Field 20. 8. 17

xxxxxxxxxxxxxxxxxxxx

1. The Battalion will march to EECKE on the 20th. inst.
Parade on road running through camp in sections of threes
Head of Column facing south west ready to march off at 1.50 p.m.
Dress - Full marching order Caps will be worn.
Order of March Scouts drums, Headquarters, W. X. Y. and Z Coys.

2. Route. Route will be Via L.13.d.4.0 - L.19.a.0.0. - L.19.c.8.0 - L.25.a.4.8. - L.31.c.6.6. - K.35.d.5.5 - GODSWAERSVELDE - Q.29.a.0.5.90 - EECKE

3. Billeting party has been sent forward. and will meet the Battali[on] at the entrance to the town.

4. Transport will accompany the Battalion.

Furbur Carriers will march in rear of "Z" Company.
O.C. Z Company will detail an O.C. Stragglers to report to the Adjutant 10 minutes before the Battalion moves off.

5. O's C Companies will take steps to ensure that present lines are in a thoroughly clean and sanitary condition before they move of[f].

All tents removed from their original sites will be replaced.
No tents or shelters will be removed from the area.
Officers' and Company Baggage will be stacked at Q.M.Stores by 12 noo[n]
6. ACKNOWLEDGE.

(Signed) M. H. FitzGerald, Lieutenant,
A/Adjutant, 1st. Royal Muns. Fusiliers.

Issued at ....

Copy No............

Copy No. 1 Commanding Officer
2 Adjutant
Copy No. 3 Intelligence Officer
Copy No. 4 O.C W Company
Copy No. 5 O.C. X Company
Copy No. 6 O.C. Y Company
Copy No. 7 O.C. Z Company
Copy No. 8 47th. Bde.
Copy No. 9 R.S. M.
Copy No. 10 Quartermaster
Copy No. 11 Transport Officer
Copies No. 12 and 13 file.

S E C R E T O P E R A T I O N O R D E R S No. 155

By

Major J. W. STACKPOOLE Comdg. 1st Bn. Royal Munster Fusiliers.

In the Field 20. 8. 17

Appendix 1 File

1. The Battalion will entrain at CAESTRE Q.32.d.1.1 21st. inst. at 2.30 p.m. Parade in column of threes in Main Street EECKE Head of column facing South outside Orderly Room ready to march off at 12.30 p.m. in following order:-
Scouts, Drums, H.Q. Coy., Y Z W and X Coys.
Dress - full marching order.
Companies will be told off into carriage parties of 30 men including N.C.O. before moving off.

2. Transport will arrive at Station 3 hours before time of entrainment and will parade in Main Street ready to march off at 10.45 a.m.

The following party will be detailed for duty at Detraining Station and will parade with transport They will report to R.T.O. immediately train arrives at destination - 25 men per Company including proportion N.C.O's 2nd. Lts. DONNELLY & WILKINSON are detailed for futy with this party.

Transport Officer will obtain a complete marching out state of Battalion shewing Number of men, horses, G.S. , Limbered G.S. and 2 wheeled wagons, hand carts and bicycles from Orderly Room before moving off which he will hand to R.T.O. on arrival at CAESTRE Furbur carts and wheeled stretchers will march with transport.

3. BILLETING PARTIES. - Lt. E. J. MAHONY is detailed to act as Billeting Ofcicer for Battalion 1 N.C.O. per Company and representatives of Transport and Quartermaster's Stores will report to him on arrival of Battalion at CAESTRE Station, where he will report to Staff Captain with party at 1 p.m.

4. ENTRAINMENT OFFICER - 2nd. Lt. HALDANE is detailed to act as Entrainment Officer for the Battalion When the head of the column reaches point Q.32.d.2.2. the Battalion will halt 2nd. Lt. HALDANE will then go forward to report to R.T.O. arrival and receive instructions as to when Battalion can enter Station. 1 Guide per Company will report to 2nd. Lt. HALDANE on arrival at Station.

5. LORRIES - - 1 Lorry will be at the disposal of Battalion for ~~a single~~ a single journey to CAESTRE from 7 a.m. to 9 a.m. Quartermaster will arrange for guide to be at Brigade Headquarters at 6.30 a.m. Officers' Valises and extra stores to be at Q.M. Stores at 6.30 a.m. Quartermaster will arrange for Guard for these stores when dumped at station and will be responsible that they are loaded on train A Limber wagon will collect valises of Z and Y Company starting with former at 5 a.m.

6. SUPPLIES - (1) P.M. rations for consumption on 21st. have been drawn to-day .
(2) Rations for 22nd. will be drawn from Railhead on 20th. by Divisional Train. . Supply wagons with these will entrain full with Battalion.

7. INSTRUCTIONS - The following will be strictly observed:-
(a). Carriage parties will be told off previous to marching off.
(b). Men are not to get out of the train or ride outside of or on top of the trucks.
(c). Officers will keep a look out during journey and check all irregularities.
(d). Men will only be allowed to get out at fixed stops and then only with permission of an Officer. A list of halts may be obtained from Adjutant at CAESTRE Station before departure of train.
(e). Y and X Coys. will find picquets for duty at each end of train ~~marking~~ during stops to prevent troops leaving.
(f). All doors of covered trucks and carriages on right hand side of train when on main line should be kept closed.
8. ACKNOWLEDGE.

(Signed) M. H. FitzGerald, Lieutenant,
A/Adjutant, 1st Royal Munster Fusiliers.

Appendix. H.

SECRET

OPERATION ORDERS No. 154

By

Major J. W. STACPOOLE Comdg. 1st. Bn. Royal Munster Fusiliers.
In the Field 24. 8. 17

1. The 47th. Infantry Brigade will relieve 110th. Infantry Brigade in Reserve Brigade Area to-morrow 25th. inst. and will come under orders of G.O.C. 21st. Division.

The Battalion will relieve the 7th LEICESTERS in SOUTHERN Camp MOYENNEVILLE (A.5.a.8.8).

2. Companies will march off on the road A.24.c.6.9 - A.16.d.7.6 - A.10.b. as follows :-

Headquarter & W Coy.	11 a.m.
X Company	11.5 a.m.
Y Company	11.10. a.m.
Z Company	11.15 a.m.

Dress - full Marching Order - Caps will be worn.

3. Officers' Valises and Company Mob. Boxes will be at Q.M. Stores by 9 a.m.

4. Lewis Gun Limbers will be loaded as usual, but will be sent to Companies immediately on arrival in new Camp.

5. Advance party of 1 N.C.O. per Company will report to Lieutenant MAHONY at Orderly Room at 8 a.m. and will proceed on bicycles to take over new Camp.

6. The following distances are to be maintained on the march when moving

(1) West of ARRAS - BAPAUME Rly. 250 yds. between Battns.
100 yds. between Coys.

(11) East of Railway - 5 minutes between Coys., unless special orders for a march are issued.

7. Completion of Relief will be reported to Bn. H. Q. immediately.

8. O's C Companies are responsible that their lines are handed over in a clean and sanitary condition. Quartermaster will hand over Camp and obtain receipt for tents etc.

9 The 47th. Infantry Brigade will relieve the 64th. inf. Bde. in the frnt line right Sector on the 26th. inst. Detailed instructions will be issued later.

Issued at

Copy No...........

Signed M. E. FitzGerald, Lieutenant,
A/Adjutant, 1st. Bn. Royal Munster Fusiliers

Copy No. 1 47th. Infantry Brigade
Copy No. 2 Comdg. Officer
Copy No. 3 2nd. In Command
Copy No. 4 Adjutant,
Copy No. 5 Intelligence Officer
Copy No. 6 Quartermaster
Copy No. 7 Transport Officer
Copy No. 8 "W" Company
Copy No. 9 "X" Company
Copy No. 10 "Y" Company
Copy No. 11 "Z" Company
Copy No. 12 O.C. H.Q. Company
Copy No. 13 R. S. M.
Copy No. 14 Medical Officer.
Copies Nos. 15 and 16 File.

Appendix N.

SECRET

OPERATION ORDERS No. 155
By
Major J. W. STACPOOLE Commanding 1st. Royal Munster Fusiliers.
In the Field 26. 8. 17

xxxxxxxxxxxxxxxxxxxxxxxxxxxxxx

Ref. Map 51 c 1/40,000
and 57 c 1/40,000

1 The Battalion will relieve the 9th. K. O. Y. L I. in support to-day 26th. instant.

2. Companies will relieve corresponding Coys. as follows:-

"W" Company 1st. R. M. Fus. will relieve "A" Coy1 9th. K.O.Y.L.I.
"X" Company 1st. R.M. Fus. will relieve "B" Coy. 9th. K.O.Y.L.I
"Y" Company 1st. R. M Fus. will relieve "C" Coy. 9th. K.O.Y.L.I.
"Z" Company 1st. R. M. Fus. will relieve "D" Coy. 9th. K.O.Y.L.I.
H.Q. Coy. 1st. R. M. Fus. will relieve H.Q. Coy.9th. K.O.Y.L.I.

Companies will march off in the above order at 5 minutes interval
Time of Marching off of 1st. Company - - - - - - - - - - - - - 2 p.m.
ROUTE - - - HAMELINCOURT - a . 12 Central - Track via b.8. Central - -b.9.a. (Reserve Battn. Camp) where guides will be in readiness at 3.15 p.m. "W" Company to arrive at b.9.a. Camp at that hour. All Movement East of a Line North and South through b.9. Central to be by platoons at 5 minutes interval.

3. All trench Stores will be carefully taken over and receipts sent to Battalion Headquarters by 3 p.m. 27th. inst.

4. Completion of relief to be reported to Battalion Headquarters in B.A.B. Code

5. RATIONS. Rations and water will be at the Support Line to-night at 8. p.m.

6. TRANSPORT. Transport on departure of Battalion will move to Lines at present occupied by Transport K.O.Y.L.I.

7. ACKNOWLEDGE.

(Signed) M.H. FitzGerald, Lieutenant,

A/Adjutant, 1st. Royal Munster Fusiliers.

Issued at .... Copy No..........

Appendix N

S E C R E T

OPERATION ORDERS No. 155

By

Major J. W. STACPOOLE Commanding 1st. Royal Munster Fusiliers.

In the Field 26. 8. 17

xxxxxxxxxxxxxxxxxxxxxxxxxxxxxxx

Ref. Map 51 c 1/40,000
and 57 c 1/40,000

---

1 The Battalion will relieve the 9th. K. O. Y. L. I. in support to-day 26th. instant.

2. Companies will relieve corresponding Coys. as follows:-

"W" Company 1st. R. M. Fus. will relieve "A" Coyl 9th. K.O.Y.L.I.
"X" Company 1st. R.M. Fus. will relieve "B" Coy. 9th. K.O.Y.L.I
"Y" Company 1st. R. M. Fus. will relieve "C" Coy. 9th. K.O.Y.L.I.
"Z" Company 1st. R. M. Fus. will relieve "D" Coy. 9th. K.O.Y.L.I.
H.Q. Coy. 1st. R. M. Fus. will relieve H.Q. Coy.9th. K.O.Y.L.I.

Companies will march off in the above order at 5 minutes interval
Time of Marching off of 1st. Company - - - - - - - - - - - - 2 p.m.
ROUTE - - - HAMELINCOURT - a . 12 Central - Track via b.8. Central - -b.9.a. (Reserve Battn. Camp) where guides will be in readiness at 3.15 p.m. "W" Company to arrive at b.9.a. Camp at that hour. All Movement East of a Line North and South through b.9. Central to be by platoons at 5 minutes interval.

3. All trench Stores will be carefully taken over and receipts sent to Battalion Headquarters by 3 p.m. 27th. inst.

4. Completion of relief to be reported to Battalion Headquarters in B.A.B. Code

5. <u>RATIONS.</u> Rations and water will be at the Support Line to-night at 8. p.m.

6. TRANSPORT. Transport on departure of Battalion will move to Lines at present occupied by Transport K.O.Y.L.I.

7. ACKNOWLEDGE.

(Signed) M.H. FitZgerald, Lieutenant,

A/Adjutant, 1st. Royal Munster Fusiliers.

Issued at .... Copy No..........

W A R   D I A R Y .

FOR   MONTH   OF   ~~AUGUST~~,   1917.

VOLUME..........

U N I T 1st Royal Munster Fusiliers

Vol 19

Instructions regarding War Diaries and Intelligence Summaries are contained in F. S. Regs., Part II. and the Staff Manual respectively. Title pages will be prepared in manuscript.

WAR DIARY
or
~~INTELLIGENCE SUMMARY.~~
(*Erase heading not required.*)

Army Form C. 2118.

1st R. Munster Fusiliers

Place	Date	Hour	Summary of Events and Information	Remarks and references to Appendices
3rd Army 6 Corps War Front	1/9		Battalion in support in RAILWAY RESERVE. CROISILLES – ECOUST ST MEIN. Headquarters in Tunnel [illegible] in support [illegible] Y Coy in RAILWAY RESERVE. X Coy [illegible]. [illegible] Revetting, draining and repairing trenches. Deepening, widening and draining and revetting KNUCKLE AVE. Carrying and Ration parties supplied to [illegible]. Light shelling. Strength O. 35, OR. 891. To Hosp. 2. Draft of 12 joined.	
"	2/9		Work continued on RESERVE and KNUCKLE AVE. Strength O. 35 OR 907. To Hosp. 3. Rejoined 2.	
"	3/9		Work continued. Erecting Elephant dugouts in RAILWAY RESERVE. erecting WATER CART STAND and repairing road. Strength. O. 35. OR 906. To Hosp. 2. To Cadet School 1.	
"	4/9		Work continued. Strength O. 35, OR. 903. To Hosp. 2. From Hosp. 2. To 2nd Bn. 1.	
"	5/9		Work continued. Strength O. 35, OR. 902. Wounded 1. (on working party.) To Hosp. 2. From Hosp. 2. From G.H.Q. School 1. Draft of 11 joined.	

Instructions regarding War Diaries and Intelligence Summaries are contained in F. S. Regs., Part II. and the Staff Manual respectively. Title pages will be prepared in manuscript.

WAR DIARY
or
~~INTELLIGENCE SUMMARY.~~
(Erase heading not required.)

2.

1 R. Muns. Fus.

Army Form C. 2118.

Place	Date 1917	Hour	Summary of Events and Information	Remarks and references to Appendices
SEE BRIGADE DIARIES	6/9		Work Continued. Strength O. 35. OR. 913. 2nd Lieuts. DICKEY, BOUCHIER, and MURROGH-BERNARD reported arrival.	
	7/9		Work Continued. Strength O. 38 OR. 913. To Hosp. 1. Draft of 7 OR joined.	
	8/9		Work Continued. Strength O. 38 OR 919. To Hosp. 3. Rejoined 2.	
	9/9		Work Continued. About 9.20 pm. enemy put over about 50 gas shells of pattern hitherto unseen – bursting in air and spreading presumably capsules of gas. No casualties. Men wore masks for 1 hour. Strength O. 38. OR. 91[?]. To Hosp. 3. Rejoined 2.	
	10/9		Work Continued. Strength O. 38. OR. 919. To Hosp. 2. Draft of 18 joined. Orders for Relief issued.	Opta. Order No 1.
	11/9		Battalion moved into Front Line, relieving 7 Leinster R.. Z Coy on Left – X Coy in centre – Y Coy on Right. W Coy in support in MAIN RESERVE. Relief completed about 11.30 pm. Strength. O. 38. OR. 935. Killed 1, wounded 5. (by Pineapple bomb among working party). Rejoined 3.	

A6945 Wt. W11422/M1160 350,000 12/16 D. D. & L. Forms/C./2118/14.

Instructions regarding War Diaries and Intelligence Summaries are contained in F. S. Regs., Part II. and the Staff Manual respectively. Title pages will be prepared in manuscript.

WAR DIARY
or
~~INTELLIGENCE SUMMARY.~~

(Erase heading not required.)

3.

1. R. Innis. Fus.

Army Form C. 2118.

Place	Date 1917	Hour	Summary of Events and Information	Remarks and references to Appendices
Front Line.	12/9		Battn in Front Line. Night quiet. 1 man wounded. Officer Patrol reported no enemy met in No man Land. Strength O. 38. OR. 932. Wounded 1. To Hosp. 1.	
	13/9		Situation quiet. A little shelling. Work on front line improving parapet – firesteps & dug outs. Strength O. 38 OR 930. To Hosp 1. Lieut. Robinson struck off strength & attached 11 Hants R. 4 NCOs struck off for instructional school.	
	14/9		Nothing unusual to report. Patrols report enemy wire good. Work on front line continued. Strength O. 37 OR 925. From Hosp. 2.	
	15/9		Orders for Relief. Battalion relieved by 6. R Ir. Regt. beginning at 9 pm. to billets at ERVILLIERS. – A Camp ENNISKILLEN CAMP. Relief complete about midnight without incident. Strength O. 37. OR. 927. To Hosp. 2, Rejoined 2. Draft of 55 joined.	Op'tn. Order No 2.
ERVILLERS.	16/9		Battn in billets (huts) in Camp. Men bathed and were refitted with clothing etc. Cleaned arms and inspect. of equipment. Strength. O. 37 OR. 983. To Hosp. 4.	

D. D. & L., London, E.C.
(A7883) Wt. W809/M1672 350,000 4/17 Sch. 52a Forms/C/2118/14

Instructions regarding War Diaries and Intelligence Summaries are contained in F. S. Regs., Part II. and the Staff Manual respectively. Title pages will be prepared in manuscript.

WAR DIARY
or
~~INTELLIGENCE SUMMARY.~~
(Erase heading not required.)

4

1 R Muns Fus.

Army Form C. 2118.

Place	Date 1917	Hour	Summary of Events and Information	Remarks and references to Appendices
ERVILLERS	17/9		Battn in camp. Training begun. Rifle & Squad drill – Bombing – Musketry – Practising attack in open. Lewis Gun team practising and Rifle Gren practice and training. Strength O. 37. OR. 987. To Hosp. 1. Rejoined 2. Draft of 7 joined.	
	18/9		Training carried on as above with different parties. Working party of 1 officer 4 Sgts. 70 OR. formed daily for work on DYSART CAMP. Strength O. 37. OR. 995.	
	19/9		Training & working party. Strength O. 37. OR. 995. To Hosp. 5. Rejoined 2. Draft of 59 OR joined. Daily parade of N.C.Os under R.S.M.	
	20/9		Training & working party & R.S.M. parades. Strength. O. 37. OR. 1054. To Hosp. 5. Rejoined 2.	
	21/9		Training & working party & R.S.M. parades. Strength O. 37 OR. 1051. To Hosp. 3. Draft of 18 joined.	
	22/9		Training – working party & R.S.M. parades. Strength O 37 OR. 1066.	Opn Order No 3
	23/9		~~Training~~ Working party ~~& R.S.M. parade~~. Strength O. 37. OR. 1066. From Hosp 4. Draft of 5 joined. Divine Service.	

D. D. & L., London, E.C.
(A7883) Wt W809/M1672 350,000 1/17 Sch. 52a Forms/C/2118/14

Instructions regarding War Diaries and Intelligence Summaries are contained in F. S. Regs., Part II, and the Staff Manual respectively. Title pages will be prepared in manuscript.

5

WAR DIARY
or
INTELLIGENCE SUMMARY.
(*Erase heading not required.*)

1 R. Muns Fus

Army Form C. 2118.

Place	Date 1917	Hour	Summary of Events and Information	Remarks and references to Appendices
ERVILLERS	24/9		Training - Working Party, + RSM. Parades. Strength O. 37 OR. 1075.	
	25/9		Training - Working Party, + RSM. Parades. Strength O. 37. OR. 1075.	
			Accidentally wounded 2 (By Bombing accident whilst training)	
			1 from Hosp. 6 Officers reported. Lieut. F.G.Y. MCDANIEL -	
			Lt. E.F. COLLINS. - Lt. H.M.J. BLAKE. - Lt. J.H.B. NIHILL -	
			2/Lt. C.W. MARSDEN - 2/Lt. G.V. HESLAM.	
	26/9		Training - Working Party + RSM Parades. Strength O. 43. OR. 1074.	
	27/9		Training - Working Party + RSM Parade. Strength O. 43 OR 1074.	
			From Hosp 2. Draft of 15 joined.	
	28/9		Training - Working Party + RSM Parades. Strength O. 43 OR. 1091	
	29/9		Training - Working Party + RSM Parades. Strength O. 43. OR 1091.	
			To Hosp. 4 Rejoined 2.	
	30/9		Divine Service. Working Party. Strength O 43. OR. 1089. Draft of	
			17 joined. Orders issued for Relief of	
			6 R. Ir. Regt. in RAILWAY RESERVE by the	
			Battn. tomorrow 1st Oct.	

J. W. Stacpoole Major
1st Ry Mun Fus
30/9/17

D. D. & L., London, E.C. (A7883) Wt. W809/M1672 550,000 4/17 Sch. 52a Forms/C/2118/14

SECRET

No I

OPERATION ORDERS

By

Lt. Col. R. H. Monck-Mason D.S.O. Comdg. 1st. R. M. Fusiliers.

In the Field 10th. Sept. '17.

xxxxxxxxxxxxxxxxxxxxxxxxxxxxxxxxxxxxxxx

1. RELIEF.
The Battalion less 1 Company will relieve the 7th. Leinster Regt. in the front line on the night of the 11/12th. September. Surplus of "W" Company minus Lewis Gun Section moving into close Support in MAN MAN RESERVE . Present positions in RAILWAY RESERVE willbe handed over tot the outgoing Battalion .

2. ORDER OF RELIEF.
Reliefs will take place in the following order:-

"Z" Coy. 1st. R.M.F. will relieve "A" and "C" Coys. 7th. Leinsters on the left.

"X" Coy. 1st R.M.F. will relive "D" Coy. 7th. Leinster Regt. in the centre

"Y" Coy. 1st. R.M.F. will relieve "B" Coy. 7th. Leinster Regt. on the right

Guides 1 per Platoon will be at Junction of PELICEN and RAILWAY RESERVE at 7.30 p.m. . Movement will be by platoon at 200 yds. distance All up traffic will be by PELICEN and down traffic by KNUCKLE. Surplus of "W" Coy. will move into MANCHESTER RESERVE Via KNUCKLE Leading platoon to enter KNUCKLE by 7.30 p.m. Movement across open to be by small parties at 200 yds. distance .

3. LEWIS GUNS.
Relief to commence at 3 p.m. 1 guide per gun will be at Leinsters H.Q. at 3 p.m. Lewis Gun Section of "W" Coy. will take part in this relief which will be carried out as follows:-
"Z" Coy. 1st. R.M.F. will relieve "A" Coy. 7th. L.R.
"W" Coy. 1st. R.M.F. will relive "C" Coy. 7th. L.R.
"X" Coy. 1st. R.M.F. will relive "D" Coy. 7th. L.R.
"Y" Coy. 1st. R.M.F. will relieve "B" Coy. 7th. L.R.
16 Lewis Guns will be taken into the line .

4. ADVANCE PARTIES.
Advance parties of 1 Officer and 1 N.C.O. per Company will be sent to take over so as to arrive at their destination at 3 p.m.

5. FRONTAGE.
After completion of relief O.C. "X" Coy. will extend his frontage to the left so ~~as~~ that his flank rests on QUEENS AVENUE .

6. REPORTS.
Completion of relief will be reported to Orderly Room in code immediately

7. TRENCH STORES.
Trench Stores will be taken over and receipts forwarded to O.Room by 12 noon on the 12th. instant O.C. "Z" Coy. will take over stores on charge of "A" and "C" Coys. 7th. L.R. . Receipts for stores handed over to representatives of 7th L.R. in RAILWAY RESERVE will be sent in with the above and also certificates that present positions have been handed over in a clean and sanitary condition.

8. RATIONS.
Rations will be drawn by Ration Parties before moving off from present position.

9. ACKNOWLEDGE.

(Sd.) M.H. FitzGerald, Lieutenant,
A/Adjutant, 1st. Royal Munster Fusiliers.

Copies to

Commanding Officer
2nd. in Command
Adjutant
O.C. "W" Coy.
O.C. "X" Coy.
O.C. "Y" Coy.
O.C. "Z" Coy.
Signalling Officer
Intelligence Officer
Transport Officer
Quartermaster
O.C. 7th. Leinster Regt.
R. S. M.
2 Copies retained.

S E C R E T   O P E R A T I O N   O R D E R S   No. 2

By

Lt. Col. R. H. Monck-Mason D.S.O. Comdg. 1st. Royal Munster Fusiliers.
In the Field 15. 9. 1917

1. The Battalion will be relieved by the 6th. Royal IRISH Regiment on the night of the 15/16th. September.

2. ORDER OF RELIEF

"B" Coy. 6th. Royal Ir. Reg. will relieve "Y" Coy. 1st. R.M.F.
"C" Coy. 6th. Royal Ir. Reg will relieve X Coy. 1st. R.M.F.
"A" Coy. 6th. Royal Ir. Reg. will relieve "Z" Coy. 1st. R.M.F.
"D" Coy. 6th Royal Ir. Reg. will relieve "W" Coy. 1st. R.M.F.

Guides 1 per platoon to be at Battalion Headquarters at 9 p.m. Movement will be by platoons at 200 yards distance.

3. LEWIS GUNS.

1 Guide per gun to be at Battalion H.Q. at 6.30 p.m.

4. Advance party

Advance parties of 1 Officer and 1 N.C.O. per Company will be sent to take over Huts near ERVILLERS occupied by the 6th. CONNAUGHT Rangers to arrive at destination at 4 p.m.

5. REPORTS

Completion of relief will be reported to Orderly Room in code immediately.

6. TRENCH STORES.

List of Trench Stores handed over to be sent to Orderly Room by 3 p.m. on the 16th. inst.

(Signed) W. F. SUGRUE, Lieutenant,
A/Adjutant, 1st. Royal Munster Fusiliers

Copies to

Commanding Officer
2nd. in Command
Adjutant,
47th. Inf. Bde.
"W" Company
"X" Company
"Y" Company
"Z" Company
Quartermaster
Transport Officer

Signalling Officer
O.C. 6th. R.I.Regt.
R. S. M.
2 Copies retained.

SECRET. OPERATION ORDERS. No.3.

By

Lt-Col.R.H.MONCK-MASON. D.S.O. Comdg. 1st.ROYAL MUNSTER FUSILIERS.

In the Field. 30/9/1917.

****

1. RELIEF.
The Battalion will relieve 6th.Royal Irish Regt. & Portion of 6th. Connaught Rangers in RAILWAY RESERVE and STRAY & MAN SUPPORT, tomorrow the 1st.prox.

2. ORDER OF RELIEF.
Relief will be carried out as follows:-
H.Q.Coy. 1/R.M.Fus. will relieve H.Q.Coy. 6th.R.I.R. in RAILWAY RES.
Time of Marching off from present camp 7-30 p.m.
"W" Coy. 1/R.M.F. will relieve "B" Coy. 6th.R.I.R. in RAILWAY RES. S.
Time of Marching off 7-35 p.m.
"X" Coy. 1/R.M.F. will relieve "A" & "D" Coys(Less 1 Platoon) 6th.R.I.R. in RAILWAY RESERVE. Time of Marching off 7-50 p.m.
"Z" Coy. will relieve "C" Coy. 6th. R.I.R. in RAILWAY RESERVE, NORTH.
Time of marching off 8-5 p.m.
"Y" Coy. will relieve ~~xxxxxxxxx~~ 1 platoon "B" Coy.6/R.I.R.in MAN SUPPORT and 3 Platoons 6th.Connaught Rangers in STRAY SUPPORT.
Time of marching off 8-20 p.m.

3. MOVEMENT.
All movements will be by platoons at 5 minutes interval. Leading platoon will not cross ST.LEGER - VRAUCOURT. Road before [illegible]-15 p.m.

4. BAGGAGE.
All Kit and stores will be stacked for removal by Transport Officer at Company H.Q. at 4 p.m.

5. RATIONS.
Rations will be at the respective dumps by 11 p.m.

6. TRENCH STORES.
All trench Stores, Working Parties will be carefully taken over, Copiesof Trench Store Receipts will be sent to Orderly Room by 12 noon 2nd.Prox.

7. COMPLETION OF RELIEF.
Completion of Relief to be reported by runner immediately to Battn. Headquarters.

8. Company Commanders will see that their lines are vacated in a clean and sanitary condition.

9. ACKNOWLEDGE.

(Sd.) M.H.FITZGERALD. Lieutenant;
A/Adjutant. 1st. Bn. ROYAL MUNSTER FUSILIERS.

No.of Copy.__________ Time of Issue.__________

No.1 Copy. Commanding. Officer.
No.2 Copy. 2nd. In Command.
No.3 Copy. Adjutant.
No.4 Copy. O.C."W" Coy.
No.5. Copy. O.C."X" Coy.
No.6 Copy. O.C."Y" Coy.
No.7 Copy. O.C."Z" Coy.
No.8 Copy. O.C.H.Q. Coy.
No.9 Copy. Transport Officer.
No.10 Copy. Quartermaster.
No.11 Copy. R.S.M.
No.12.6th.Royal Irish Regt.
No.13.6th.Connaught Rangers.
No.14.H.Q.47th.Brigade.
No.15. Intelligence Officer.
No.16 & 17 Copies. retained.

W A R D I A R Y

FOR MONTH OF OCTOBER, 1917.

UNIT 1st Bn. Munster Fusiliers

VOLUME NUMBER

Vol 20

Army Form C. 2118.

Instructions regarding War Diaries and Intelligence Summaries are contained in F. S. Regs., Part II. and the Staff Manual respectively. Title pages will be prepared in manuscript.

WAR DIARY or ~~INTELLIGENCE SUMMARY.~~

(Erase heading not required.)

I

1 R Munster Fus

Place	Date	Hour	Summary of Events and Information	Remarks and references to Appendices
	1917			
ENNISKILLEN	OCT. 1.		Battn preparing to move into Support. First party marched	Bde Optn
CAMP.			at 7.30 pm Relieved 6 R. I. R in Support in RAILWAY RESERVE	Order No
ERVILLERS.			Relief complete at 11 pm.	162.
IN SUPPORT	2		W - X & Z Companies in RAILWAY RESERVE. Y Coy in STRAY	Optn
ECOUSTE			SUPPORT with 1 Platoon in MAN SUPPORT. Work on dugouts in	Order
SECTOR.			RAILWAY RESERVE begun and work in progress taken over.	No 3.
			Working Parties for R.E. work in front line detailed as	
			per Brigade programme	
	3.		do.	
	4		do	
	5		do	
	6		do Y Coy relieved by Z Coy in STRAY SUP & MAN SUPPORT.	
	7		do	
	8		do	
	9		Battn less 1 Coy relieved the 6 Leinster R. in Front line	Optn
			as follows:- W Coy on Right, X Coy in Centre, Y Coy on Left.	Order No 4

D. D. & L., London, E.C. (A7883) Wt. W809/M1672 350,000 4/17 Sch. 52a Forms/C/2118/14

Instructions regarding War Diaries and Intelligence Summaries are contained in F. S. Regs., Part II. and the Staff Manual respectively. Title pages will be prepared in manuscript.

WAR DIARY
or
~~INTELLIGENCE SUMMARY.~~
(*Erase heading not required.*)

II

Army Form C. 2118.

1. R. Munster Fus

Place	Date	Hour	Summary of Events and Information	Remarks and references to Appendices
	1917 Oct. 10		Nothing of interest to report in line. Work continued on trenches.	
	11		Enemy shelled heavily all day. No damage to front line. Our batteries in rear of Batt. H.Q. were shelled and some damage done.	
	12		Gas attack made from our front by projectors. 500 gas projectiles put over on enemy front opposite QUEENS LANE at 8 p.m. Very successful – enemy appeared to be taken by surprise. He shelled wildly for 30 minutes. No damage. 500 gas projectiles put over on FAG. ALLEY front at midnight. Retaliation weak. 4 gas cylinders fell short in our front line causing 3 slight casualties on reoccupying line.	
	13		Left of our line badly shelled and damaged. Several casualties. All work continuing.	
	14		Enemy sent many light T.Ms and pineapples on our left. Work continuing.	

D. D. & L., London, E.C. (A7883) Wt W809/M1672 350,000 4/17 Sch. 52a Forms/C/2118/14

Instructions regarding War Diaries and Intelligence Summaries are contained in F. S. Regs., Part II, and the Staff Manual respectively. Title pages will be prepared in manuscript.

III

Army Form C. 2118.

WAR DIARY
or
~~INTELLIGENCE SUMMARY.~~
(Erase heading not required.)

1. R. Munster Fus.

Place	Date	Hour	Summary of Events and Information	Remarks and references to Appendices
	1917 Oct. 15		Nothing to report. All work continuing. Artillery preparation	
	16		6 Leinster R. took over our Centre section at 1 a.m. and raided Enemy line at 2.10 a.m. Objective MARS and TUNNEL TRENCH. Our barrage good. Coloured lights sent up by us on all our front. 2 Prisoners taken. MARS was strongly held. Leinster casualties 6. 1 killed. Gas attack by us on extreme left in afternoon.	
	17		Battalion relieved by 6 R. Ir. R. at 7 p.m. Relief complete at 11.30 p.m. Battalion marched to DYSART CAMP (B13 b7.7.)	Bde Order 166
DYSART CAMP. ERVILLERS	18 19 20 21 22 23 24		Work started on Camp. Companies inspection, Kit and clothing. Baths and training. Fatigue parties found for Brigade Rifle Range. Brick fireplaces built in huts, huts, officers quarters and messes. Drains dug and brick paths made. Cross Country Race — Boxing and Dopes for Corps entries.	Battn Opti Order No 5.

D. D. & L., London, E.C. (A7883) Wt. W809/M1672 350,000 4/17 Sch. 52a Forms/C/2118/14

Instructions regarding War Diaries and Intelligence Summaries are contained in F. S. Regs., Part II. and the Staff Manual respectively. Title pages will be prepared in manuscript.

WAR DIARY
or
~~INTELLIGENCE SUMMARY.~~

(Erase heading not required.)

IV

1. R. Munster Fus.

Army Form C. 2118.

Place	Date	Hour	Summary of Events and Information	Remarks and references to Appendices
	1917 Oct			
DYSART CAMP	25 to 31.		Camp improving & training and inspection continued. Visit of Cardinal Bourne to the Battalion	Strength and Casualty return. Officers joined and drafts.

H. P. Goodland Major
1 R. Muns. Fus.

D. D. & L., London, E.C.
(A7883) Wt. W809/M1672 350,000 4/17 Sch. 52a Forms/C/2118/14

SECRET. OPERATION ORDERS. No.3

By

Lt-Col.R.H.MONCK-MASON. D.S.O. Comdg. 1st.ROYAL MUNSTER FUSILIERS.

In the Field. 30/9/1917.

****

1. RELIEF.
The Battalion will relieve 6th.Royal Irish Regt. & Portion of 6th. Connaught Rangers in RAILWAY RESERVE and STRAY & HAM SUPPORT, tomorrow the 1st.prox.

2. ORDER OF RELIEF.
Relief will be carried out as follows:-
H.Q.Coy. 1/R.M.Fus. will relieve H.Q.Coy. 6th.R.I.R. in RAILWAY RES. Time of Marching off from present camp 7-30 p.m.
"W" Coy. 1/R.M.F. will relieve "B" Coy. 6th.R.I.R. in RAILWAY RES. S. Time of Marching off 7-35 p.m.
"X" Coy. 1/R.M.F. will relieve "A" & "D" Coys(Less 1 Platoon) 6th.R.I.R. in RAILWAY RESERVE. Time of Marching off 7-50 p.m.
"Z" Coy. will relieve "C" Coy. 6th. R.I.R. in RAILWAY RESERVE. NORTH. Time of marching off 8-5 p.m.
"Y" Coy. will relieve ~~xxxxxxxxxx~~ 1 platoon "B" Coy.6/R.I.R.in HAM SUPPORT and 3 Platoons 6th.Connaught Rangers in STRAY SUPPORT. Time of Marching off 8-20 p.m.

3. MOVEMENT.
All movements will be by platoons at 5 minutes interval. Leading platoon will not cross ST.LEGER - VRAUCOURT. Road b fore 7-15 p.m.

4. BAGGAGE.
All Kit and stores will be stacked for removal by Transport Officer at Company H.Q. at 4 p.m.

5. RATIONS.
Rations will be at the respective dumps by 11 p.m.

6. TRENCH STORES.
All trench Stores, Working Parties will be carefully taken over, Copies of Trench Store Receipts will be sent to Orderly Room by 12 noon 2nd.Prox.

7. COMPLETION OF RELIEF.
Completion of Relief to be reported by runner immediately to Battn. Headquarters.

8. Company Commanders will see that their lines are vacated in a clean and sanitary condition.

9. ACKNOWLEDGE.

(Sd.) M.H.FITZGERALD. Lieutenant;
A/Adjutant. 1st. Bn. ROYAL MUNSTER FUSILIERS.

No.of Copy.__________ Time of Issue.__________

No.1 Copy. Commanding. Officer.
No.2 Copy. 2nd. In Command.
No.3 Copy. Adjutant.
No.4 Copy. O.C."W" Coy.
No.5. Copy. O.C."X" Coy.
No.6 Copy. O.C."Y" Coy.
No.7 Copy. O.C."Z" Coy.
No.8 Copy. O.C.H.Q. Coy.
No.9 Copy. Transport Officer.
No.10 Copy. Quartermaster.
No.11 Copy. R.S.M.
No.12.6th.Royal Irish Regt.
No.13.6th.Connaught Rangers.
No.14.H.Q.47th.Brigade.
No.15. Intelligence Officer.
No.16 & 17 Copies. retained.

SECRET

OPERATION ORDERS No. 4
By
Lt. Col. R. H. Monck-Mason D.S.O. Comdg. 1st. Royal Fus.
In the Field 9. 10. 17.

1. RELIEF

The Battalion less 1 Company will relieve the 7th Leinster Regt. in the front line on the night of the 9/10th. inst. . Present position in RAILWAY RESERVE will be handed over to the outgoing Battalion .
Z Company will remain in their present position in [illegible] SUPPORT and MAY SUPPORT.

2. ORDER OF RELIEF.

Y Coy. 1st. R. M. F. will relieve "A" Coy. 7th. Leinsters in LEFT SECTOR
X Coy. 1st. R. M. F. will relieve "C" Coy 7th. Leinsters in CENTRE SECTOR
W Coy. 1st. R. M. F. will relieve "D" Coy. 7th. Leinsters in RIGHT-SECTOR
Guides from advance parties will meet their own Coys. in Front Line

3. ROUTE.

W Coy. will relieve RIGHT SECTOR by PELICAN
Leading party to enter PELICAN by 5 p.m.
X Coy. will relieve CENTRE SECTOR by QUEENS AVENUE leading party to enter LEG LANE by 6 p.m.
Y Coy. will relieve LEFT SECTOR by KNUCKLE
Leading party to enter LEG LANE by 6.30 p.m.
All movements to be by small parties at 200 yards distance.

4. LEWIS GUNS.

Reliefs to commence at 2 p.m. . 1 Guide per Sector will meet teams as follows:-
L and C Sector at Junction of RLY RESERVE and LEG LANE at 2 p.m.
RIGHT SECTOR at Junction of RLY RESERVE and PELICAN at 2 p.m.
L.G. Section from Z Coy. will take part in this Relief.
16 Lewis Guns will be taken into the Line.
Advance parties of 1 Officer and 1 N.C.O. per Coy. will be sent to take over from 7th L.R. so as to arrive at their destination at 2 p.m.

5. REPORTS.

Completion of relief will be reported to Battalion Headquarters in code immediately.

6. TRENCH STORES.

~~Taken~~ Trench stores will be taken over and receipts forwarded to Battalion Headquarters by 12 Noon on 10th. instant.
Receipts for Stores handed over to rep. of 7th. L. R. in RLY RESERVE will be sent with the above, also certificates that present positions have been handed over in a clean and sanitary condition.

(Signed) C. H. Corrigan, Captain,
Adjutant 1st. Royal Munster Fusiliers.

S E C R E T

O P E R A T I O N   O R D E R S   No. 5

By

Lt. Col. R. H. MONCK-MASON D.S.O. Comdg. 1st. Royal Muns. Fusiliers

In the Field 16. 10. 17

XXXXXXXXXXXXXXXXXXXXXXXXXXXX

1. RELIEF

The Battalion will be relieved in the front line by the 6th. Royak Irish Regiment on the evening of the 17th. October commencing at 7 p.m.

"B" Coy. 6th. Royal Irish Regt. will relieve "W" Coy. 1st. R.M. Fus. in Right Sector as far as No. 16 Post (exclusive)
"C" Coy. 6th. Royal Irish Regt. will relieve "X" Coy. 1st. R.M.Fus. in Centre Sector from No. 16 Post (inclusive) to NOB SAP (exclusive)
"D" Coy. plus 2 platoons "A" Coy. 6th. Royal Irish Regt. will relieve "Y" Coy. in Left Sector from NOB SAP (inclusive) to the left boundary.
Coy. Headquarters plus 2 platoons "A" Coy. and 2 platoons 6th. Connaught Rangers will relieve "Z" Coy. 1st. R. M. Fus. in MAN SUPPORT and STRAY SUPPORT the 6th. Connaught Rangers in STRAY SUPPORT.

On completion of relief Companies will move independently to Camp at B.13.b.7.7.
Relief will be reported to Battalion Headquarters by wire.

2. LEWIS GUNS.

The Lewis Gun Teams 1st. R. M. F. will be relieved by incoming teams at 6 p.m.

3. Advanced Parties.

1 N.C.O. per Coy. and 1 N.C.O. H.Q. Coy. will report to 2nd. Lt. WALSH at Battalion H.Q. at 2 p.m.

5. Trench Stores.

Companies will hand over trench stores as they stand. The necessary adjustment between Coys of the 6th. Royal Irish Regt will be made afterwards Receipts for Trench Stores will be forwarded to Battalion Headquarters by 10 a.m. the 18th. instant, also certificates that trenches are handed over in a clean and sanitary condition.

4. WORKING PARTIES.

All working parties found by 1st R. M. Fus. will be taken over by 6th. Royal Irish Regiment.

5. TRANSPORT

Transport will be at CRUX CIRCUS at 6 p.m. for Lewis Gun Stores.

6. ACKNOWLEDGE.

(Signed) C. H. CARRIGAN, Captain,
A/Adjutant, 1st. Royal Munster Fusiliers.

Copy No. 1. Commanding Officer
Copy No. 2. Adjutant,
Copy No. 3 Intelligence Officer
Copy No4 O.C. H. Q. Coy.
Copy No. 5 O. C. "W" Coy.
Copy. No. 6 O.C. "X" Coy.
Copy No. 7 O.C. "Y" Coy.
Copy No. 7 O.C. "Z" Coy.
Copy No. 8 47th. Inf. Bde.
Copy No. 9 6th. Royal Irish Regt.
Copy No. 10. 6th. Connaught Rangers.
Copy No. 11 R. S M.
Copy No. 12 Transport Officer
Copy No. 13 Quartermaster
Copies 14 and 15 File.

Issued at ....

W A R   D I A R Y

FOR MONTH OF NOVEMBER, 1917.

VOLUME :-

U N I T : - 1st Royal Munster Fusiliers

Vol 21

Instructions regarding War Diaries and Intelligence Summaries are contained in F. S. Regs., Part II. and the Staff Manual respectively. Title pages will be prepared in manuscript.

WAR DIARY
or
INTELLIGENCE SUMMARY. 1 R. Munster Fus.
(Erase heading not required.)

Army Form C. 2118.

Place	Date	Hour	Summary of Events and Information	Remarks and references to Appendices
	1917 Nov			
DYSART CAMP.	1.		In Camp. Bde orders rec'd to go to line	Bde Ord. 169.
ERVILLERS.	2.		Battalion relieved 6 R. Ir. Regt. in line in left Sub-Sector with One	Batt Ord.
HENDECOURT			Coy (W) in front line. One Coy (X) in support, and 2 Coys Y & Z in Reserve.	No 6.
SECTOR.			Relief completed at 9 pm.	
CROISILLES – ECOUST LINE	3		In line. Working parties from X Y & Z Coys at work repairing [illegible] trenches. Work on Dugouts [illegible]	
	4		In line. Daily working parties from [illegible] All work in hand continued. Lt Col [illegible] returned from leave and re-assumed command from Major Goodeve.	
	5		In line. All work continued. Major [illegible] returned from leave.	
	6		In line. All work continued. [illegible]	
	7		In line. All work continued. W & X Coys relieved by Y & Z Coys.	
	8		In line. All work continued.	
	9		In line. All work continued.	
	10		In line. All work continued.	
	11		In line. All work continued. Y Coy relieved by X Coy in front line.	

D. D. & L., London, E.C.
(A7883) Wt. W809/M1672 350,000 4/17 Sch. 52a Forms/C/2118/14

Instructions regarding War Diaries and Intelligence Summaries are contained in F. S. Regs., Part II, and the Staff Manual respectively. Title pages will be prepared in manuscript.

WAR DIARY
or
INTELLIGENCE SUMMARY.
(*Erase heading not required.*)

1 R. Munster Fus.

2

Army Form C. 2118.

Place	Date	Hour	Summary of Events and Information	Remarks and references to Appendices
	1917			
Left Sector	Nov. 12		In line. Bde orders recd for relief	Bde order 72
	13		Battalion relieved by 6 R. I. Regt. and marched to DURROW CAMP	Batt. order
DURROW CAMP	14		In Camp. W & X Coys. refitting clothing and bathing	No 7
	15		W & X Coys to Training ground to practice attack. Y & Z bathe etc.	
	16		W & X Coy to Training ground	
	17		W & X Coys to Training ground.	
	18		Battalion less Y Coy marched to line and relieved 6 R. I. Regt in front line, Z Coy in front line, W & X in support. Relief completed at 8 pm.	Batt. order No 8
Left Sector	19		W and X Coys fully equipped with extra S.A.A., Bombs, tools etc for operation on 20th. All arrangements completed and [illegible] explained [illegible]. Bde H.Q. moved to RAILWAY RES. Batt. HQ moved to [illegible] SUNKEN [illegible]	
	20		Operations began. Zero 6.20 a.m. German front line attacked and taken. Y Coy moved up and employed digging new communication trench and carrying. Z Coy digging new communication trench across old No man's Land. W & X Coys holding new front line in TUNNEL TRENCH	Report on Operations

D. D. & L., London, E.C. (A7883) Wt. W809/M1672 350,000 4/17 Sch. 52a Forms/C/2118/14

3

Instructions regarding War Diaries and Intelligence Summaries are contained in F. S. Regs., Part II, and the Staff Manual respectively. Title pages will be prepared in manuscript.

WAR DIARY
or
INTELLIGENCE SUMMARY.
(Erase heading not required.)

Army Form C. 2118.

1. R. Munster Fus.

Place	Date	Hour	Summary of Events and Information	Remarks and references to Appendices
	1917			
TUNNEL TRENCH	Nov. 21		W & X Coys holding and consolidating the newly gained trench. Fairly heavy shell fire and some sniping. An S.O.S. on left brought down our barrage, but no enemy action appeared.	
	22		Still holding trench and at 9.40 pm relieved by the 6 R. Ir. Regt. and marched to DURROW CAMP arriving there at 1 am.	Batt. order No 9.
DURROW CAMP	23	}	Battalion resting and refitting. Brig. Gen. Pereira left.	
	24	}		
	25	}		
IN LINE.	26		Battalion relieved 6 Connaught Rangers in line in old Front line. Relief complete at 8 pm.	Batt. order No 12
	27		All Coys on working parties repairing battered trenches and carrying to new front line	
	28		Coys working. Heavy enemy barrage on old & new lines at 6 pm.	
	29		Heavy enemy barrage at 6 am for 30 min. No action followed. Battn changed front and line readjusted. Part of 3 Div line taken over. Readjustment complete at 10 pm. Hants Pioneers assisting in digging new trenches.	Batt. order No 13

D. D. & L., London, E.C.
(A7883) Wt. W809/M1672 350,000 4/17 Sch. 52a Forms/C/2118/14

Instructions regarding War Diaries and Intelligence Summaries are contained in F. S. Regs., Part II, and the Staff Manual respectively. Title pages will be prepared in manuscript.

WAR DIARY
or
INTELLIGENCE SUMMARY.
(*Erase heading not required.*)

4

Army Form C. 2118.

1 R Munster Fus

Place	Date 1917	Hour	Summary of Events and Information	Remarks and references to Appendices
	NOV 29		Contd. 2 Coys. 6 Conn. Rgrs moved up to RAILWAY RES as supports.	
			Lt Col. Monck-Mason went on leave. Major Goodland assumed command.	
			Hants. Pioneers in Ry. RES. Work. W Coy took up the OG GOG & MAGOG Line, posts and BURG TR. old German line.	
	30		Heavy enemy barrage at 5.50 am. S.O.S. sent up on our Right. Our Artillery opened. No action followed. At 11 am enemy put down another barrage on both new and old front lines. Our Artillery replied. No action followed. Very little damage done considering intensity of bombardment of enemy. Wiring and digging at night on OG GOG & MAGOG Line.	

[illegible] Goodland Major
Cmdg 1st R Munster Fus

D. D. & L., London, E.C. (A7883) Wt. W809/M1672 350,000 4/17 Sch. 52a Forms/C/2118/14

Instructions regarding War Diaries and Intelligence Summaries are contained in F. S. Regs., Part II, and the Staff Manual respectively. Title pages will be prepared in manuscript.

WAR DIARY or ~~INTELLIGENCE SUMMARY.~~

(*Erase heading not required.*)

Army Form C. 2118.

5

1. R. Muns Fus.

Summary of Events and Information

Daily Strength & Casualty Return.

Place	Date 1917 Nov	Hour	Officers.	O. Ranks	To Hospital	Killed	Wounded	Missing	Joined	Left	Remarks and references to Appendices
	1		46	1111					3 (Drafts) 2 From Hosp.		
	2		46	1116	4					1 (Commission) Sgt. Gurnell. 3 (To Base) 4 (Struck off)	
	3		46	1104	5				1 Hosp.		
	4		46	1102		1	1				
	5		46	1100	3				1 Hosp 3 Draft.		
	6		46	1101		1	1			1 (Commission) Sgt. Hogg.	
	7		46	1098	1	1	6		1 Hosp.		
	8		46	1091	2					1 (Transferred)	
	9		46	1088	2		1				
	10		46	1085	1		2		2 Hosp.		
	11		46	1084	2						
	12		46	1082	4				2 Hosp.		
	13		46	1080					1 Hosp.		
	14		46	1081					1 Hosp.		
	15		46	1082					1 Hosp.	1 (2/Lt. S[illegible]) R.F.C.	
	16		45	1083	2				1 Hosp.		

D. D. & L., London, E.C.
(A7883) Wt. W809/M1672 350,000 4/17 Sch. 52a Forms/C/2118/14

Instructions regarding War Diaries and Intelligence Summaries are contained in F. S. Regs., Part II. and the Staff Manual respectively. Title pages will be prepared in manuscript.

WAR DIARY
or
~~INTELLIGENCE SUMMARY.~~

(*Erase heading not required.*)

6.

Army Form C. 2118.

1 R Muns. Fus

Summary of Events and Information

Daily Strength & Casualty Return

Place	Date	Hour	Officers	O Ranks.	To Hospital	Killed	Wounded	Missing	Joined	Left	Remarks and references to Appendices
	1917										
	17		45	1082	2				1 Hosp.		
	18		45	1081							
	19		45	1081							
	20		45	1081		OFFICERS 3	O.R.	OFFICERS 1			
	20					Lt. MacDaniel 2/Lt Ennis 2/Lt Blake		2/Lt Whitay [uncertain]			
	20					O.R. 9	59	O.R. 5			
	21		41	1008						1 (2/Lt Reidy) invalided	
	22		40	1008	5						
	23		40	993	2				1 (Capt Tomlinson)		
	24		41	991							
	25		41	991	2				2 Hosp.		
	26		41	991	4		1		2 Hosp.		
	27		41	988	2				1 T.M. By.		
	28		41	987	1			1		1 (2/Lt Heslam)	To R.F.C.
	29		40	985							
	30		40	985							

H. J. [illegible] Major 1 RMF

D. D. & L., London, E.C. (A7883) Wt. W809/M1672 350,000 4/17 Sch. 52a Forms/C/2118/14

SECRET. **O P E R A T I O N O R D E R S.** No.6.

By

Lt-Col.R.H.MONCK-MASON D.S.O. Commanding 1st.Bn.ROYAL MUNSTER FUS.

In the Field. 1/11/1917.

****

The Battalion will relieve the 6th.Bn.ROYAL IRISH REGIMENT in the L ine tomorrow evening the 2nd.instant., in the left Sub-sector. Lewis Gunners under 2/Lieut.J.E.WALSH will relieve Lewis Gunners of 6th.R.I.R. by 3 p.m.

All movements will be by platoons at 5 minutes interval.

"W" COMPANY will relieve "C" COMPANY & 1 Platoon "B" COMPANY, 6th. R.I.R. in Front line from U.14.c.23.89. to QUEENS LANE via CRUX CIRCUS & LEG LANE. First Platoon "W" Coy. will leave Camp at 6 p.m.

"X" COMPANY:- will relieve 3 Platoons " B" COMPANY 6th.R.I.R. in STRAY SUPPORT via CRUX CIRCUS & LEG LANE. The remaining Platoonx will be accomodated at Bn.H eadquarters. 1st.Platoon "X" Coy.will leeave 5 Minutes after the last platoon "W" Coy.has left camp.

"Y" C OMPANY.will relieve "A" COMPANY 6th.R.I.R.in RAILWAY RESERVE, via MAIDA VALE. First Platoon "Y" Coy.will leave 5 Minutes after last platoon of "X" Coy. has left Camp.

"Z" Company.:- will relieve "D" COMPANY 6th.R.I.R. in RAILWAY RES. via MAIDA VALE , First Platoon "Z" Coy.will leave 5 Minutes after thelast platoon of "Y" Coy. has left Camp.

"H.Q.COMPANY- will relieve H.Q.COMPANY 6th.R.I.R. in RAILWAY RESERVE (LEFT). 1st.Half Company will leave Camp at 5 p.m. 2nd.Half Company will leave 10 minutes after last man of First Half Coy.has left Camp.

O.C."W" Company will take over two extra Lewis Guns (Six in all) but must provide their own teams.

ADVANCE PARTIESof 1 Officer & 1 N.C.O.per Company & 1 N.C.O.for H.Q. Company will parade at Orderly Room at 2 p.m.to proceed to take over trench stores etc.

LISTS OF TRENCH STORES taken over will be rendered to Orderly Room by 10 a.m.on the 3rd.instant.

Completion of Relief will be immediately reported to Bn.H.Q. in Code.

ACKNOWLEDGE.

(Signed.) C.W.MARSDEN. Lieutenant ;
A/Adjutant. 1st.Battalion.Royal Munster Fusrs.

Issued at ____________

Copy No.__________

No.1 Copy. Commanding Officer.
No.2 Copy. Second in Command.
No.3 Copy. Adjutant.
No.4 O.C."W" Coy.
No.5.Copy O.C."X" Coy.
No.6 Copy. O.C."Y" Coy.
No.7 Copy. O.C."Z" Coy.
No.8 Copy.O.C.H.Q. Coy.
No.9 Copy Intelligence Officer.
No.10 Copy.47th.Infy.Bde.
No.11. 6th.Bn.Royal Irish Regt.
No.12 Copy.R.S.M.
No.13 Copy. Quartermaster.
No.14 Copy. Transport Officer.

Copies 15 & 16 FILE.

SECRET. OPERATION ORDERS. No.7.

by

Lt-Colonel; R.H.MONCK-MASON D.S.O. Commanding. 1st.Bn.ROYAL MUNSTER FUSILIERS

In the Field. 13/11/17.

"W" "X" & "Y" Coys. will be relieved by the 6th.Bn.ROYAL IRISH REGIMENT, tonight the 13th.instant.

"Y" COY.will be relieved in the FRONT LINE by "A" Coy. R.I.REGT.& part of "B" Coy.R.I.REGT.
1 PLATOON "W" COY IN [illegible] will be relieved by part of "D" Coy.R.I.REGT.
"W" COY.will be relieved in STRAY SUPPORT by 2 platoons "D" Coy.R.I.REGT.
& 1 Platoon "B" COY.R.I.REGT.
"X" COY.will be relieved by 3 Platoons "B" Coy.R.I.R. in RAILWAY RESERVE.

LEWIS GUNNERS will be relieved at 3 p.m.

RELIEF COMPLETE will be sent to Bn.H.Q.in Code as soon as possible.

LEWIS GUN LIMBERS will be at CRUX CIRCUS at 6 p.m.
4Limbers will be at CRUX CIRCUS at 6 p.m.
On Relief the Companies will proceed to BURROW CAMP.

ACKNOWLEDGE. (Signed) G.?.MARSDEN. Lieutenant;
A/Adjutant. 1st.Bn.ROYAL MUNSTER FUSILIERS.

Copy No.______________ Issued at ______________

No.1 Commanding Officer.
Copy No.2. 2nd.in Command.
Copy No.3 Adjutant.
Copy No.4 Intelligence Offr.
Copy No.5 O.C."W" Coy.
Copy No.6 O.C."X" Coy.
Copy No.7 O.C."Y" Coy.
Copy No.8 O.C."Z" Coy.
Copy No.9 R.S.M.
Copy No.10 Quartermaster.
Copy No.11 Transport Officer.
Copy No.12 6th.Royal Irish Regt.
Copy No.13 47th.Bde.H.Q.
Copies 14 & 15 FILED.

OPERATION ORDERS. No.8.

By

Lt-Col.R.H.MONCK-MASON D.S.O.Commanding. 1st.Bn.ROYAL MUNSTER FUSRS.

In the Field. 17/11/17.

The Battalion Less "Y" Company will relieve the 6th.Bn.ROYAL IRISH REGIMENT in the Line on the 18th.instant.

"Z" Company. will relieve "A" Coy.& 2 platoons "D" Coy.6th.ROY.I. REGT.in front Line(Boundary QUEEN'S LANE to Left.) at 4 p.m. 1st.Platoon to pass 6th.R.I.R.Hd.Qrs.RAILWAY RESERVE AT 3-45 p.m. Platoons at 10 Minutes intervals. Men to go over the ground from RAILWAY RESERVE to entrance of LEG LANE in groups of 4 at 50 yards interval.

"W" & "X" COMPANIES will relieve 2 platoons "D" Company R.I.R. & 1 platoon "B" Coy.R.I.R. in STRAY SUPPORT.

H.Q.COMPANY will leave Camp at 4 p.m.

Platoons will move off at 5 Minutes interval. "W" Coy.after "H.Q.Coy. "X" Coy.after "W" Coy.

"Y" COMPANY.will stay on in DURROW CAMP.

Officers' Kits are to be cut down to Mobilization Weight. Extra Kit to be sent to Quartermaster's Stores by 3 p.m. and marked"extra kit." All Officers' Kit for the Line to be stacked at Orderly Room by 3 p.m.

Relief Complete to be reported in Code to Bn.H.Q. as soon as possible.

Lists of Trench Stores taken over to be rendered to Orderly Room by 10 a.m.19th.instant.

ACKNOWLEDGE.

(Sgd.) C.W.MARSDEN. Lieutenant;
A/Adjutant. 1st.Bn.ROYAL MUNSTER FUSILIERS.

Copy No.______ Issued at 9-50 p.m.

Copy No.1. Commanding Officer.
Copy No.2. 2nd.in Command.
Copy No.3 Adjutant.
Copy No.4 Intelligence Officer.
Copy No.5.O.C."W" Coy.
Copy No.6.O.C."X" Coy.
Copy No.7.O.C."Y" Coy.
Copy No.8. O.C."Z" Coy.
Copy No.9. R.S.M.
Copy No.10.Quartermaster.
Copy No.11.Transport Officer.
Copy No.12.6th.Royal Irish Regt.
Copy No.13.47th.Bde.H.Q.
Copies 14 & 15. Retained.
Copy No.16.O.C.H.Q.Company.

OPERATION ORDERS. No.9.

By

Lt-Col. R. H. MONCK-MASON D.S.O. Commanding. 1st. Bn. ROYAL MUNSTER FUS.
In the Field. 18/11/1917.

1. The 47th. Infantry Brigade will capture & Consolidate TUNNEL TRENCH from JOVE (U.20.b.50.70.) to SAP at U.14.a.68.12. (incl.) Blocks will be established at about U.14.a.98.05. and U.20.b.58.78.

2. The 6th. CONNAUGHT RANGERS are attacking on the Right and will Capture TUNNEL TRENCH from JOVE to U.14.d.20.30.
The 1st. ROYAL MUNSTER FUSILIERS will attack from U.14.d.10.30. to SAP at U.14.a.68.12.

3. The attack will be carried out by "W" & "X" Companies.
"W" Coy. from U.14.d.10.30. to U.14.c.92.75.
"X" Coy. from U.14.c.92.75 to SAP at U.14.a.68.12.

4. DISPOSITIONS FOR THE ATTACK.
The attack will be carried out in two waves. Strength of Platoons will be 30 men per Platoon. Each platoon will attack with 2 sections in the Front wave and two in close support.
The attached Diagram explains the method of attack.
In each platoon the sections will be composed as follows, except where otherwise stated:-
4 Riflemen, 2 Bombers, 1 Carrier, and 1 Rifle Grenadier.
Platoons will advance in Line of Sections, in File, at about 25 to 30 yards interval. The Fourth Section in each Platoon consists of Lewis Gunners.
Distance between waves 20 to 25 yards.
Each Company will supply a party of 1 Officer & 12 Other Ranks who will clear the TUNNEL working from North to SOUTH, commencing on the Northern Flank of their Company Front.
"X" Coy. will furnish a Party of 1 N.C.O. & 6 men to accompany the officer in Charge of the Tunnelling party in reconoitring the TUNNEL. This party will work along the TUNNEL after it has been cleared, commencing from the Northern entrance, in the Brigade FRont at about U.14.a.70.10. Every man employed in TUNNEL clearing will carry an Electric Torch.
Section No.22 & No.24 (Lewis Gun Section) of No.6 Platoon, will form a Double Block in FAG ALLEY.
No.22 Section will be composed as follows :- 4 Bombers, 2 Rifle Grenadiers, & 2 Carriers.
Sections 7 & 12 (Lewis Gun Section.) & 23 & 28 (Lewis Gun Section) will form the Covering parties for the wirers.

At Zero the Artillery Bombardment Starts.
At Zero plus 2 Minutes the Infantry will advance to the attack.

5. On arrival at the enemy's Trench all mine shaft entrances will have sentries posted over them.
O.C. Platoons will arrange as soon as possible, to construct firesteps at selected points in the paradore, the reverse side of traverses is generally the best. Lewis Gun Teams will prepare L.G. Positions on arrival in Tunnel Trench.

6. Lewis Gun Positions will be prepared by Lewis Gunners assisted by details of 156 Coy. R.E. at about U.14.d.1.5. and North of FAG ALLEY at about U.14.a.75.05.
Nos.4 & 28 Sections (Lewis Gun) will furnish those posts. Remaining Lewis Guns will occupy temporary Posts covering our front.

OPERATION ORDERS. No. 9. dated 18/11/1917. (Continued.) SHEET 2.

7. DRESS.

Fighting Order, with full water Bottle, Haversack Rations, Irin Rations, and 170 Rounds S.A.A. Bayonets & Equipment to be dulled.
Every man will carry 2 Mills Grenades, 1 in each side pocket, 1"P" Grenade, 3 Sandbags folded lengthways & carried in the Belt, 1 Very Light & 2 flares in the Pocket.
Each Company will carry 45 Shovels & 15 Picks., every alternate man carrying either a pick or a shovel.
Every Bomber will carry 8 Bombs. Every Carrier will carry a Bucket containing 16 Bombs & 8 on the person 2
Rifle Grenadiers will carry 6 Mills Rifle Grenades and 2 Phosphurous Rifle Grenades. Each Company will take 12 S.O.S. Rockets.
Officers' Observers will each carry a Watson Fan.

8. A Communication Trench will be dug from S.E. Corner of BEAUMANS LOOP (U.14.b.46.75.) and a Point in TUNNEL TRENCH about 50 yards S. of FAG ALLEY. (U.14.c.90.80.). Length 250 - 270 yards. True Bearing from U.14.c.46.57. 63 deg. 30 Min. This will be dug under supervision of 156 Company R.E. "Y" Company will supply this party consisting of 2 Officers 5 N.C.Os. & 50 men., with 35 Shovels & 15 Picks. The Party will be accomodated in Beaumans Dugouts. The Orders to commence Work will be given by the R.E. Officer in charge. Work should commence as soon after Zero as possible.
"Y" Coy. will also supply a party of 3 N.C.Os. & 30 men for carrying wire, under the orders of O.C. 156 Coy. R.E. "Y" Coy. will hold in readiness a Party of 1 N.C.O. & 15 Men for carrying stores to the attacking Coys. Companies will send direct to O.C. "Y" Coy. stating their requirments.

9. "Z" Coy, will be in close support & will commence to occupy the Front Line with 2 platoons at Zero plus 5 Minutes, and 2 platoons accomodated in deep dugouts in KNUCKLE AVENUE. The remainder of "Y" Coy. will be in Reserve in STRAY SUPPORT.

10. After Consolidation the new Line occupied by the Battalion will be held by 4 Lewis Gun Posts & 2 Bombing Posts.

11. An advanced Battalion Ammunition Dump will be established at MEBUS No. 8. containing 6 Boxes S.A.A. 24 Boxes Mills Grenades, 4 Boxes Very Lights, 6 Boxes S.O.S. Rockets.

12. R.E. DUMPS.
(1) U.14.d.61. (Off KNUCKLE AVENUE. Wire, Pickets, 3 Scaling Ladders, Explosives, Picks & Shovels, Baby Elephants, Sheeting.
(2) U.14.c.40.45. (Off BEAUMANS SUPPORT) Pickets, Trench Boards, Scaling Ladders, Explosives.
(3) U.14.c.3.5. (Off BEAUMANS SUPPORT). Trench Boards, "A" Frames, Corrugated Iron Sheets X.P.M..

13. Assembly positions will be our front line trench.
Support Coy. "Z" Coy. Dugouts in KNUCKLE AVE. & STRAY SUPPORT.
RESERVE (Part of "Y" Coy.) STRAY SUPPORT.

14. Positions of H.Q.
47th. Infantry Brigade RAILWAY RESERVE. U.25.a.65.55.
Bn. H.Q. STRAY SUPPORT U.19.b.88.38.
Coy. H.Q. "W" & "X" Coys. U.14.c.64.08. "Y" & "Z" Coys. U.20.a.05.65.

15. Men must be warned on no account to touch or move anything in the TUNNEL, or to collect Souvenirs, in order to avoid the risk of exploding a Booby Trap mine.

16. Regimental Police., will furnish a stragglers post at the junction of KNUCKLE & STRAY SUPPORT, composed of 2 Police.

17. There will be a runners' Post at the Coy. H.Q. at the North end of KNUCKLE AVENUE. U.14.c.64.08.

Z hour will be notified later.

Operation Orders. No. 9. dated 18/11/17. (CONTINUED.) SHEET 3.

19. All prisoners will be checked by 2/Lieut. J.E. WALSH at Bn.H.Q. and evacuated to the Cage at Bde.H.Q. T.28.a.60.50. All Captured Maps & Documents must be taken off prisoners at once & sent to Bn.H.Q. in Sandbags, with escort.

20. Brigade H.Q. will open at U.25.a.65.55. at 6 p.m. on the 19th.inst. 10th.ROYAL DUBLIN FUSRS.H.Qrs.(Bn.on Left) will be in German Dug-out at U.13.b.70.30.

21. "Y" Coy. will detail 1 N.C.O. & 10.Men to report at H.Q.47th.T.M.B. in RAILWAY RESERVE at 9 a.m. 19th.instant.

22. White Flares will be carried, They will be lit when called for by Contact Aeroplanes. They will not be required in the initial attack. Contact Aeroplanes will be marked as follows :- A Black Band one foot wide on the lower side of each wing 6 feet from the fuselage. A Rectangular Streamer 18" to 2! Long in prolongation to these bands

23. ACKNOWLEDGE.

(Signed.) C.W.MARSDEN. Lieutenant;
A/Adjutant. 1st.Bn.ROYAL MUNSTER FUSRS.

Copy No.________________.

Issued at 10- 30 p.m.

No.1. Commanding Officer.
No.2. 2nd.in Command.
No.3. Adjutant.
No.4. Intelligence.Officer.
No.5. Signalling Officer.
No.6. Major H.T.Goodland.
No.7. O.C."W" Coy.
No.8. O.C."X" Coy.
No.9. O.C."Y" Coy.
No.10. O.C."Z" Coy.
No.11. Qr.Mr.& T.O.
No.12 R.S.M.
No.13. O.C.6th.Connaught Rgrs.
No.14. H.Q.47th.Inf.Bde.
No 15. O.C.10th.R.D.F.
No.16 & 17 Retained.

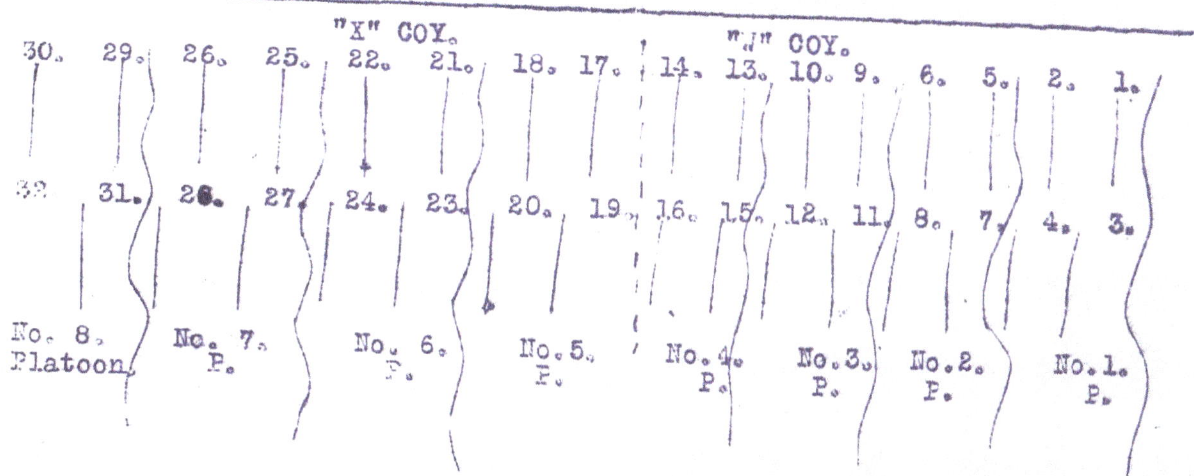

OPERATION ORDERS. No. 9. (Continued).
By
Lt-Col. R.R. MONCK-MASON D.S.O. Commanding. 1st. Bn. ROYAL MUNSTER FUSRS.
In the Field. 19/11/17.

1. Companies will be in their positions of assembly by 5-30 a.m. on the 20th. November 1917. When in Position, Companies will report to Bn. H.Q. by Runner.
The Party of 2 Officers 5 N.C.Os.& 50 Men of "Y" Coy. detailed for digging the communication trench will be in BEAUMANS LOOP DUGOUTS by 3 a.m. on the 20th. instant. The Balance of "Y" Coy. will move up to STRAY SUPPORT by 5 a.m.

2. At ZERO plus 5 Minutes "Z" Coy. will move up & occupy our Front Line from KNUCKLE AVENUE to the N. Ende of BEAUMANS LOOP with 2 plat oons. "Z" Coy. H.Q. will move up to the Dugout at the N.E. end of KNUCKLE U.14.c.60.08.

3. 2/Lieut. C.S. BOUCHIER will superintend the Stragglers' Post in KNUCKLE AVENUE. All unwounded men will be collected & sent back to their Coys The names of All men wounded or otherwise belonging to any unit, will be taken, with the name of the unit against their name. All escorts to prisoners in exess of 1 to every 10 prisoners will be sent back.

4. Between 10 & 11 p.m. on ZERO day the S.O.S. LINE will be pushed beyond the SUNKEN ROAD running through U.14.b.& U.15.c. to U.21.b. if the Situation is quiet. Strong Patrols under Ofcers will move up at 10 p.m. and reconnoitre the SUNKEN ROAD, taking the usual precautions against surprise or being cut off. They will avoid becoming engaged in a Fight. They will endeavour to find out if the enemy has evacuated the SUNKEN ROAD, and must be back in our lines by 11 p.m. Should the S.O.S. Signal go up between 10 & 11p.m. it will keep 200 to 300 yards East of SUNKEN ROAD for 20 minutes to give the patrols time to at once return to our line. After 20 minutes the S.O.S. Line will be switched back to its original line W. of the Sunken ROAD. "W" & "X" Coy. will each send out a patrol of 1 Officer & 12 O.R.

5. All officers are to be warned to be very careful about sending up the S.O.S. If sent up without due cause it wastes ammunition & is liable to draw heavy retaliation on our lines.

6. In the event of steel doors being found in the TUNNEL this must be reported to the nearest sapper of 156 F. Coy. R.E.

7. Communications will be as follows:-
Battn. H.Q. to Brigade. Fullerphone. Visual via Central Exchange.
Battn. H.Q. to Coy. H.Q. Fullerphones.
Assaulting Coys. Fullerphones Power) Accompany "W" Coy.
Buzzer & Amplifier)
"W" Coy. 1 Pair Pigeons.
"X" Coy. 1 Pair Pigeons
Signal Section 1 Pair Pigeons.
RUNNERS. Runners post at Coy. H.Q. N.E. End. of Knuckle.
Company Runners will carry from Front Line to this post.
Post will supply runners to Battalion H.Q.

8. Officers will be provided with special map U.1. to C.C. No. other maps are to be taken. No papers or orders will be taken into TUNNEL TRENCH.

(Signed.) C.V. MARSDEN. Lieutenant;
A/Adjutant. 1st. Bn. ROYAL MUNSTER FUSILIERS.

Copy No.__________. Issued at __________.

Secret

OPERATION ORDERS No.10.
By
Lt-Col.R.H.MONCK-MASON D.S.O.Commanding, 1st.Bn.ROYAL MUNSTER Fus.
In the Field. 19/11/17.

1. Company H.Q.will be established as follows by 5-30 p.m.19th.inst.
   "W" and "X" Coys.:- Dugout N.E.end of KNUCKLE AVENUE.U.1[illegible].c.60.08.
   "Y" & "Z" Coys.:- Dugout S.W.end of KNUCKLE AVENUE.U.20.a.05.65.
   Battn. H.Q.:- STRAY SUPPORT U.19.b.88.38.

2. "W" Coy.will relieve part of "Z" Coy.From KNUCKLE AVENUE to the Junction of BEAUMANS LOOP and BURGH TRENCH.
   "X" Coy.will relieve part of "Z" Coy.in BEAUMANS LOOP. The part of "Z" Coy.holding the Front Line from QUEENS LANE to KNUCKLE AVENUE will withdraw when relieved by the 6th.CONNAUGHT RANGERS.
   "Z" Coy.will withdraw to STRAY SUPPORT.
   "Y" Coy.will be accomodated in RAILWAY RESERVE near present Bn. H.Q., & will leave DURROW CAMP at 5 p.m.19th.instant.
   Battalion H.Q. will move to STRAY SUPPORT at 5 p.m.

3. Relief Complete will be sent by Code Word "PAT" to new Bn.H.Q.

4. ACKNOWLEDGE.

(Sgd.) C.[illegible]MARSDEN. Lieutenant;
A/Adjutant, 1st.Bn.ROYAL MUNSTER FUSILIERS.

Copy No. 16.

Issued at 12-15 p.m.

Copy No.1. Commanding Officer.
Copy No.2. 2nd.in Command.
Copy No.3. Adjutant.
Copy No.4. Major H.I.Goodland.
Copy No.5. Intelligence Officer.
Copy No.6. Signalling Officer.
Copy No.7. O.C."W" Coy.
Copy No.8. O.C."X" Coy.
Copy No.9. O.C."Y" Coy.
Copy No.10. O.C."Z" Coy.
Copy No.11. Transport Officer.
Copy No.12. Quartermaster.
Copy.No.13.6th.CONNAUGHT RANGERS.
Copy No.14. R.S.M.
Copy.No.15.47th.Infantry Brigade.
No.16 & 17. Retained.

S E C R E T

O P E R A T I O N   O R D E R S   No. 12'

By

Lt. Col. R. H. MONCK-MASON D. S. O. Comdg. 1st. Royal Muns. Fusiliers.

In the Field 26. 11. 17

****

The Battalion will relieve 6th. Bn. Connaught Rangers and one Company 7th. Leinster Regt. in the Line to-day, 26th. Instant.

"W" Coy. will Relieve "D" Coy. 7th. Leinster Regt.
2 Platoons MAIN SUPPORT 2 Platoons QUEEN'S LANE Deep Dugout.
"X" Coy. will relieve "A" and "B" Coy 6th. C.R. in RAILWAY RESERVE South.
Y Coy. and Z Coy, will relieve "D" Coy. 6th. C. R. in Old Front Line from U,20.[illegible].9.4 to U.14.c.6.1.
"Z" on Left "Y" on right.
Train will be at MORY Siding at 4 p.m. All Companies will be at the Entraining Point by 3.30 p.m.
Detraining Point will be Top of MAIDA VALE.
"W" Company on Front of Train, Y and Z Coys. next H.Q. and "X" Compani in rear.
All Kits for Q.M. Stores will be stacked at Orderly Room by 2 p.m. and "W" Coys. kits will be called for at 2.15 p.m.

All Kits for the Line to be stacked at Orderly Room by 3 p.m.
"W" Company 2.45 p.m.

List of Trench Stores taken over to be rendered to Orderly Room by 10 a.m. 27th. instant.

Completion of Relief to be reported in code to Battalion Headquarters as soon as possible.

A C K N O W L E D G E.

(Signed) G. [illegible] MARSDEN, Lieutenant,

A/Adjutant, 1st. Royal Munster Fusiliers.

Copy No. 1 Commanding Officer
Copy No. 2 2nd. in Command
Copy No. 3 Adjutant
Copy No. 4 Major Goodland
Copy No. 5 Intelligence Officer
Copy No. 6 Signalling Officer
Copy No. 7 O.C. "W" Coy.
Copy No. 8 "X" Coy.
Copy No. 9 "Y" Coy.
Copy No. 10 "Z" Coy.
Copy No. 11 Transport Officer
Copy No. 12 Quartermaster
Copy No. 13 6th. Connaught Rangers
Copy No. 14 7th. Leinsters
Copy No. 15 R. S. M.
Copy No. 16th. 47th. Infantry Brigade.
Copy Nos. 17 and 18 retained.

S E C R E T

O P E R A T I O N   O R D E R S   No. 13
By
Major H. T. GOODLAND Comdg. 1st. Royal Munster Fusiliers.
In the Field 29. 11. 17
****

1On the night of the 29/3 0th. November "W" Coy. 1st. R. M. Fus. will relieve the following details of 1st. GORDON HIGHLANDERS .

(a) 1 Platoon in VALLEY TRENCH from U.21.c.5.1. - U.20.d.9.4.
(b). 1 Platoon in Old German Front Line from U.21.c.98.70 -U.21.a.80. 05.
(c). Post of Lewis Gun and 12 men at U.21.b.1.1.

2. Disposition of "W" Company 1st. R. M. Fus. after relief will be as follows:-

(a). 1 Platoon holding four Posts in front VALLEY TRENCH on OG, GOG, and MAGOG line.
(b). 1 Platoon in VALLEY TRENCH from U.21.c.5.1 - U.2 0.d.9.4.
(c). 1 Platoon from U.21.c.98.70 to U.21.a.8 0.05 with bombing Post at U.21.a.85.12.
(d). 1 Platoon forming 2 posts.
(a) At U.21.a.99.25.
(b) At U.21.b.1.1. (See 1 (a) above)
Company Headquarters at U.21.c.35.10. Receipts for all Trench Stores will be forwarded to Battalion Headquarters by 10 a.m. 30th. instant.

3. Relief to commence at 5 p.m.
1st. Battalion Gordon Highlanders to supply three guides They will be at entrance to NEW NEW PELICAN AVENUE at 5 p.m.

4. When "W" Company is in position Code Word BEEF will be wired to Battalion Headquarters and to Headquarters 1st. Gordon Highlanders. On receipt of this message 1st. Gordon Highlanders willtake up their New Positions.

A C K N O W L E D G E .

(Signed) C. W. MARSDEN, Lieutenant,

A/Adjutant, 1st. Royal Munster Fusiliers.

SECRET

OPERATION ORDERS No. 14

By

Major H. T. GOODLAND Comdg. 1st. Royal Munster Fusiliers.

In the Field 29. 11. 17

****

1. 3 Platoons Z Company will occupy Old Front Line Between QUEEN'S LANE and BEAUMAN'S LOOP and 1 Platoon in STRAY SUPPORT

2. Y Company will occupy Old Front Line from QUEEN'S LANE to U. 20.d.9.4.

3. 2 Platoons of X Coy. will take over Position in MAN SUPPORT and 2 platoons will remain in present position in RAILWAY RESERVE All Dispositions to be completed by 6.30 p.m.
When Companies are in position code word COW will be wired to Battalion Headquarters.

4. Z Coy. and the left platoon of Y Company in case of attack will come under orders of O. C. 6th. Royal Irish Regt.

5. Any Trench Stores in MAN and STRAY Supports will be taken over by X and Z Coys. respectively.

(Signed) C. W. MARSDEN, Lieutenant,

A/Adjutant, 1st. Royal Munster Fusiliers.

Report on Operation North of BULLECOURT

Part taken by [illegible] Royal Munster Fusiliers.

The Battalion on the 14th. 15th. 16th. and 17th. November trained for the attack over [illegible] ground.

On the 18th. November the Battalion moved into the line.

On the 19th. November all preparations for the attack were completed and arrangements made for the supply of food, water, ammunition etc..

Each section commander was shown his position of assembly by daylight and given a point to march on. The jumping off places were marked with pieces of broad white tape with the number of the section on it, and ladders placed where required.

During the night the necessary gaps were cut in our own wire.

At 5.30 a.m. on the 20th. November 1917 W and X Companies were in their assembly positions in [illegible] TRENCH (our front line) W Company on the right resting on [illegible] AVENUE and X Company on the left of [illegible] SAP. The 6th. Battalion the Connaught Rangers on our right and 10th. Royal Dublin Fusiliers of the Brigade on our left.

[illegible] communication trenches were also [illegible].

At zero 6.20 a.m. the barrage opened.

At zero plus [illegible] minutes the front wave left our trenches followed in perfect order by the second wave at a distance of about 25 yards. The formation being lines of sections in single file at about 30 yards interval, in two waves. At about 50 yards from the objective the line halted for the barrage to lift, and then advanced to the objective without the loss of a single man. The barrage was absolutely perfect. At 6.26 the first wave entered the German Trench followed closely by the second wave.

The advance worked like clockwork and the sections, each of which had been allotted a definite task arrived as near as possible at their right positions. The charge for the enemy's trench was made so swiftly and with such dash that no time was given the enemy to man his parapet or get his machine guns in position and only one gun was able to come into [illegible] action. This was on W Company front about 30 yards to the right of the junction of FAG ALLEY and TUNNEL TRENCH. This was practically a strong point and was at the entrance to the Company Headquarters. It was here that a stubborn fight took place, 2nd. Lt. [illegible] attacked this party on the right and was killed, Captain [illegible] attacked them on the left and the blocking party who had been detailed to form a Block in FAG ALLEY not being able to get up FAG ALLEY owing to the fighting that was going on went over the parados and established the block and in so doing cut off the enemy's means of retreat. This fight lasted about 20 minutes, the enemy finding themselves cut off surrendered. While this was going on all the tunnel entrances had been picketed and the parties for clearing the tunnel had descended and the work underground proceeded with great rapidity the party driving the enemy up the entrances as they went along, there was very little fighting in the tunnel itself but the entrances were defended from below in one or two cases by firing M.G. up it was by one of these guns that Lt. MACDANIEL was killed. Sections detailed for the purpose in the meantime advanced over the TUNNEL TRENCH firing with rifles and L.G's on some of the enemy who were retreating over the open and commenced at once to prepare positions for defence.

On the right the fighting was less severe, in only a few instances did parties of the enemy make any strenuous resistance, all these cases were rapidly dealt with

A ladder wire, Fuller phone and Power Buzzer accompanied the party and proved invaluable and communication was maintained throughout.

At 7.5 a.m. Report came through that TUNNEL TRENCH was clear and that all leads and wires had been cut

At 7 a.m. consolidation ~~[illegible]~~ commenced and continued all day and the Block in FAG ALLEY was completed by filling the trench for some distance with loose wire taken from the old German Front Line.

50 men of Y Company under [illegible] supervision followed the advance and commenced digging a communication trench from the [illegible] corner of

BEAUMAN'S LOOP to a point near the entrance of PAG ALLEY. 2nd. Lt. BLAKE one of the Officers with this party was dangerously wounded and died before reaching the Aid Post.
At 10 p.m. two patrols went out, one from each Company to reconnoitre the SUNKEN ROAD and report as to whether it was occupied ~~[illegible]~~ under 2/Lt. Cahil.
X Company patrol returned safely and reported SUNKEN ROAD occupied. W Company Patrol under Lt. WHITBY was less fortunate, only 1 N.C.O. and 2 men returned. Details of what exactly happened are not available but apparently Lt. WHITBY came on the SUNKEN ROAD suddenly right on a party of the enemy, he called to the men to scatter and withdraw. The probability is that the Officer was killed.
During the following day consolidation was carried on and work on communication trenches continued.

Throughout the whole time the Battalion occupied the trenches the enemy's fire was very poor.

At 9.44 a.m. on 22nd. November 1917 the two companies in the Front Line were relieved by two Companies of the 6th. Royal Irish Regt. and the Battalion Relief was complete by 10.55 p.m.

Great credit is due to the Officers Commanding the Attacking Companies for the completeness in which the attack was carried out and also to Captain GOODLAND who controlled the situation in TUNNEL TRENCH establishing a report centre. There were several very gallant actions performed. Recommendations for immediate awards have already been submitted.

Casualties	Killed	Wounded	Missing
Officers	3	1	1
Other Ranks	9	59	5

Prisoners	Officers	O.R.
Checked at Bn. H.Q.	2	148
Passed to 48th. Bde Cage	1	16
Total	3	164

R Monck-Mason Lt. Colonel,

Commanding 1st. Bn. Royal Munster Fusiliers.

27. 11. 17

WAR DIARY,

FOR MONTH OF DECEMBER, 1917.

VOLUME :-

UNIT:- 1st Royal Munster Fusrs.

Vol 22

Instructions regarding War Diaries and Intelligence Summaries are contained in F. S. Regs., Part II. and the Staff Manual respectively. Title pages will be prepared in manuscript.

WAR DIARY
or
~~INTELLIGENCE SUMMARY.~~
(*Erase heading not required.*)

1

Army Form C. 2118.

1 R Munster Fusiliers

Place	Date	Hour	Summary of Events and Information	Remarks and references to Appendices
	1917			[illegible]
Bullecourt	Dec 1		Battalion in line on night and occupying the new [illegible] TRENCH	BO No 179
[illegible]			connecting OG-OGG & MAGGS [illegible] [illegible] completed on this trench	
FRONT			W Coy relieved by X Coy. [illegible] on night. Quiet day	BO 180
	2		Orders for Relief. Battalion relieved by 1 G R Welch Fusiliers. Relief com-	Batt order
			plete at 11.30 pm. March to 10 Trees for [illegible] marched to [illegible]	No 15
			and took lorries for GOMMECOURT. [illegible]	
	3		Marched with full transport at 1.45 pm. Arrived BEAULENCOURT	
			via BAPAUME at 6 pm. Battalion in huts. Weather very cold but men	
			in good shape	
BEAULEN-COURT	4		Remained at BEAULENCOURT	
	5		Remained at BEAULENCOURT	
	6		Battalion marched at 9.30 am for TINCOURT via RUQUIGNY–	Batt orders
			TEMPLEUX-LA-FOSSE. Arrived TINCOURT at 6 pm. Battalion disposed in	No 16
			billets and Adrian Huts. Whole Brigade at TINCOURT	
TINCOURT	7		In billets	
	8		In billets. New line reconnoitred by C.O.	

D. D. & L., London, E.C.
(A7883) Wt. W809/M1672 350,000 4/17 Sch. 52a Forms/C/2118/14

Instructions regarding War Diaries and Intelligence Summaries are contained in F. S. Regs., Part II, and the Staff Manual respectively. Title pages will be prepared in manuscript.

WAR DIARY
or
INTELLIGENCE SUMMARY.
(Erase heading not required.)

Army Form C. 2118.

2

1. R Munster Fusiliers.

Place	Date 1917	Hour	Summary of Events and Information	Remarks and references to Appendices
	DEC			
TINCOURT	9		C.O. inspected new line and LEMPIRE. Line occupied by 8/9 DUBLINS	
			Divisional H.Q. at VILLIERS-FAUCON.	
"	10		Major General Hickie inspected billets etc and men.	
"	11		Battalion entrained at HAMEL siding for line. Detrained at 4 p.m.	Bn order
			and relieved the 8/9 Dublins in the Left sub-Sector of Right Section	No 17.
			with front from TOMBOIS FARM on left to a point 100^x east of CAUSEWAY	
			LANE in DANIEL TR. Z Coy on left to COCHRANE AVE. Y Coy on right.	
			W Coy. 1 Platoon at LEMPIRE EAST. – 2 Platoons in DOLEFUL POST	
			1 Platoon with Batt H.Q. X Coy. at SART LANE dugouts	
LINE.	12		Work started on repairing trenches. Batt H.Q. LANCASTER HOUSE. LEMPIRE.	
LEFT SUB.	13		New trench started to make SART LANE a Strong Point. Wiring started	
SECTOR.			to protect left at TOMBOIS FARM. Heavy shelling of front line.	
	14.		Work continued but forced to stop in daylight by shelling observed by	
			great enemy aeroplane activity. Casualties in CAUSEWAY LANE.	
	15		Work continued at night. Company relief. W & X Coys in front	
			line. Z to SART LANE and Y to LEMPIRE & DOLEFUL POST. Name of this post changed to WRAFTER POST. Much work on this post done.	

D. D. & L., London, E.C.
(A7883) Wt. W809/M1672 350,000 4/17 Sch. 52a Forms/C/2118/14

3

Army Form C. 2118.

Instructions regarding War Diaries and Intelligence Summaries are contained in F. S. Regs., Part II. and the Staff Manual respectively. Title pages will be prepared in manuscript.

WAR DIARY
or
INTELLIGENCE SUMMARY.

(Erase heading not required.)

1 R Munster Fusiliers.

Place	Date	Hour	Summary of Events and Information	Remarks and references to Appendices
	1917 Dec.			
IN LINE	16		Enemy Artillery very active shelling front line and Village. Our tunnellers started work enlarging chamber in WRATTER POST.	
			Snow and cold	
	17		Relieved at 7.30 pm by 6 Connaught Rangers. Battn moved to LEMPIRE VILLAGE occupying areas as follows A-Y Coy, B-X Coy, C-Z Coy, D-W Coy.	Batt. orders No. 18
LEMPIRE	18		Work started wiring the Posts and defences. Village divided into 4 areas, containing from 4 to 6 strong points each.	
	19		Work continued on defences under R.E.	
	20		Work continued on defences.	
	21		Work continued on defences. Heavy shelling. The left section reconnoitred by Coy Officers.	
	22		Work continued on defences.	
	23		Battalion relieved by 7/8 Inniskilling Fusiliers. Heavy enemy artillery during relief. Relief complete at 7.30 pm. Marched to ST EMILIE by Platoons to entrain for TINCOURT. Arrived	Batt. orders No. 19.

D. D. & L., London, E.C.
(A7883) Wt. W809/M1672 350,000 4/17 Sch. 52a Forms/C/2118/14

Instructions regarding War Diaries and Intelligence Summaries are contained in F. S. Regs., Part II. and the Staff Manual respectively. Title pages will be prepared in manuscript.

WAR DIARY
or
~~INTELLIGENCE SUMMARY.~~

(Erase heading not required.) 1 R Munster Fusiliers

4

Army Form C. 2118.

Place	Date 1917	Hour	Summary of Events and Information	Remarks and references to Appendices
	Dec			
TINCOURT	24		Battalion in billets at TINCOURT. Preparing for Christmas and cleaning up.	
	25		CHRISTMAS DAY. Battalion Church Parades RC at 10. C of E 11. am Dinners served the men at 2 p.m. Roast Pork, vegetables & Pudding. Beer given out and Comforts from Irish Womens Assocn and Xmas Comforts fund of RMF given out Tobacco & cigarettes etc. Very successful and cheery day for the men. Officers and C.O. visited all Companies Officers dinner in evening. Band in attendance. Most successful	
	26		Companies to Baths and clothes changing	
	27		W and X Companies inspected on parade ground by C.O	
	28		Y and Z Companies inspected on parade ground by C.O	
	29		Battalion paraded for the Line at 2.15 pm and entrained at 3 pm Relieved the 8/9 Dubs in the Right sub-sector of Left Section. W Y & Z Companies in front line, X Coy in Posts and support. 40 men of X Coy to Hants Pioneers. Relief complete at 7.55 pm. Very cold weather. Fairly quiet night.	Batt orders No 20

D. D. & L., London, E.C. (A7883) Wt. W809/M1672 350,000 4/17 Sch. 52a Forms/C/2118/14

5

Instructions regarding War Diaries and Intelligence Summaries are contained in F. S. Regs., Part II, and the Staff Manual respectively. Title pages will be prepared in manuscript.

WAR DIARY
or
~~INTELLIGENCE SUMMARY.~~
(Erase heading not required.)

Army Form C. 2118.

1. R. Munster Fusiliers

Place	Date 1917	Hour	Summary of Events and Information	Remarks and references to Appendices
	Dec			
IN LINE	30		Battalion in line. Trenches very bad & full of snow. GRAFTON POST	
Right-Sub-Sec			heavily shelled from 3 to 6 pm. Much wire put out in evening	
of Left Section			and work on trench shelters started. Inclined to thaw.	
	31		Heavy shelling on our front line at 6 am, and spasmodic shelling	
			of road & ST PATRICKS TR during day. Colder. A few salvoes	
			of 4.2 near Batt HQ during night. Wiring continued by Hants	
			Pioneers along front of GRAFTON. POST to TOMBOIS.	

signed. H. S. Goodland Lt Col
Comdg 1 R.M.F.

D. D. & L., London, E.C.
(A7883) Wt. W809/M1672 350,000 4/17 Sch. 52a Forms/C/2118/14

Instructions regarding War Diaries and Intelligence Summaries are contained in F. S. Regs., Part II, and the Staff Manual respectively. Title pages will be prepared in manuscript.

WAR DIARY
or
~~INTELLIGENCE SUMMARY.~~

(Erase heading not required.)

Army Form C. 2118.

6

1 R Munster Fus.

STRENGTH RETURN & CASUALTIES

Place	Date 1917	Hour	OFFICERS	O.R.	TO HOSP.	OFFICERS K	OFFICERS W	OFFICERS M	O.R. K	O.R. W	O.R. M	REJOINED		DRAFTS.	REMARKS.
	Dec 1		40	992	2										2 to Cadet Sch.
	2		40	988								2	Hosp.		
	3		40	990	5							2	"		
	4		40	987	1									5	8 Struck off.
	5		40	983								2	Hosp.		
	6		40	985	2										1 to Cadet Sch.
	7		40	982	2										
	8		40	980	6							2	Hosp		1 to Commission Sec Lt J. P. Morrough struck off Sec Lt G. D. Boudain joined
	9		40	975											
	10		40	975	3										
	11		40	972	2										
	12		40	970	2					1		3	Hosp		
	13		40	970	2				2	5					6 to T. M. Batty.
	14		40	955	1										
	15		40	954	6					1		2	Hosp		
	16		40	949	5				1	1		1	"		

D. D. & L., London, E.C.
(A7883) Wt. W809/M1672 350,000 4/17 Sch. 52a Forms/C/2118/14

Instructions regarding War Diaries and Intelligence Summaries are contained in F. S. Regs., Part II. and the Staff Manual respectively. Title pages will be prepared in manuscript.

WAR DIARY
or
INTELLIGENCE SUMMARY.
(*Erase heading not required.*)

7

Army Form C. 2118.

1. R Munster Fus.

Place	Date 1917 Dec	Hour	Summary of Events and Information: OFFICERS	O.R.	TO HOSP.	OFFICERS R	OFFICERS W	OFFICERS M	O.R. K	O.R. W	O.R. M	REJOINED		DRAFTS	REMARKS	Remarks and references to Appendices
	17		40	843	1					1					2Lt. H.A. Brown Joined; Lt S.B Holmes I.A.	
	18		40	941	6							1	Hosp.		Maj Stacpoole to U.K.; 2Lt Murphy Joined	
	19		40	936	4							2	"			
	20		40	934	2											
	21		40	932	6							3	Hosp.			
	22		40	929	5										Capt I.C.C. Lee Sick [illegible]; " Grenier do	
	23		38	924	1										Capt Henn joined	
	24		39	923	3							3	Hosp.			
	[illegible]		39	923	1											
	26		39	922	2											
	27		39	920	7											
	28		39	913	3							4	Hosp.			
	29		39	914	7											
	30		39	907	3									16	2Lt. Wil[illegible] [illegible]	
	31		38	920												

Signed [illegible] Lt Col Comdg 1 R.M.F.

D. D. & L., London, E.C. (A7883) Wt. W809/M1672 350,000 4/17 Sch. 52a Forms/C/2118/14

SECRET

OPERATION ORDERS No. 15.

By

Major H. T. GOODLAND Comdg. 1st. Royal Munster Fusiliers.

In the Field 2. 12. 17

****

On the night of 2 /3rd. December the 1st. Bn. Royal Muns. Fuslrs. will be relieved in the Right Sub Sector by the 19th. Bn. Royal Welsh Fusiliers .

"D" Coy. R. W. F. will relieve "X" Coy. 1st. R.M.F. from MAGOG exclusive to the right

"C" Coy. 19th. R. W. F. will relieve "Y" Coy. 1st. R.M.F. from QUEEN'S AVENUE to MAGOG Inclusive

"B" Coy. 19th. R. W. F. will relieve "Z" Coy. 1st. R.M.F. from STH. BEAUMAN'S LOOP to QUEEN'S LANE Inclusive

2 Platoons "A" Coy. R. W. F. plus Coy. H.Q. will relieve 2 Platoons "W" Coy. 1st. R. M. F. plus H.Q. in RAILWAY RESERVE SOUTH

2 Platoons "A" Coy. 19th. R. W. F. will relieve 2 platoons "W" Coy. 1st. R. M. F. in MAN SUPPORT

Relief will take place about 7.3 0 p.m.

1 Guide from each platoon 1st. R. M. Fus. will report at once to Battalion H. Q. and will proceed from there to DURROW CAMP as guides to the platoons r(respectively) of the Royal Wels Fus, and conduct these platoons back to the line.

Transport Officer R. M. Fus. will see that Guides are sent up with R.W.F. rations to CRUX CIRCUS.

All Trench Stores will be handed over and copy receipts sent to Battalion H. Q. by 1 0 a.m. December 3rd.

Certificates of cleanliness etc., will be obtained from R.W. Fus. and handed in to Battalion H. Q. at 10 a.m. 3rd. December.

No troops will be withdrawn until they have been properly relieved.

On completion of Relief Code Word "BUG" will be sent to Battalion Headquarters by wire.

On relief complete Companies will proceed via MEAIDE VALE to rendezvous at TEN TREES where they will await further orders.

All trenches must be handed over absolutely clean and clear

(Signed) C. W. MARSDEN Lieutenant,

A/Adjutant, 1st. Royal Munster Fusiliers.

Copy No. 12.

Issued at 12.45. PM.

Adjutant

O P E R A T I O N   O R D E R S   No. 16

by

Major [illegible] GOODLAND Comdg. 1st. Royal Muns. Fusiliers.

In the Field 5. 12. 17

****

1. The Battalion will move from BEAULANCOURT to TINCOURT on Decr. 6th, Via. ROCQUIGNY, MANANCOURT, NOISLANDS, TEMPLEUX-LA-FOSSE. Distance about 14½ miles.

2. Battalion will parade ready to march off at 9 a.m.

3. Company Officers will inspect their Coys. at 8.30 a.m. and see that all men are clean and see that no superfluous kit is carried.

4. Order OF March will be :-

Signallers and Scouts Y Z Drums W X and H.Q. Coys.

5. 1 Sgt. from each Coy. including H.Q. Coy will report to 2nd. Lt. WALSH at the Officers' Mess at 6.45 a.m. as an advance party.

6. All 1st. Line Transport will march with the Battalion

Strict march discipline will be observed and the Regulation ten minutes halt at ten minutes to each clock hour will also be observed.

Dinners will be cooked on route and served at arrival in camp.

7. Camps must be left spotlessly clean. Coy, Officers will be held responsible for their part of the Line.

8. Packs and Steel Helmets will be worn.

9. The Brigadier will inspect the Battalion as it marches past the Starting Point at N.24.c.1.9.

10. All baggage, kit blankets etc. will be dumped at Q.M. Stores by 8 a.m.

(Signed) C. W. MARSDEN Lieutenant,

A/Adjutant, 1st. Royal Munster Fusiliers.

Copy No..............   Issued at ....

O P E R A T I O N O R D E R [illegible]

By

Lt. Colonel H. T. GOODLAND Comdg. 1st. Bt. Royal Munster Fusiliers.

In the Field 10. 12. 17

Ref. Trench Map 1/10,000 62.c. N.E. 2

1. The Battalion will relieve the 8/9th. R. Dublin Fusiliers in the Left Subsection on the night of the 11/12th. Dec. 1917

2. "Z" Coy. will relive "A" Coy. 8/9th. R. D. F. from (TOMBOIS FARM) to COCHRAN AVENUE with three platoons and 1 Platoon in LONDON ROAD
"Y" Coy. will relieve "B" Coy. 8/9th. R. D. F. from COCHRAN AVENUE to F.12.c.Central.
"W" Coy will relieve "C" Company 8/9th. R. D. F. as follows:-
1 Platoon LEMPIRE (with Battalion Headquarters)
1 Platoon LEMPIRE EAST . 2 Platoons DOLEFULL POST
"X" Coy. will relieve "D" Coy. 8/9th. R. D. F. in SART LANE F.17.a.4.8.
"Z" Coy. will relieve by FLEECEALL LANE
"Y" Coy. will relieve by POMPOMEOUS LANE

3. Battalion Headquarters will be at LEMPIRE .
Brigade Headquarters will be at St. EMILIE

4. Defence Schemes and Trench Maps will be taken over .
Trench Store Lists will reach Battalion H.Q. by 10 a.m. 12th. instant.
Companies will arrange to hand over their Billets to Companies of the 8/9th. R. D. F. and obtain clean Certificates for same.
These certificates will reach Battalion Headquarters by 10 a.m. 12th. inst.

5. Advance Parties of 1 N.C.O. per Platoon of all Companies will proceed to the Line at 8 a.m. 11th. inst. to take over.

6. All Billets must be cleaned up by 12 noon ready to be handed over and will be inspected by the C.O. at this time.

7. Company Guides of 8/9th. R.D. F. will be at E.24.a.9.1.at 5.30 p.m.
Platoon Guides of 8/9th. R.D.F. will be at E.21.c.2.9 at 6 p.m.

8. Coys. will parade ready to march off at the following times:-
"Z" Coy. .... 3.45 p.m.
"Y" Coy. ....4.0.p.m.
"W" COY. .... 4.10 p.m.
"X" Coy ....4.20 p.m.

9. Route will be via MARQUAIX and ROISEL.

On relief complete following code word will be sent to Battalion H.Q. at once "SPLENDID"

10. Baggage and Transport Orders will be issued later.

(Signed) C. W. MARSDEN, Lieutenant,

A/Adjutant. 1st. B. Royal Munster Fusiliers.

18

[illegible]

O P E R A T I O N   O R D E R S   No. 17

by

Lt. Col. [illegible] Comdg. 1st. Royal Munster Fusiliers.

In the Field 16. 12 17

---

1. The Battalion will be relieved by the 6th Bn. C.R. in the left subsector on evening 17th. December 1917.

2. '[illegible]' Coy. will be relieved by 'A' Coy. 6th Conn. Rgrs.
'X' Coy. will be relieved by 'B' Coy. 6th. Conn. Rgrs.
'Y' Coy. will be relieved by 'D' Coy. 6th. C. R. as follows:-
1 platoon in [illegible], 1 platoon in [illegible], 2 platoons in GRAFTER POST.
'Z' Coy. will be relieved by 'C' Coy. 6th. C. R. in HART LANE
1 Guide per platoon will report at 6th. C R Bn HQ at 3 p.m.

3. Relief will commence at [illegible] p.m.

4. Lewis Guns will be relieved at [illegible] p.m.

5. Companies will send 1 Sgt. to reconnoitre new dispositions in [illegible] where the Battalion will ~~xxxxxx~~ proceed to on relief. These N.C.O's will report at 6th. Conn Rgrs. Battalion H.Q. at 2.30 p.m.

6. Guides for Lewis Guns will report at ~~xxxxxxx~~ C.R. Battalion H.Q. at [illegible].15 p.m. to guide their Lewis Guns up to the line.

7. All Trench Stores and work etc., will be handed over. Copies of Trench Stores Receipts will be handed into Orderly Room by 10 a.m. 18th. instant.

8. All trenches will be cleaned up by noon 17th. inst. ready to hand over.

9. Completion of relief will be sent to Battalion H.Q. by code word "SON".

10. N.C.O's referred to in para. 5 as soon as they have reconnoitred the new positions will report back to Bn. H.Q. 1st. R. M. Fus. and await as guides to their Companies.

11. A C K N O W L E D G E.

(Signed) G. [illegible]. Mar[illegible]. Lieutenant.

A/Adjutant. 1st. Royal Munster Fusiliers.

SECRET OPERATION ORDERS No. 19

By

Lt. Colonel H. T. GOODLAND Commanding 1st. Bn. Royal Munster Fus.

In the Field [illegible].[illegible].17

1. The Battalion will be relieved by the 7/8th. Inns. Fus. on the night of 23rd. December 1917.

2. Y Coy will be relieved by "A" Coy. 7/8th. Inns. Fus.
"Z" Coy. " " " " "B" Coy. do do
W Coy. " " " " "C" Coy. do do
X Coy. " " " " "D" Coy. do do

3. Relief will take place about 6 p.m. Companies will proceed to St. EMILIE to an entraining point to be notified later. Platoons will be at 5 minutes interval.

4. Advance party of 1 Officer and 1 Sgt. from each Company will report at Battalion H.Q. at 10 a.m. tomorrow to proceed to HAMEL to take over billets from the 7/8th. Royal Inns. Fus. which will be the same as last time. They will pay particular attention to the cleanliness of the Camp. The usual receipts will be handed over by them to the 7/8th. Royal Inniskilling Fusiliers.

5. Blankets and packs will be found in Billets on arrival. Lewis Guns and all Magazines will be carried to the Train, thence to billets.

6. Mess Kit and Baggage will be stacked at each Company H.Q. by 4 p.m. 1 Limber will be between X and Z Coy. H.Q. for their use at 5 p.m.. 1 Limber will go to Y Coy. H.Q. first and load up their half at 5.30 p.m. and then back to W Coy. H.Q. to load up other half Limber. 1 Limber will be at Battalion H.Q. at 5 p.m., mess and Maltese Cart at Battalion H.Q. at 4.30 p.m.

7. Trench Stores will be handed over and usual receipts obtained for same.

8. Company Commanders will see that their Billets and the lines around them are spotlessly clean by noon.

9. Relief complete will be wired to headquarters by the code word "TURKEYS".

10. Company Officers will report to Battalion H.Q. as soon as the men are all in their Billets.

11. Disposition of Battalion H.Q. at HAMEL will be as before.

12. A C K N O W L E D G E.

(Signed) C. [illegible]. MARSDEN, Lieutenant,

A/Adjutant, 1st Bn. Royal Munster Fusiliers.

WAR DIARY

FOR MONTH OF JANUARY, 1918.

VOLUME :-

UNIT :- 1st R. Munster Fusiliers

Army Form C. 2118.

Instructions regarding War Diaries and Intelligence Summaries are contained in F. S. Regs., Part II, and the Staff Manual respectively. Title pages will be prepared in manuscript.

WAR DIARY
or
INTELLIGENCE SUMMARY. / R Munster Fusiliers

(Erase heading not required.)

Place	Date 1918	Hour	Summary of Events and Information	Remarks and references to Appendices
RIGHT SUB ~~LEFT~~ SECTOR OF	JANY. 1st		Battalion in the line, with W Coy. Adv HQ and MULE TRENCH. –	
LEFT			X Coy ZEBRA & YAK POSTS and SANDBAG ALLEY – Y Coy HEYTHROP POST	
SECTOR.			Z Coy. GRAFTON POST. Weather very cold and deep snow. All work	
LEMAIRE			confined to trench shelters.	
SECTION.	2.		At 4.20 am after a heavy barrage on HEYTHROP & GRAFTON	
			POSTS and MULE TR, the enemy attempted to raid our line at	
			HEYTHROP, but failed to enter, being repelled by our Lewis Gun	
			fire. Trenches badly damaged and owing to frost, hard to repair.	
			8 men wounded. Signal wires cut by shell fire before Artillery	
			could be called, and our Artillery did not fire. Work on	
			shelters continued.	
	3		Battn. relieved by 6 Connaught Rangers. Complete at 9 pm.	Battn
			Battn. marched to ST EMILLE Railway Cutting shelters. Some	orders
			shelling during relief.	No 1.
	4		Battn. provided working parties for R.E. Wiring and Hants Pioneers digging trench N of MALLASSES FARM.	

D. D. & L., London, E.C.
(A7883) Wt. W809/M1672 350,000 4/17 Sch. 52a Forms/C/2118/14

Instructions regarding War Diaries and Intelligence Summaries are contained in F. S. Regs., Part II. and the Staff Manual respectively. Title pages will be prepared in manuscript.

WAR DIARY
or
~~INTELLIGENCE SUMMARY.~~
(*Erase heading not required.*)

2.

Army Form C. 2118.

1 R Muns Fus

Place	Date 1915	Hour	Summary of Events and Information	Remarks and references to Appendices
	JAN			
ST EMILLE	5		Working Parties provided. Snowed again.	
	6		Working Parties. 2 Coys working Front line with Hants Pioneers	
	7		Working Parties. 2 Coys digging trenches with Pioneers at night.	
	8		Working Parties.	
	9		Working Parties	
	10		Battn relieved from Reserve by 7/8 Inniskilling Fusiliers	Battn
			during day. Battn marched to Hamel. Thaw starting.	order
HAMEL	11		Battn in good billets. Cleaning up. 1 Coy daily to Div. for fatigue.	No 2
	12		Programme for Battn training made. Platoons started training	
			Average 2 Coys on working parties daily.	
	13		Training and working parties	
	14		do	
	15		do	
	16		do	
	17		do	
	18		Brigadier inspected Battn.	

D. D. & L., London, E.C.
(A7883) Wt. W809/M1672 350,000 4/17 Sch. 52a Forms/C/2118/14

Instructions regarding War Diaries and Intelligence Summaries are contained in F. S. Regs., Part II. and the Staff Manual respectively. Title pages will be prepared in manuscript.

3.

WAR DIARY
or
~~INTELLIGENCE SUMMARY.~~
(Erase heading not required.)

1 R. Muns. Fus.

Army Form C. 2118.

Place	Date 1918	Hour	Summary of Events and Information	Remarks and references to Appendices
	JAN.			
HAMEL	19		Training and Working Parties. Com. of W & X changed.	
	20		SPORTS in afternoon. Battn. Tug of War team beat team of 2 Leinsters.	
	21		Training and Working Parties	
	22		Battn. paraded for line and relieved 2 R. Dublin Fus in original out sector TOMBOIS FARM etc. HQ at LANCASTER HO. Entrained at 5 pm. relief complete 9 pm. W & X front line, Y at SART FARM W at LEMPIRE.	Battn order No 3
LEFT SUB-SECTOR of	23		Battn. in line. Trenches in terrible condition owing to thaw. Work started on fire bays in posts.	
RIGHT ~~Sub~~ SECTOR.	24		Work continued on reclaiming fire bays & posts. Lieut AMORY of U.S. Army attached for instruction. Inter-Coy relief ordered every 48 hours by Coys. Y & Z relieved W & X.	
	25		Work continued. Active patrol made. dead enemy found. Very foggy weather	
	26		Still foggy. Work continued. W & Y relieved Z & X.	

D. D. & L., London, E.C. (A7883) Wt. W809/M1672 350,000 4/17 Sch. 52a Forms/C/2118/14

4.

Instructions regarding War Diaries and Intelligence Summaries are contained in F. S. Regs., Part II, and the Staff Manual respectively. Title pages will be prepared in manuscript.

WAR DIARY
or
~~INTELLIGENCE SUMMARY.~~
(*Erase heading not required.*)

Army Form C. 2118.

1 R. Muns Fus.

Place	Date 1918	Hour	Summary of Events and Information	Remarks and references to Appendices
	JAN			
LEFT SUB SEC	27		Work on trenches and Posts continued. Situation better. Foggy weather allowing wire repair from front.	
	28		Relieved by 6 Conn. Rangers. Complete at 8 pm. Battn moved to	Batt
LEMPIRE			LEMPIRE and took over area. W in D – X in A – Y in B – Z in C. H.Q. in old billets.	order No 4
	29		Battn provides 351 men daily for working parties under R.E.	
	30		Working Parties. 2 Coys digging trench in front line.	
	31		Working Parties. 2 Coys digging. Corps. General inspected defences.	

N. D. Goodland Lt. Col.
Commdg 1 R. Mun. Fus.

D. D. & L., London, E.C.
(A7683) Wt. W809/M1672 350,000 4/17 Sch. 52a Forms/C/2118/14

APPENDIX A

Army Form C. 2118.

WAR DIARY

or

~~INTELLIGENCE SUMMARY.~~

STRENGTH AND CASUALTY RETURN.

(Erase heading not required.)

1 R Muns Fus

Instructions regarding War Diaries and Intelligence Summaries are contained in F. S. Regs., Part II. and the Staff Manual respectively. Title pages will be prepared in manuscript.

Place JANY	Date 1918	Hour	OFFICERS	O.R.	HOSPITAL	OFFICERS K	OFFICERS W	OFFICERS M	O.R. K	O.R. W	O.R. M	FROM HOSP	JOINED	OFFICERS JOINED AND LEFT	Remarks and references to Appendices
1			38	920	9							2	16	Joined Capt. W.F. Hehir	Draft
2			39	929	6					[illegible]		1			
3			39	924						7		2			
4			39	919	4										
5			39	915	3							1			
6			39	913	4					1		2			
7			39	910	4										
8			39	906	8							4			
9			39	902											
10			39	902	2										
11			39	900	3										
12			39	897	1							2		Left Lt Col Monck-Mason	Struck off
13			38	898	1							1			
14			38	898	5							1	8	Joined 2Lt. Malone " O'Donnell	Draft
15			40	902	4							3			
16			40	901	3							1		1 O.R. to Base	

D. D. & L., London, E.C.
(A7883) Wt. W809/M1672 350,000 4/17 Sch. 52a Forms/C/2118/14

Instructions regarding War Diaries and Intelligence Summaries are contained in F. S. Regs., Part II. and the Staff Manual respectively. Title pages will be prepared in manuscript.

WAR DIARY
or
INTELLIGENCE SUMMARY.

(Erase heading not required.)

Army Form C. 2118.

Place	Date	Hour	Summary of Events and Information													Remarks and references to Appendices
JAN'Y	1918		O	O.R.	To Hospital	Officers K	Officers W	Officers M	O.R. K	O.R. W	O.R. M	From Hosp	Joined	Officers Joined [illegible]		
17			40	898	4							4	4			Draft
18			40	902	3							2				
19			40	901	1							5				
20			40	905	2							1	8			Draft
21			40	912	3							1				
22			40	910	9											
23			40	901	3							2	4		2 OR to Base	Draft
24			40	898	6							2				
25			40	894								1				
26			40	895	4							1				
27			40	892	8							3				
28			40	887	2							2	3			Draft
29			40	890	3							4				
30			40	891	2					2		2				
31			40	889												

A.D. Gosland Lt Col
Cmdg 1R Mun Fus
2.2.18

D. D. & L., London, E.C.
(A7883) Wt. W809/M1672 350,000 4/17 Sch. 52a. Forms/C/2118/14

SECRET

OPERATION ORDERS No. [illegible]

By

Lt. Col H. [illegible] GOODLAND Comdg. 1st Bn. Royal Munster Fusiliers

In the Field 3. 1. 1916

1. The Battalion will be relieved by the 6th. Bn. Conn. Rgrs. tomorrow 4th. Jany. 1916 about 5.30 p.m.

2. Z Coy. 1st R. M. Fus. will be relieved by "A" Coy. 6th. Conn Rgrs.
Y Coy. 1st R. M. Fus. will be relieved by B" Coy. 6th. Conn Rgrs.
" " Coy " " " " C Coy. " " "
X Coy " " " " D Coy. " "

3. Advance party of 1 Officer, 1 Sgt., and 4 O.R. from each Company will report to Intelligence Officer at Battalion Headquarters at 1[illegible]a.m. tomorrow and proceed to RAILWAY CUTTING ST. [illegible] to take over from the 6th. Bn. Connaught Rangers. 1 Guide from each platoon will report at Battalion headquarters. at 5 p.m. to lead 6th. Bn. Conn R

4. 2 Limbers to convey Lewis Guns down the Line will report to Battalion Headquarters 6.3[illegible] p.m. . Transport Officer will arrange for conveyance of Officers' Kits and Company and Orderly Room Stores down the Line. Limbers to be at Battalion Headquarters by 6.3[illegible] p.m.

Trench Stores will be handed over. Copies Receipts will be sent to Orderly Room by 1[illegible] a.m. 5th. instant.

5. All Working Parties , work proposed and in progress will be handed over.

Completion of Relief will be wired to Battalion Headquarters by Code Word "[illegible]" .

6. On Relief Companies will proceed to Railway Cutting St. [illegible] by following route:-
To Rly Stn St. [illegible] by the same route as coming into the trenches from thence along Rly. Line to the cuting.

ACKNOWLEDGE.

(Signed) C. [illegible], Lieutenant,

A/Adjutant, 1st. Royal Munster Fusiliers.

S E C R E T

OPERATION ORDERS No. 2

By

Lt. Colonel H. T. GOODLAND Comdg. 1st. Royal Munster Fusiliers.

In the Field 9.1.18

1. The Battalion will be relieved by the 8/9th Royal Inns. Fus. tomorrow morning 10th. inst.

W Coy. will be relieved by B Coy 8/9th. R. Inns. Fus.
X Coy. will be relieved by C Coy. 8/9th. R. Inns. Fus.
Y Coy. will be relieved by A Coy. 8/9th. R. Inns. Fus.
Z Coy. will be relieved by D Coy. 8/9th. R. Inns. Fus.

Relief will commence about 12 noon.

2. All Work in progress, working parties etc., will be handed over.

3. Guides of 1 N.C.O. per platoon will report to R.S.M. at bottom of stairs leading up to Orderly Room at 11.30 a.m.

4. The Transport Officer will arrange for following Transport :-

2 Limbers for Lewis Guns to be at Bn. H.Q. at 11.30 a.m.
1 Limber for Orderly Room Kit and H.Q. Officers' Kit at 11.30 a.m.
Maltese Cart and Mess Cart at 12 noon
G.S. Wagons to report at Bn. H.Q. at 11.30 a.m.
1 blnaket per man and all Company Kit will be stacked outside Orderly room at 11 a.m.

5. On Relief complete the Battalion will proceed to HAMEL.
Dress - full marching Order and 1 Blanket.
Route via ROISEL and MARQUAIX.

6. The Quartermaster will meet the Staff Captain at Town Major's Office TINCOURT at 11 a.m. 10th. instant.
Advance party of following will meet 2nd. in Command at old Battalion Headquarters HAMEL at 12 noon and will then have their billets allotted.

1 Officer per Company and 1 N.C.O. per Platoon
2 N.C.O's for Headquarter Company.

7. All Shelters and Company Lines will be cleaned up by 11 a.m.

Certificates of cleanliness for same will be obtained from 8/9th. Royal Inniskillings and will be handed in to Orderly Room by 10 a.m. 11th. instant.

8. Completion of Relief will be sent by runner to Battalion H.Q. as soon as possible.

9. A C K N O W L E D G E.

(Signed) C. .. Marsden, Lieutenant,

A/Adjutant, 1st. Bn. Royal Munster Fusiliers

S E C R E T . O P E R A T I O N O R D E R S No. 3

By

Lt. Colonel H. T. GOODLAND Comdg. 1st. Royal Munster Fusiliers.

In the Field 21. 1. 18

The Battalion will relieve "B" Battalion Royal Dublin Fusiliers in the front line Left Subsection tomorrow evening 22nd. instant.

"W" Coy. will relieve "B" Coy. R.D.F. and 1 Platoon "C" Coy. R.D.F. from F.12.a.4.3 to F.12.c.6.7 & EGG POST F.11.d.9.6
"X" Coy. will relieve "D" Coy. R.D.F. F.12.a.3.2 to F.11.a.7.6
"Y" Coy. will relieve "A" Coy. R.D.F. 2 Platoons SART POST F.17.a.7.9 2 Platoons GRAFTER POST F.17.b.6.6.
"Z" Coy. will relieve "C" Coy. R.D.F. 1 Platoon LEMPIRE EAST 1 Platoon LEMPIRE CENTRAL 2 platoons & Coy. H.Q. F.16.a.9.7.

2. Battalion will parade ready to march off in CALAIS STREET . Head of Column at Cross roads by Via. 112th. Field Ambulance at 4.15 p.m. in the following Order:-

"W" "X" Y Z and Headquarter Company

3. Battalion will entrain at HAMEL SIDING at 4.30 p.m. and will detrain at ST. EMILIE. 2nd. Lt. L.C. BOYD will be in charge of entraining.
Battalion will move from S . EMILIE by Companies at 500 yards interval along overland route to LANCASTER HOUSE.

4. Folloing advance parties will proceed to the Front Line at 9 a.m. 22nd. Instant to reconnoitre and take over.
1 N.C.O. Headquarter Company, 1 Officer, 1 Sgt., Nos 1 Of Lewis Guns, 4 Guides from each Company. The guides after reconnoitring Route from Battalion Headquarters (LANCASTER HOUSE) to their respective platoons in the line will report at LANCASTER HOUSE to 2nd. Lt. HIGGINS who will be in charge of them, at 5.30 p.m. . 1 Guide from Each Company "B" Royal Dublin Fusiliers will also report at this time.
The Companies will be guided to the Line by them.

5. Anti-aircraft Lewis Guns Protecting wagon Lines will be relieved by 48th. Infantry Brigade by 12 noon 22. 1. 18 and will proceed to join their Companies at HAMEL at this time. Lewis Guns and ammunition will be taken on the train.

6. The following will be taken over:-
1. All trench Stores. 2. Written Defence Schemes. 3. All Documents (except air photographs) connected with theline. 4. All Work in Progress and proposed (in writing) 5. Trench Maps (if any).
Copy of Trench Stores Lists to reach Orderly Room by noon 23. 1. 18.

7. All Billets will be left scrupulously clean and certificates obtained Advance Parties of 48th. Infy. Bde. should arrive about 2.30 p.m. . The Quartermaster will hand over the present Billets to incoming Unit and obtain a clean Certificate for same, which will be forwarded to Battalion H.Q. by 9 a.m. 23rd. inst.

8. Battalion Headquarters will be at LANCASTER HOUSE F.16.a.8.6.

9. All Packs and Blankets will be stacked at Battalion Headquarters by 10 a.m. to-morrow. All Officers' Kits for ~~Tra~~ Transport Lines by 11 a.m.

10. 2 Limbers report Battalion Headquarters at 2 p.m. to take Company Officers' Kit etc. to the Line. Half a Limber to each Company.
1 Limber for Orderly Room Kit at Battalion Headquarters 2 p.m.

11. Guides for Ration Parties must report Battalion Headquarters as soon as the Relief is complete.

12. Completion of relief will be sent by Code word "LEAVE" as soon as possible.

A.C.K.N O W L E D G E .

(Signed) C. A. MARSDEN, Lieutenant,
A/Adjutant 1st. Bn. Royal Munster Fusiliers.

S E C R E T

O P E R A T I O N   O R D E R S   No. ~~12~~ 4

By

Lt. Colonel A. T. GOODLAND Comdg. 1st. Royal Munster Fusiliers.

In the Field 27. 1. 17

XXXXXXXXXXXXXXXXXXXXXXXXXXXXXXXX

The Battalion will be relieved by the 6th. Battalion Connaught Rangers tomorrow 28th. January about 5 p.m.

"W" Coy. will be relieved by C Coy. 6th. Bn. Conn. Rangers.
"X" Coy. " " D Coy. " " " "
"Y" Coy. " " A Coy. " " " "
"Z" Coy. " " B Coy. " " " "

3. An advance party of 1 Sgt. 4 O.R's (Platoon Guides) from each Company will report to the Intelligence Officer at Bn. Hd. Qrs. at 1.30 p.m. tomorrow and proceed to LEMPIRE to take over from 6th. Connaught Rangers as follows:-

"W" Coy. to take over from/"A" Coy. ~~xxxxxxBn~~. 6th. Conn Rgrs.
"X" Coy. to take over from "B" Coy. 6th. Conn Rgrs.
"Y" Coy. to take over from "D" Coy. 6th. Conn Rgrs.
"Z" Coy. to take over from "C" Coy. 6th. Conn Rgrs.

4. Transport Officer will arrange for following:-

Maltese Cart to be up at Barrier at 5 p.m.
1 G.S Limbered Wagon for Orderly Room & Officers' Kit to be at Bn. H.Q. at 5 p.m.

5. Trench Stores will be handed over
Receipt copies to be sent to Orderly Room by 1 p.m. 29th. inst..

6 All working parties, work in progress and defence shhemes will be carefully checked and handed over.

7. Company dispositions in LEMPIRE ~~xxxLEMPIRE~~ defences will be as followsxx (~~being~~ which are the same as occupied during the last tour in that Sector)
~~xxxxxxxxxxxxx~~

"W" Company in D Area
"X" Company in A Area
"Y" Company in B Area
"Z" Company in C Area.

Company Commanders must arrange rendezvous for their Platoon Guides so that they can direct their respective Platoons to their Billets.

9. Completion of relief will be wired to Bn. H.Q. by code word "RATS"

10. A C K N O W L E D G E.

(Sd.) J.G. MORROUGH_BERNARD, Lieutenant,
A/Adjutant, 1st. Bn. Royal Munster Fusiliers

W A R   D I A R Y .

FOR   MONTH   OF   FEBRUARY, 1918.

VOLUME:-

UNIT:- 1st Btn Ro. Munster Fusiliers

WO 24

SECRET

OPERATION ORDERS No. 5

By

Colonel H. T. GOODLAND Comdg. 1st. Bn. Royal Munster Fusiliers

In the Field 2. 2. 18

XXXXXXXXXXXXXXXXXXXXXX

1. The Battalion will relieve the 6th. Connaught Rangers tomorrow night 2. 2. 18 in the left subsection.

"W" Coy. 1st. R.M.F. will relieve "A" Coy 6th. Conn. Rgrs. in SART LANE
"X" Coy. " " " " "B" " " " " in LEMPIRE
"Y" Coy. " " " " "C" " " " " on Rt. Front Line with a Lewis Gun & Team of "W" Company.
"Z" Coy. 1st. R.M.F. will relieve "D" Coy. 6th. Conn. Rgrs. on Left Front Line with Lewis Gun and Team of "X" Company.

Battalion Headquarters will be at LANCASTER HOUSE.
Relief will commence at 5 p.m. in the following Order :-
Z Y X W Companies
Platoons will move up to the Line at 5 minute intervals.

2. The following advance party will be at LANCASTER House at 2.15 p.m. tomorrow to take over from 6th. Bn. Conn. Rgrs.
1 Offr. , 1 Sgt. and 3 O.R. from each Company
1 Offr. , 1 Sgt. from Headquarter Company.

3. All work in progress, Trench Stores and defence Schemes will be carefully taken over in writing. Trench Store Lists to reach Bn. Headquarters by 11 p.m 3rd. inst.

4. TRANSPORT

The Transport Officer will arrange for the following :-
Maltese and Mess cart to be at Bn. H.Q. RONSSOY by 4.30 p.m.
1 G.S. Limbered Wagon for Orderly Room & Officers' Kit to be at Bn. Headquarters same time.
2 G. S. Wagons for blankets to be up in RONSSOY by 4 p.m. .

5. BLANKETS.

Headquarter and W Companies to have blankets at Orderly Room by 3 p.m.
"X" "Y" and "Z" Coys. to have blankets dumped at their respective H.Q's by 3 p.m.

6. All Billets, shelters and dugouts to be cleaned by 2 p.m. and certificates of cleanliness to be obtained from 6th. Conn. Rgrs. and sent to Bn. H.Q. by 1 p.m. 3rd. inst.

7. The following patrols , strength 1 Officer 20 O.R. will be sent out from "Y" and "Z" Coys. on their respective fronts from dusk until 11 p.m. to cover Relief. The above must be sent up to the Line in daylight.

8. Rations will be up about 6.30 p.m. . Company Commanders must see that Ration parties are ready at that time.

9. Completion of Relief to be wired to Battalion H.Q. by Code word "GRAINGER".

10. ACKNOWLEDGE.

(signed) J.C. Morrough-Bernard, Lieutenant,

A/Adjutant, 1st. Bn. Royal Munster Fusiliers

FILE

S[illegible]

OPERATION ORDERS No. 7

By

Lt. Colonel H.T. GOODLAND Comdg. 1st. Royal Munster Fusiliers.

In the Field 7. 2. 18

xxxxxxxxxxxxxxxxxxxx

1. The Battalion will be relieved in the left sub-section by the 6th. Connaught Rangers tomorrow evening 8. 2. 18 about 5.30 p.m.

W Coy. 1st. R.M.F. will be relieved by C Coy. 6th. Conn. Rgrs.
X Coy. 1st. R.M.F. will be relieved by D Coy. 6th. Conn. Rgrs.
Y Coy. 1st. R.M.F. will be relieved by A Coy. 6th. Conn. Rgrs.
Z Coy. 1st. R.M.F. will be relieved by B Coy. 6th. Conn. Rgrs.

2. On Completion of relief Companies will proceed to LEMPIRE .

3. The following advance parties - 1 Sgt. H.Q. Coy., and 1 Sgt. and 3 O.R's per Company will report to the Intelligence Officer at Battalion Headquarters at 2 p.m. to-morrow and will proceed to LEMPIRE to take over from the 2nd. Battalion Leinster Regiment as follows :-

W Coy. 1st. R.M.F. will take over from B Coy. 2nd. Leinsters
X Coy. 1st. R.M.F. will take over from A Coy. 2nd. Leinsters
Y Coy. 1st. R.M.F will take over from C Coy. 2nd. Leinsters
Z Coy. 1st. R.M.F. will take over from D Coy. 2nd. Leinsters.

(The above Companies' positions are as before)

All Trench Stores, Defence Schemes and work in progress must be taken over in writing.

4. 1 Guide per platoon will report at Battalion Headquarters LANCASTER HOUSE at 5.15 p.m. to guide Conn. Rgrs. into positions

5. All work in progress and proposed, trench stores and defence schemes must be handed over in writing.

Trench Store receipts to reach Battalion Headquarters by 10 a.m. 9th. instant.

6. Patrols consisting of 1 Officer 20 O.R's will be sent out by front line Companies of 6th. Conn. Rgrs. from about 5 p.m. to protect relief from surprise.

7. Platoons will move down to LEMPIRE at 500 yards interval.

8. The transport Officer will arrange for following :-

Maltese Cart to be at Barrier by 4.30 p.m.
Mess Cart and 1 G.S. Limbered wagon to be at Battalion H.Q. by 4.30 p.m.

The Quartermaster will arrange that the Compaies' Blankets are brought up with rations on the night of 8. 2. 18.

9. Relief complete will be wired to Battalion Headquarters by code word "RABBIT".

10. ACKNOWLEDGE.

(SD.) J.G. Morrough-Bernard, 2/Lieutenant,

A/Adjutant, 1st. Bn. The Royal Munster Fusiliers.

S E C R E T   O P E R A T I O N   O R D E R S   No. 8

By

Lt. Colonel R.R. KANE D.S.O. Comdg. 1st. Royal Munster Fusiliers
In the Field 11. 2. 18

1. The Battalion will relieve the 2nd. Battalion Leinster Regt. in the right Subsection on night of February 12th. 1918

W Coy. will relieve A Coy. 2nd. Leins. Regt. (Left)
X Coy. will relieve B Coy. 2nd Bn. Leins. Regt. (Right)
Y Coy. will relieve C Coy. 2nd. Bn. Leins. Regt. (Close Support)
C Company 8/9th. R.Inns. Fus. will relieve D Coy. 2nd. L.R. (Bn. H.Q.)

2. Companies will proceed to the Line at undermentioned times. Guides from 2nd. Bn. Leins. Regt. having previously being sent to them.
W Coy. 5. 30 p.m. X Coy. 5.45 p.m. Y Coy. 5.55 p.m.
C Coy. R.Inns. Fus. and Bn. H.Q. 6.20 p.m.

3 Advance Parties of 1 Officer Nos. 1 Of Lewis Guns and 1 N.C.O. per Company will proceed to the line at 2 p.m. tomorrow to take over. 2nd. Lt. J.G. Burrough Bernard will take over Battalion Headquarters and Orderly Room Documents.

4. All work in hand and proposed, trench stores and Defence Scheme will be taken over. Copies of Trench Stores to reach Orderly Room by 10 a.m. 13. 2. 18.

5. Present Billets will be cleaned up by 10 a.m. tomorrow, and when handed over a certificate of cleanliness will be obtained. All trench sotres will be handed over, copies of same to reach Orderly room by 10 a.m. 13. 2. 18.

6Blankets will be stacked outside Company H.Q. by 10 a.m. 1 Limber will report to W & Y Coys. 1st. R.M.F. and C Coy. R.I.F. at this time, and 1 Limber to X Company at 4.30 p.m. to take blankets to the Stores.
Transport Officer will arrange for the following:-
1 Limber (Orderly Room and H.Q. Officers' Kits).
Maltese Cart and Mess Cart at Battalion H.Q. at 4 p.m.

7 Patrols consisting of 1 Officer and 20 O.R's from both W and X Coys. will be at F.16.D.45.25. to meet guides from 2nd. Leinster Regt. at 3.30 p.m.. These patrols will protect Battalion Frontage during relief .

8. Ration Guides will report at New Battalion H.Q. (F.17.A.3.C.) as soon as possible after relief is complete .

9. Completion of relief will be wired to Battalion H.Q. by code word "REPEAT".

10. A C K N O W L E D G E.

(SD) C. W. MARSDEN, Lieutenant,

A/Adjutant, 1st.Bn. Royal Munster Fusiliers.

68

SECRET OPERATION ORDERS No. 9

By

Lt. -Colonel R. R. KANE D.S.O. Comdg. 1st. Royal Munster Fusiliers.

In the Field 20. 2. 18

****

1. The Battalion will be relievec by 6th. Bn. Conn. Rgrs. tonight 20th. inst.
2. Y Coy. will be relieved by "A" Coy. 6th. C.R.
   D Coy. 6th. C. R. willbe relieved by C Coy. 6th. C.R.
   X Coy. will be relieved by "B" Coy. 6th. C.R.
   W Coy. will be relieved by "D" Coy. 6th. C.R.
   Relief will commence about 6.30 p.m.
3. On completion of relief companieswill proceed to same billets as before in LEMPIRE . Z Company will come up from TINCOURT (Train arrangements to be notified later) and proceed to their billets in LEMPIRE.
4. Advance parties of 1 Officer, 1 N.C.O. per company will proceed to LEMPIRE and take over Billets etc. by 4 p.m.. All work in progress and on hand will be taken over and all trench stores.
5. All work in hand and in progress, defence shhemes and trench stores will be handed over. Copies of trench Stores to reach Orderly Room by 10 a.m. 21st. instant.
6. Transport Officer will make arrangements for the undermentioned Transport
   Mess Cart at Bn. H. Q. at 5 p.m.
   1 Limber (Orderly Room) at Bn. H.Q. 5.30 p.m.
   Maltese Cart GILLEMONT R.E. DUMP at 6 p.m.
7. Completion of relief will be wired at once to Bn. H.Q. by Code word "SUCCESS".
8. Arrival in LEMPIRE will be wired to Bn. H.Q. (New) LEMPIRE) by code word "PERHAPS"

(Sd.) C.W. MARSDEN, Lieutenant,
A/Adjutant, 1st. Royal Munster Fusiliers.

SECRET OPERATION ORDERS No. 10
By
Lt. Colonel R R.KANE D. S.O. Comdg. 1st. Royal Muns. Fusiliers.
In the field 23. 2. 18
****

1. The Battalion will relieve 2nd. Bn. Leinster Regt. in the left subsection on night 24th. February. Relief will commence at 6 p.m.

2. W Coy. will relieve D Coy. 2nd. Leinster Regt. (Left front Line)
Z Coy. will relieve A Coy. 2nd. Leinster Regt. (Right Ft. Line)
Y Coy. will relieve C Coy. 2nd. Leinster Regt. (LEMPIRE EAST)
X Coy. will relieve D Coy. 2nd. Leinster Regt. (SART FARM)

3. Companies will leave Billets at the following times
W and Z 6 p.m. X 6.15. p.m. Y 6.30 p.m. H.Q. 6.30 p.m.

4. Patrols consisting of 1 Offr. and 20 O.R's from both W and Z Coys. will report at 2nd. Leinster Bn. H.Q. LANCASTER HOUSE) at 2 p.m. and will proceed from there to the Line. They will protect the Battalion front during relief.

5. Advance parties of 1 Officer Nos 1 Of the Lewis Guns and 1 N.C.O from each Company will proceed to the Line at 3 p.m. to take over and reconnoitre. These N.C,O's will act as Coy. Guides and will report after reconnoitring the line to 2nd. Lt. J F. PULLIN MC at LANCASTER HOUSE at 5.30 p.m.. They will guide their Companies to the line

6. All work in hand and proposed, trench stores and Defence Schemes will be handed over in LEMPIRE and taken over in the Line. Copies of Trench Store Lists to reach Orderly Room by 10 a.m. 25. 2. 18

7. Transport Officer will arrange for the undermentioned Transport
Mess Cart and Maltese Cart at Bn. H.Q. 5 p.m.
1 Limber (for X and Z Coys.) at X Coy. H.Q. 6 p.m. (for blankets)
1 Limber (W and Y Coys.) at Y Coy. H.Q. 6 p.m. do
1 Limber (O. Room Kit etc.) at Bn. H.Q. 5 p.m.

8. All Billets etc., will be cleaned up by noon tomorrow , a certificate of cleanliness of same will be obtained by each Coy. Commander and handed into O.Room by 10 a.m. 25. 2. 18.

9. Completion of Relief will be wired to Bn. H.Q. by Code word "DOLPHIN" .

ACKNOWLEDGE.

(Sd.). C. W. MARSDEN, Lieutenant,
A/Adjutant, 1st. Royal Munster Fusiliers.

Issued at ..6.p.m....

Copy No. 1 to Commanding Offr.
Copy No. 2 to O.C. W Coy.
Copy No. 3 to O.C. X Coy.
Copy No. 4 to O.C. Y. Coy.
Copy No. 5 to O.C. Z Coy.
Copy No. 6 to O.C 2nd. Leinster Regt.
Copy No. 7,to O.C. 6th. Conn. Rangers
Copy No. 8 to 47th. Infy. Bde. H.Q.
Copy No. 9 to Signalling Officer
Copy No. 10 Medical Officer
Copy No. 11 R.S.M.
Copy No. 12 to Quartermaster
Copy No. 13 to Transport Officer
Copies Nos. 14 and 15 file.

File

File

S E C R E T O P E R A T I O N O R D E R S No. 11
By
Lt. Colonel R. R. KANE D S.O. Comdg. 1st. Royal Muns. Fus.
In the Field 27. 2. 18

****

1. The Battalion will be relieved by the 1st. Bn. Lincoln Regt. on the night of February 18/Mar. 1st. 1918.

C Company Lincoln Regt. will relieve Y Coy. 1st. Bn. R.M.Fus.
D Company " " " " X " " " "
A Company " " " " Z Coy " " "
B Company " " " " W Coy. " " "

2. On relief complete the Battalion will proceed to MOISLANS by following route . :-
(A). By-road via RONSSOY to St. EMILIE Siding (F.13.C.)
(b). By second train to MOISLANS
2nd. Lt. J. F. FULLIN MC will be in charge of entraining at ST EMILIE.

3. An advance party of 1st. Bn Lincoln. Regt. consisting of 1 Officer and 20 O.R's will proceed to the Line to both Y and X Companies at 6 p.m. 27th instant to reconnoitre and take over the Line. These parties will be billeted in the trenches.

4. The following will be handed over and receipts obtained :-
(a). All Trench Stores.
(b). Written defence Schemes.
(c). All maps and documents connected with the Line.
(d). Air Photogr phs..
(e). Work in progress and proposed (in writing)
Copies of Trench Store Lists to reach Battalion Headquarters MOISLANS) by noon 1. 3. 18.

5. GUIDES (a). 1 N.C. O. per company will report to 2nd. Lt. J. F. FULLIN MC at Bn. H.Q. at 4 p.m. 28.th. inst.
(b). 1 N. C. O. per platoon will report to 2nd. Lt. L.C. BOYD at Battalion H. Q. at 6 p.m. 28th. inst.

6. PATROLS of 1 Officer and 20 O.R's from both Y and X Coys. will be sent out on night of 28th. inst. , to protect relief. These patrols will be withdrawn as soon after relief complete as possible in order the they may get down to ST. EMILIE for entraining.

7. Transport Officer will make arrangements for the undermentioned Transport :-
Mess Cart and Maltese Cart at Bn. H.Q. at 6 p.m.
1 Limber (Orderly Room & H.Q. Offrs' Kits) at Bn. H.Q.6.30 p.m.
2 Limbers (1 for W and Z Coys., and 1 for Y and X Coy.)
at Bn. H. Q. at 8 p.m.

8. All men on detachments will report to their companies at MOISLANS on 1. 3. 18

9 Battalion Headquarters will close at lancaster house and open at MOISLANS as soon after relief complete as possible.

10. Completion of relief will be wired to Bn. H.Q. by code word "CHEERS". Arrival in Billets at MOISLANS will be reported to Battalion H. Q. by runner.
ACKNOWLEDGE.

(Sd.). C. W. MARSDEN, Lieutenant
A/Adjutant, 1st. Royal Munster Fusiliers

P. T. O.

Issued at ....

Copies to

No. 1 Commanding Officer
No. 2 2nd. in Command
No. 3 Quartermaster
No. 4 Transport Officer
No. 5 Intelligence Officer
No. 6 Signalling Officer
No. 7 O. C. W Company
No. 8 O. C. X Company
No. 9 O. C. Y Company
No. 10 O. C. Z Company
No. 11 H.Q. 47th. Infantry Brigade.
No. 12 O.C. 1st. Bn. Lincoln Regt.
No. 13 Medical Officer
No. 14 to R. S.M.
No. 15 and 16 War Diary
No. 17 File

1st Battalion Royal Munster Fusiliers
16th Division

Sheet No 1

Army Form C. 2118.

Instructions regarding War Diaries and Intelligence Summaries are contained in F. S. Regs., Part II. and the Staff Manual respectively. Title pages will be prepared in manuscript.

WAR DIARY
or
~~INTELLIGENCE SUMMARY.~~
(Erase heading not required.)

Place	Date	Hour	Summary of Events and Information	Remarks and references to Appendices
EMPIRE (Left Sub-sector, Right Sector)	1.2.18 to 8.2.18	—	Battalion in line the whole of this period, which was very quiet & nothing of any importance occurred.	
"	7.2.18		Lt. Colonel R. R. G. Kane D.S.O. assumes command of the Bn, Lt. Col. H. T. Goodland proceeding on leave pending appointment under Canadian Govt. Bt Major G. W. Nightingale, MC 1st Royal Munster Fusiliers reported his arrival & took over the duties of 2nd in Command from Major Carrigan MC who assumes command of "Y" company. New Bde formation taken into effect. There are now only three Bns in the 47th Inf. Bde. 1st RMF, 2nd L.R., 6th C.R.	
	8.2.18	7pm	Battalion relieved in the Right Sector by the 6th Battn Connaught Rangers, & proceeded to Support billets in RONSOY.	
	12.2.18		Battalion relieved the 2nd Bn Leinster Regt. in the Right Subsection (LEMPIRE) after 4 days in Support — during all of which everything was quiet. On the 10.2.18, "Z" company proceeded to billets in TINCOURT to train for one week for a raid against the enemy. The following officers proceeded with the company: Major G. W. Nightingale MC, in charge of the detachment; Capt Lawlor MC, OC Coy; Lt Reynolds, and 2nd Lt Bourchier & Higgins. Lt Dickie also accompanied the party for two days, as Intelligence Officer.	
			A draft of 64 NCOs & men from the 7/8th Royal Irish Fusiliers joined the Bn on the 10th inst. & were taken on the strength from that date	

G. W. Nightingale Major
1st R Munster Fusiliers

A6945 Wt. W11422/M1160 350,000 12/16 D. D. & L. Forms/C./2118/14.

1st Bn Royal Munster Fusiliers
16th Division.

Sheet No 2

Instructions regarding War Diaries and Intelligence Summaries are contained in F. S. Regs., Part II. and the Staff Manual respectively. Title pages will be prepared in manuscript.

WAR DIARY
or
INTELLIGENCE SUMMARY.
(Erase heading not required.)

Army Form C. 2118.

Place	Date	Hour	Summary of Events and Information	Remarks and references to Appendices
LEMPIRE (Right Subsection)	18.2.18	5.45 pm	"Z" company, which has been out training since 11.2.18, left TINCOURT on lorries to proceed to the front line to undertake a raid against the enemy in WILLOW TRENCH & LONE TREE TRENCH.	
		7pm	Z Company arrived at S. EMILIE & sustained first casualty (one man slightly wounded) by enemy bombs from aircraft.	
		12 midnight	Raiding party proceeded to RONSOY. Further operations described in detail in attached report.*	Appendix
			The weather throughout the training & on the night of the raid was dry & cold. The raid took place at 4am (zero hour) & the company was reported in about one hour later, having captured 5 of the enemy, killed a considerable number offering resistance & only sustaining casualties themselves to the amount of 1 officer wounded (Capt [illegible]) & 16 other ranks. One man was killed.* There was very little response from the enemy's artillery.	Pte H... KLEM [illegible]
	19.2.18		Z company proceeded to TINCOURT to billets. The remainder of the Bn holding the same sector as before. Very quiet & normal. Weather still cold & fine. Bombing at night by enemy aeroplanes is becoming very frequent. Capt J. Shea reported his arrival back from leave & took over the duties of P.R.I.	
	20.2.18	7pm	The Bn was relieved by the 6th Connaught Rangers & proceeded to the support billets in Ronssoy. During the relief a concentration [illegible] fire on V[illegible] took place with a certain amount of retaliation on the part of the enemy ~~[illegible]~~, causing a few casualties to the Connaught Rangers. The effect of this raid on the enemy seems to [illegible]	

A6945 Wt. W11422/M1160 350,000 12/16 D. D. & L. Forms/C./2118/14.

G.W. Nightingale Major
1st R Munster Fusiliers

1st Bn Royal Munster Fusiliers

Sheet No 3

WAR DIARY
or
INTELLIGENCE SUMMARY.
(Erase heading not required.)

Army Form C. 2118.

Instructions regarding War Diaries and Intelligence Summaries are contained in F. S. Regs., Part II. and the Staff Manual respectively. Title pages will be prepared in manuscript.

Place	Date	Hour	Summary of Events and Information	Remarks and references to Appendices
LEMPIRE	20.2.18		be that he has realized there are more troops & superior artillery opposite him than he at first imagined. On the two days following the raid he showed no willingness to retaliate, but, by bombing his own wire & being constantly on the alert, gave the impression that he was decidedly nervous & jumpy. Any little activity on our part at once caused him to appeal to his artillery for support.	
	21.2.18	4.30am	Heavy artillery firing & machine gun fire caused the Bn to stand to in its battle positions. The firing was in the direction of EPÉHY, but by 5.30 am had completely died down. RONSSOY was not shelled but our troops holding the front line were seen to put up the S.O.S. signal. During the day, which was clear, there was intermittent shelling & registering by the enemy & our guns. There was much aerial activity. The Bn was on fatigue during the whole day, under the OC LEMPIRE Defences.	
	22.2.18		Very quiet all day. Misty weather & no artillery fire or aerial work. The new scheme for having an Advanced & rear Bn HQ Quarters came into force today. The Commanding Officer & Adjutant remained at Advanced Bn HQ & dealt with all "G" work. Major [illegible] MC & Capt Shea, PRI. proceeded to the Transport lines at VILLERS FAUCON, where rear Bn HQs are situated to deal with all "Q" work.	
	23.2.18		[illegible] & O'Farrell & 6 ORs proceeded to [illegible] to attend an Infantry Training Course.	
	24.2.18		The Battalion [illegible] [illegible] LEMPIRE [illegible]	

D. D. & L., London, E.C. (A7883) Wt. W809/M1672 350,000 4/17 Sch. 52a Forms/C/2118/14

[illegible], Major
1st R Munster Fusiliers

1st Royal Munster Fusiliers

Sheet No 4

WAR DIARY
or
INTELLIGENCE SUMMARY.
(*Erase heading not required.*)

Army Form C. 2118.

Instructions regarding War Diaries and Intelligence Summaries are contained in F. S. Regs., Part II. and the Staff Manual respectively. Title pages will be prepared in manuscript.

Place	Date	Hour	Summary of Events and Information	Remarks and references to Appendices
LEMPIRE E	24/8 (contd)		The relief [illegible] H.Q. are established at LANCASTER HOUSE	
	25/8		Observation had a very bitter activity [illegible] the artillery [illegible] took over [illegible]	
			of the [illegible] the line held by the [illegible]	
	26/8	1.30 am	Patrol of 1 NCO + 6 O.R. sent out to reconnoitre. The enemy's wire [illegible] FAG TRENCH	
	27/8		Operation orders received for suggested move to MOISLAINS [illegible] shelling, aircraft [illegible]	
			1 W.O. + 13 O.Rs reported their arrival [illegible] duty, posted to coys [illegible] on his arrival off leave	
	31/8		All orders regarding the relief of the Bn [illegible] to MOISLAINS cancelled. [illegible] quiet all day, except	
			for intermittent shelling. An inter company relief took place in the line, the dispositions now being as	
			follows:– X + Y coys in front line, Z coy in support + W company in reserve. The Quarter Master's	
			Stores moved to TINCOURT, i.e. all surplus stores.	
			The following is the strength of the Bn at the end of the month	
			39 Officers 893 other ranks (Full strength)	
			24 Officers 708 other ranks (Fighting strength)	

[illegible] Major
[illegible] 1st R. Munster Fusiliers

D. D. & L., London, E.C.
(A7883) Wt. W809/M1672 350,000 4/17 Sch. 52a Forms/C/2118/14

PATROL ORDERS
By
Lt. Colonel R. R. KANE D.S.O. Comdg. 1st. Royal Munster Fusiliers.
In the Field 26. 2. 18

****

A patrol of 1 N. C. O. and 6 O.R's will leave our linestonight at 7.30 p.m. from F.11.B.55.68.

<u>OBJECT</u>
To reconnaitre enemy wire and NO MAN'S LAND in front of FAG TRENCH and to locate position of advanced Hostile Post in COCHRANE AVENUE They will return by F.12. B.65.85. at about 9.30 p.m.

Pass word "DODO".

(SD) C. W. Marsden, Lieutenant,

A/Adjutant, 1st Bn. The Royal Munster Fusiliers.

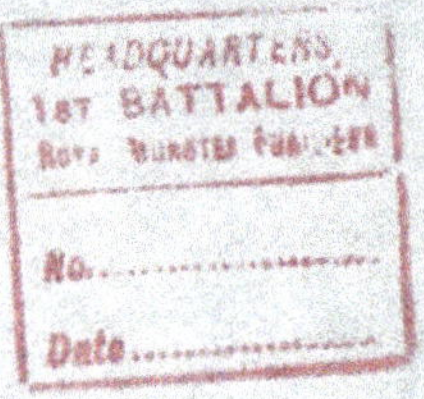
HEADQUARTERS,
1st BATTALION
Royal Munster Fusiliers

No. ....

Date ....

File

47th Brigade.

16th Division.

1st - BATTALION

ROYAL MUNSTER FUSILIERS

M A R C H 1 9 1 8

Page 1

1st Bn Royal Munster Fusiliers

47/16 March

Vol 25

Army Form C. 2118.

WAR DIARY
or
INTELLIGENCE SUMMARY.
(Erase heading not required.)

Instructions regarding War Diaries and Intelligence Summaries are contained in F. S. Regs., Part II, and the Staff Manual respectively. Title pages will be prepared in manuscript.

Place	Date	Hour	Summary of Events and Information	Remarks and references to Appendices
LEMPIRE			Battalion holding the left sub-sector of the right sector from CART FARM to TOMBOIS FARM	
ST EMILE				

D. D. & L., London, E.C. (A7883) Wt W809/M1672 350,000 4/17 Sch. 52a Forms/C/2118/14

Page II. 1st Royal Munster Fusiliers

Instructions regarding War Diaries and Intelligence Summaries are contained in F. S. Regs., Part II. and the Staff Manual respectively. Title pages will be prepared in manuscript.

WAR DIARY
or
INTELLIGENCE SUMMARY.

(*Erase heading not required.*)

Army Form C. 2118.

Place	Date	Hour	Summary of Events and Information	Remarks and references to Appendices

D. D. & L., London, E.C.
(A7883) Wt. W809/M1672 350,000 4/17 Sch. 52a. Forms/C/2118/14

Page III 1st Royal Munster Fusiliers

Army Form C. 2118.

Instructions regarding War Diaries and Intelligence Summaries are contained in F. S. Regs., Part II, and the Staff Manual respectively. Title pages will be prepared in manuscript.

WAR DIARY
or
INTELLIGENCE SUMMARY.
(*Erase heading not required.*)

Place	Date	Hour	Summary of Events and Information	Remarks and references to Appendices
DOINGT				

D. D. & L., London, E.C. (A7883) Wt. W809/M1672 350,000 4/17 Sch. 52a Forms/C/2118/14

Pale IV   1st Royal Munster Fusiliers

Army Form C. 2118.

WAR DIARY
or
INTELLIGENCE SUMMARY.
(Erase heading not required.)

Instructions regarding War Diaries and Intelligence Summaries are contained in F. S. Regs., Part II. and the Staff Manual respectively. Title pages will be prepared in manuscript.

Place	Date	Hour	Summary of Events and Information	Remarks and references to Appendices
DOINGT	23/3	1 pm	1st [illegible] Infantry Bde, [illegible] through DOINGT & PERONNE [illegible] to BIACHE [illegible]	
			Division [illegible] ordered to [illegible] [illegible]	
			[illegible]	
			[illegible] Capt [illegible] [illegible]	
			[illegible] Major H.R. [illegible]	
			[illegible] 5 officers & 110 men.	
		7 pm	[illegible]	
			[illegible] CAPPY [illegible]	
			[illegible]	
BRAY	24/3	6 am	[illegible] BRAY [illegible]	
			[illegible]	
		4 pm	[illegible] MORECOURT [illegible]	
			[illegible]	
			[illegible]	
			[illegible]	

D. D. & L., London, E.C. (A7883) Wt W809/M1672 350,000 4/17 Sch. 52a Forms/C/2118/14

Page V

1st Royal Munster Fusiliers

Instructions regarding War Diaries and Intelligence Summaries are contained in F. S. Regs., Part II. and the Staff Manual respectively. Title pages will be prepared in manuscript.

WAR DIARY
or
INTELLIGENCE SUMMARY.
(*Erase heading not required.*)

Army Form C. 2118.

Place	Date	Hour	Summary of Events and Information	Remarks and references to Appendices
MORECOURT	25 3/18	6am	The company on outpost duty was relieved after stand to by Capt Carrigan's company, in support. Returning with the Quartermaster, Major Baxter arrived up at 11am having spent the night looking for the Batt[n]. There were no signs of the enemy's cavalry & the same report came from the 49th Brigade on our left & the 2nd Leinsters & Connaughts on our right who were at ~~[illegible]~~ CERISY.	
"	"	4PM.	The B[n] received orders to proceed at once to MÉRICOURT, a village 3 miles East of our present position, & there take up an outpost position covering the bridge head.	
MERICOURT		8PM	The B[n] in position at MÉRICOURT. Capt Carrigan's company finding the outpost & Capt Nibel's coy in support in billets in the village.	
	26 3/18	6am	By orders from the C.R.E. all the bridges over the Somme were blown up. The Battalion was withdrawn & received orders to proceed to PROYART & hold the line of a railway cutting covering the village. Capt Nibel's company went on ahead to dig some sort of a line, as the information said the 66th Division would fall back through us.	
PROYART	"	1PM.	The B[n] holding the line of the railway. The 48th B[de] on the left & the Connaught Rangers on the right. Very quiet except for shellfire. Good position. Rations up in the night.	
"	27 3/18	8am	After a quiet night, during which a patrol of 3 of the enemy were caught by a patrol of Capt Carrigan's coy, the enemy showed signs of activity. There was heavy firing on both flanks & a great number of machine-guns	

D. D. & L., London, E.C.
(A7883) Wt. W809/M1672 350,000 4/17 Sch. 52a Forms/C/2118/14

Page VI 1st Royal Munster Fusiliers

Instructions regarding War Diaries and Intelligence Summaries are contained in F. S. Regs., Part II. and the Staff Manual respectively. Title pages will be prepared in manuscript.

WAR DIARY
or
INTELLIGENCE SUMMARY.

(*Erase heading not required.*)

Army Form C. 2118.

Place	Date	Hour	Summary of Events and Information	Remarks and references to Appendices
PROYART	27/3/18	8 a.m.	bullets began to enfilade our trenches from the left flank. A short time after this a great number of the enemy were seen advancing in our left rear, where apparently they had turned the flank of the 48th Bde, or crossed the SOMME behind us. Capt Carrigan formed a defensive flank by dropping back half his coy. & 3 Lewis Guns, supported by two Machine Guns attached to the Bn. These did good work, catching the enemy as he debouched in mass from a wood & forcing him to retire under cover. No orders could be obtained from the Bde, who had fallen back to a new H.Q. [illegible]. After holding the railway cutting for an hour, by which time the enemy had come on in great numbers & was well round the village in our left rear, it was decided to withdraw to a ridge the other side of the village where the position would come under less enfilade fire, as the railway cutting was now being swept by enfilade machine gun fire from enemy guns in a wood on our left bank. This movement was successfully carried out, each coy. covering the other & the last coy. to go covering the first coy. of the CONNAUGHT RANGERS, who also had to fall back.	
		11 a.m.	Unfortunately, when the Bn fell back to the new position W of the village of PROYART, Capt Carrigan's coy, with the Commanding officer, the Adjutant & Bn H.Q. [illegible], went to their left rear, while Capt Nihill's coy with Major Nightingale went to their right rear, & the two coys became separated. Both parties came under the orders of Brigadier General BELLINGHAM who commanded a Bde of the 39th Division.	

D. D. & L., London, E.C.
(A7883) Wt. W809/M1672 350,000 4/17 Sch. 52a Forms/C/2118/14

Page VII 1st Royal Munster Fusiliers

Instructions regarding War Diaries and Intelligence Summaries are contained in F. S. Regs., Part II. and the Staff Manual respectively. Title pages will be prepared in manuscript.

WAR DIARY
or
INTELLIGENCE SUMMARY.
(*Erase heading not required.*)

Army Form C. 2118.

Place	Date	Hour	Summary of Events and Information	Remarks and references to Appendices
PROYART	27/3/18		The Bn now attached itself to the 39th Division which was holding a ridge across the main road half way between PROYART & LAMOTTE. Half the Bn under Lt Col Kane was on the extreme left flank of the Division, while the other half Bn under Major Nightingale, with Capt Fitchell's coy were on the extreme right. Both half Battalions took part in a successful counter-attack which drove back the enemy about 2 miles & retook the villages of HARBONNIERES & FRAMVILLE. With both parties were detachments of the CONNAUGHT RANGERS & LEINSTER REGT. The party with Major Nightingale were under the command of Lt Col FIELDING the Commanding Officer of the CONNAUGHT RANGERS, until he was wounded. When Major Nightingale took over command of all 16th Divisional troops on the right flank, while Lt Col Kane did the same on the left flank. The situation remained so throughout the night.	
FRAMEVILLE	28/3/18	2am.	At 2 am. Brig: General Bellingham sent for all Commanding Officers & informed them that he was afraid the force was completely surrounded & cut off by the enemy ~~at~~ since 3 pm. on the previous day. No traffic of any description had come through from LAMOTTE, which lay immediately in our rear, about 3½ miles, & on patrols being sent out, it was found the enemy were occupying it in force. There was a chance that there might possibly be a gap in the enemy line due South of our position, & he had decided to withdraw the force under cover of darkness & force a way through due South & reach the French lines which were in that direction. The force under Gen: Bellingham consisted of	

D. D. & L., London, E.C.
(A7883) Wt. W809/M1672 350,000 4/17 Sch. 52a Forms/C/2118/14

Page VIII   1st Royal Munster Fusiliers

Army Form C. 2118.

Instructions regarding War Diaries and Intelligence Summaries are contained in F. S. Regs., Part II. and the Staff Manual respectively. Title pages will be prepared in manuscript.

WAR DIARY
or
INTELLIGENCE SUMMARY.
(*Erase heading not required.*)

Place	Date	Hour	Summary of Events and Information	Remarks and references to Appendices
FRAMERVILLE	28/3/18	2 AM.	about 1100 officers & men & 4 Field guns, which had covered the counter-attack. The original idea	
			was to withdraw at 3 am under cover of darkness but information was received that a counter-	
			attack was going to be made on LAMOTTE at dawn, which if successful, would probably extricate	
		10 am.	us. This however failed & at 10 am the force commenced to withdraw, covered by various units	
			in turn. The enemy soon realised what was happening & a heavy barrage was put down in the rear	
			while on both flanks the enemy opened machine gun fire. The majority of the Bn succeeded in getting	
CAIX			away, but all wounded had to be left. At CAIX the two half Bns met & Lt. Col. Kane took over command of	
			the whole Bn, which numbered approx. 5 officers & 170 men. The Bde. Hdqrs were lost & orders were received to rejoin	
			the 16th Division, but no one knew where it was, so the Bn marched to DEMUIN, where the Commanding Officer	
DEMUIN.	28/3/18		reported to General Daly commanding the 24th Division, who gave the Bn rations & told them to proceed to CASTEL	
			where he understood the 16th Division now was.	
CASTEL	"	4 pm.	The Bn marched to CASTEL & went into billets. The Bde Major ascertained that the 16th Division was at	
			BOVES, to which place the Bn was to proceed to refit.	
	29/3/18	8 am.	The Bn marched to BOVES, where Lt. Col. Jackson, G.S.O. 1 of the Division instructed Major Nightingale to collect	
BOVES			& march all 16th Divisional details to AUBIGNY. The details reached BLANGY-TRONVILLE at 2 pm where	
			found the 16th Division Transport. After an hour's halt during which the Bn got a hot meal, Major Nightingale	

D. D. & L., London, E.C.
(A7883) Wt. W809/M1672 350,000 4/17 Sch. 52a Forms/C/2118/14

Page IX   1st R Munster Fusiliers

Instructions regarding War Diaries and Intelligence Summaries are contained in F. S. Regs., Part II. and the Staff Manual respectively. Title pages will be prepared in manuscript.

WAR DIARY
or
INTELLIGENCE SUMMARY.
(Erase heading not required.)

Army Form C. 2118.

Place	Date	Hour	Summary of Events and Information	Remarks and references to Appendices
AUBIGNY	29.3.18	6 PM.	Marched the details to Aubigny, where he handed over all men of the 48th & 49th Bde to Lt Col: Moore, 1st RDF & had the men of the 47th Bde including the Bn billeted in the village.	
"	30.3.18		The whole day was spent resting & refitting the Bn. The Brigadier General & all Commanding officers were remaining at BLANGY-TRONVILLE until the Bn was sufficiently rested to go up to the line at HAMEL, Major Nightingale being left in command of the 47th Inf: Bde details at AUBIGNY. Rations, ammunition, box respirators & steel helmets were made up & the Bn reorganized into two coys, one consisting of those men of W & X that remained, under Capt Tickell, & those of Y & Z under Capt Carrigan. The Brigade Major was attached to the Bn to deal with the Brigade details.	
AUBIGNY	31.3.18		The day was spent much the same as the previous day. Most of the Bn now fitted out & getting fairly rested. Brigadier Gen. Gregory returned & took over the Bde. Strength of Bn 5 officers & 190 other ranks in Aubigny & 3 officers & 40 other ranks at Blangy-Tronville. A few stragglers & reinforcements from the Base continue to come in daily.	

D. D. & L., London, E.C.
(A7883) Wt. W809/M1672 350,000 4/17 Sch. 52a Forms/C/2118/14

Appendix I

Officer Casualties 21st & 22nd Mar 1918.

Killed. Lieut G. Donnelly
2 Lieut J. F. Fuller M C

Wounded Capt C H Stamforth MC.
" J H Lawlor MC.
" J F Shea
2nd Lt L. C. Boyd.
2nd Lt. J. G. Murrough Bernard
" P A Malone

Missing Capt T G. Cahill MC
" J G Russell MC RAMC
" T F Duggan (Chaplain)
2nd Lt C B. Boucher MC.
" H W R Humbley

1/ R Munsters

~~March~~ April 1918

Went to 57 Div

April 1918.

divisions. *

* Hely d'Oissel's detachment (5th Cavalry Division and two infantry regiments of the IX. Corps) de Mitry's detachment (6th and 7th Cavalry Divisions and the 87th Territorial Division), the XXXII. Corps (38th and 42nd Divisions, the 89th Territorial Division and the garrison of the Dixmude salient, viz. two battalions of Fusilier Marins, one Belgian battalion, one Senegalese in the bridgehead east of the river and the remaining four battalions of Admiral Ronarc'h's brigade and a second Senegalese battalion west of the river). (Ronarc'h, p.117).

Heralded by heavy bombardment, which opened at 1 a.m. and reached its maximum about 5 a.m. the German infantry left its trenches at 1 p.m. the four Allied battalions at Dixmude, attacked on three sides by twenty battalions of 4th Ersatz and 43rd Reserve Divisions,+ with six battalions in reserve, were about 4 p.m., after hand-to-hand fighting, driven over the river.** But as they destroyed the bridges across the Yser, the enemy could not immediately follow, although a small

\+ "Ypres 1914" pp. 106 and 108.

** "Ypres 1914" p.107 claims that the German attackers were "not numerically superior", but admits and shows on a map that two whole divisions were engaged.

1 R Mun Fus Vol 26

War Diary, 1st. Royal Munster Fusiliers.

Place / Date	Hour	Summary
Aubigny 1/4/18.	1 a.m.	Received orders from the Brigade to move the Bn. at 6.30 a.m. to the Bois de Vaire in close support to the Cavalry Division holding the line between Villiers-Bretonneux and Hamel. Bn. in position by 8 a.m. and remained there all day without being required.
Bois de Vaire	6 p.m.	Orders received for the Bn. to return to Hamelet and billet there for the night, and remain under ½ an hours orders to support either the Cavalry Division or the 16th. Division.
Hamelet 2/4/18.		The Bn. remained in Hamelet all day, and suffered slight casualties from shelling. Brigade Hd. Qrs. moved to the same village, and all Commanding Officers returned to their units, Lt.Col. Kane taking over again from Major Nightingale.
Hamelet 3/4/18.	3 p.m.	Orders received that the 16th. Division would be relieved to-night and that the 47th. Brigade would be relieved at 4 p.m.
Hamelet 3/4/18.	6 p.m.	The Bn. marched to Blangy-Tronville and were conveyed from there in busses to Saleux, arriving about midnight.
Saleux. 4/4/18.		Bn. entrained at 11 p.m.
Blangy 5/4/18.	9.30 a.m.	Bn. arrived at Blangy at 9.30 a.m. and marched 4 miles to Le Translay where they were billeted in the Village.
Le Translay 6/4/18.		The Bn. spent the day reorganizing, resting and refitting. The transport turns up at 4 p.m.
Le Translay 7/4/18.		Church parades and issue of clothing all day.
Le Translay 8/4/18.		The Bn. did parades all the morning and some training in the afternoon.
St.Quentin 9/4/18.	8 a.m.	The Bn. marched to St. Quentin arriving at 3 p.m. and remained in billets until midnight.
Eu. 10/4/18.	1 a.m.	The Bn. marched to Eu, where it entrained at 3 a.m.
Arques 10/4/18.	3 p.m.	Arrived at Arques, and after the men had had tea, the Bn. marched to Heuringhen, 2½ miles distant, and were billeted in the village.
Heuringhen 11/4/18	11 a.m.	The Bn. marched to Merck St. Levien, about 10 miles, arriving at 3 p.m. and were billeted in the village.

(Continued).

Place	Date	Time	Entry
Merck St.Levien	12/4/18.	3 p.m.	The Bn. was ordered to fall in and certain platoons told off to go to the Connaught Rangers and Leinster Regt. This order was cancelled later, and the Bn.was told to join with the 2nd. R.M.F. and proceeded to Le Bouquet.
Le Bouquet	13/4/18.		The 1st. and 2nd. Bns. joined up. Hd. Qrs. and 100 men of 1st.Bn. under Lt.Col.Kane proceeded to Wovrans. The remainder under Lt.Col.Tonson-Rye and the 2nd.Bn.proceeded to Ailette.
Wovrans	14/4/18.		Hd.Qrs. 1st. Bn. remained at Wovrans.
	15/4/18.		The Bn., less Hd.Qrs., marched to Steenbeke where it was billeted in the village, and came under the orders of the 16th. Divisional composite Infantry Brigade.
Steenbeke	16/4/18.		The Bn. spent the morning settling down in billets, and at 1 p.m.commenced digging a line of trenches on the western edge of the Foret de Nieppe due west of Merville.
"	17/4/18.	9 a.m.	The Bn. continued its digging till 5 p.m.
"	18/4/18.	9 a.m.	the Bn. digging all day till 3 p.m.
"	19/4/18.	9 a.m.	Digging on the line continued till 3 p.m.
"	20/4/18.	8.30 a.m.	The 1st. and 2nd. Bns amalgamated and,made up to 960 strong, with a detachment of 10th. R.D.F.,proceeded in motor busses and lorries, under Lt. Col.Kane, to Pas. Hd.Qrs. 2nd. Bn. & Lt.Col. Tonson-Rye with 10 Officers and 50 other ranks remained at Steenbeke to form the nucleus of a training Bn.
Pas.			
Henu.	21/4/18.		The Bn. billeted in Henu. The Bn. is now in the 172nd. Bde. of the 57th. Division. For the remainder of the month the Bn. went into training, after being organized into the old 4 Coy.basis.
Henu.	30/4/18.		A draft of 9 Officers and 92 other ranks arrived.

Strength of Battalion on April 30th. 1918.

Officers.....39. Other ranks.....1111.

(Sd) P.R.Kane Lieut-Colonel
1st. R.M.Fusiliers, 5/5/18.

Certified true copy.

E.W.Rase Colonel
A.O.i/c Records, No.12 District.

CORK 21/6/1918.

advance, though the Staffs had arrived several days before the troops, had not by the morning of the 10th been sufficiently completed to satisfy its commander. With the concurrence of General von Linsingen, and after arrangement with the neighbouring troops, the offensive was put off until the 11th. The postponement, however, seems to have applied only to divisions of the Sixth Army; for the Fourth Army acted on the original instructions: at any rate, the greater part of it, its centre, the III Reserve Corps, 9th Reserve Division,* XXII.

* "Ypres 1914" p.109. It had just come from the Verdun area.

and XXIII. Reserve Corps - the XXII. now composed of the 43rd Reserve and 4th Ersatz Divisions, and part of the Marine Division - a little over seven divisions in all, made a desperate attack on the French front from Langemarck to Dixmude, held by five divisions two of them Territorial and three cavalry

www.ingramcontent.com/pod-product-compliance
Lightning Source LLC
Chambersburg PA
CBHW080845230426
43662CB00013B/2030